ODD ONE OUT

GENEVIEVE MCKAY

____

Chapter 1

____

Kira

"Kira, you're up," Anna calls from her spot near the center of the ring. She tugs her ball cap lower to shield herself from the relentless sun. Her dark sunglasses are firmly in place but I can still feel her watching me. "Do you know your course?"

It's a throwaway question we both know the answer to. I *always* know my course.

I nod anyway, tuning the rest of the world out and focusing between Tessa's sharply pricked ears.

I can already feel the way the course will ride; the corner Tessa will go wide in, that roll-back where she'll sit and practically spin on her haunches like a cow-horse, the tight combination she'll love.

Tessa interprets my slight movement in the saddle as a signal to surge forward, powering up immediately into her just-barely-under-control canter. Her nose is in the air, eyes and ears already searching for the first jump.

Wait for it, I think, keeping my breathing steady and my body relaxed.

Tessa waits, barely, showing her impatience with a tiny grunt of irritation. She is addicted to jumping and will go for anything, and I do mean *anything*, in front of her if I'm not careful. I circle her one more time until she softens and then I point her eager nose at the blue-striped vertical.

Her whole body goes rock hard in anticipation and she pushes slightly against the bit. It's a question, not a demand, and in response I let her go.

"Not so fast, slow her down," Anna calls out in warning.

I like my coach Anna a lot. She's talented, extremely nice and she practically *gave* me Tessa two years ago. But there are times, like now, when she's wrong.

Tessa rockets down the long side, powering over the three-foot-six jumps like they don't even exist. She knows what she's doing and so do I. Oxer, vertical, three-stride-in-two, bounce, bounce, bounce. Roll back to the wall and deep into the corner. I don't slow her down and we move through the air so fast that the wind blurs my vision.

I sit as quietly as I can, not interfering, fingers feather-light on the reins, letting her back rise up to meet me over every jump. I'm just there to show her where to go, give the occasional suggestion, and stay out of her way.

Eight jumps, ten jumps, no more. It's done but I want to go again and again and again. We do our final circle with me standing in the stirrups, one hand patting Tessa's sweaty neck. We drop down to a trot and Tessa flattens her ears, making a face at Isla Merchant's oversized bay Hanoverian mare, Hilty, who is standing half-asleep in the upper corner of the ring.

The other rider in our lesson, Rebecca, is there too, hiding in the only patch of shade left in the ring, waiting for her final turn to jump.

"Watch it," Isla snaps, but I ignore her like I always do. Still, a little of the euphoria from my ride fades away just looking at her sulky expression.

"Well, that was a quarter brilliant and three-quarters terrifying," Anna says, wiping a hand across her forehead. "You're going to give me a heart attack one day, Kira."

"Terrifying?" I say in astonishment. "It was wonderful."

Someone snickers and I take a deep breath, willing myself to stay calm. My dad keeps reminding me that some people do not appreciate it when I bluntly state *obvious*, undeniable facts. Personally, I think that's their problem and not mine. But not everyone agrees.

"I'm not trying to brag," I correct carefully. "I meant that the round *felt* wonderful to ride. It was in no way scary. Tessa and I knew what we were doing."

There's another snicker, probably Isla, and I groan inwardly in frustration.

"I *meant*..." I start again, wondering why getting the simplest of points across is so exhausting.

"Okay, we'll talk about it once you've had a chance to go over the video," Anna says quickly, motioning in the direction of my phone, which is perched on a corner post nearby recording everything. "Isla, you're up next."

I walk Tessa in circles at the top of the ring to keep her muscles warm while Isla and Hilty take an uninspiring trip with one slow-motion stop that *anyone* halfway competent could have seen coming from a mile away.

"Good try, Isla," Rebecca calls from her spot in the corner. I look over at her incredulously, marvelling at how easily she can lie. It wasn't a good try at all. Anna is already walking over to the middle of the ring with her hands planted on her hips, ready to give Isla a list of the exact same corrections she always gives her.

"What?" Rebecca asks, catching my eye. She reaches down to scratch the itchy spot under Rio's neatly pulled mane. "It's called being supportive, Kira, you should try it."

"No thank you." I move Tessa further away.

Rebecca seems nice enough. She hasn't been boarding Rio at Three Sisters long, but she's a decent rider and it's obvious that she cares about her horse. But she's also really friendly with Isla and that makes me automatically distrust her.

Be nice to everyone, try to fit in, and make friends, is what my dad would say. He's always anxious that I don't have enough friends, especially after what happened at my last school. But he doesn't understand that I'd much prefer to be a complete hermit rather than make friends with lying, manipulative people like Isla.

The sun beats down overhead and I feel a bead of sweat trickle down my back. This is the last ride of the morning. Nobody wants to ride in the heat of the day anymore. Lessons start right at dawn, pause, and then start back up again in the early evening.

I used to take lessons in the mornings, but now those spots are reserved for the riders who will be heavily competing all summer. Most everyone will be going away next week for the big spring show on the mainland. Not me and Tessa, though; that is not our scene.

My lesson today is made up of leftovers. There is me, who hates everything to do with showing; Isla, who can't pilot Hilty successfully around a course to save her life; and Rebecca, with her very young Swedish Warmblood, Rio, who isn't ready to compete heavily yet.

The two of them will still be doing some small local competitions with Anna's assistant coach, Samantha, who teaches the beginners and those who lack the talent, or the money, to ride in the big shows.

Now that it's not my turn to ride anymore, I'm bored and I wish I could go do some flat work in the dressage ring next door until the others have finished. There is only one other rider using it today: the strange neighbour girl who has the draft horses.

I don't know much about her except that she wears weird clothes sometimes and she's usually riding one of the heavy horses, the Shires, that her family breeds. Three Sisters doesn't usually allow outside riders here, but this girl is friends with the farm owners so she pretty much shows up whenever she likes.

Today she's not riding a draft horse; she's riding the big chestnut, Paddington, who belongs to one of the owners.

I sigh, wishing I could be riding in the ring with her. Anna is a fantastic coach, but her idea of schooling on the flat is just the bare minimum of trotting and cantering in both directions before the real action, the jumping, begins.

Not that I blame her; jumping is my favourite part of riding too. Flying over a course is where the magic happens, after all. I can't imagine a life without it.

But last season Tessa and I rode in a clinic with the new dressage coach, Elliot, and it sort of changed the way I look at schooling. I hadn't even wanted to ride in the clinic in the first place. But Anna is always trying to find random non-showing opportunities to keep me motivated and she urged me to give it a try. It turned out that I'd loved it. Especially since I'd learned some new skills to help Tessa.

Tessa has a habit of becoming stiff and unresponsive when she gets nervous or excited. In the past, I'd just circled her until she calmed down, but Elliot had shown me something better. She'd taught me how to use exercises to gently mobilize Tessa's stiff body from her jaw right to her tail to get her to relax. Almost like doing the lightest of yoga. I'd never even heard of anything like that before. But I use the exercises she gave me all the time whenever Tessa gets tense or overexcited and it seems to work really well.

The other thing I like about Elliot is that she'd told me flat out during the clinic that I'd make a great trainer one day. Which is something I've always secretly wanted to do with my life even though it's completely impractical. I love figuring out what makes horses tick. And the more difficult they are, the more interesting I find them.

It's not something that I tell many people, since they usually either laugh at me or list off all the reasons why becoming a trainer won't work for someone like me. My dad said flat out that there's no future in training horses and that I need to pick something more practical that will earn me a decent income.

Even Anna, who was usually pretty supportive, had agreed with him.

"It's a hard way to make a living, Kira. And trainers need to work with *people* as well as horses," she'd told me sympathetically, "and they need to be able to go to shows and meet with sponsors and clients. Those are all things you'd hate. You should stick with riding horses as a hobby."

But Elliot hadn't said any of that and, since Anna will be away showing for half the summer, I'd convinced my dad to let me take dressage lessons for a few months.

I look longingly at the schooling ring where the neighbour girl is now cantering Paddington around on a loose rein, wondering if Anna would even notice if I just snuck over there to work on a few things by myself.

"All right, Rebecca, you're up," Anna calls. "Are you watching, Kira? Don't forget you can learn a lot from watching each other's rounds, girls."

I sigh and move Tessa into the now-vacant shady spot, pretending to watch Rebecca ride Rio around a lower, modified version of the course I'd just jumped. I don't like group lessons at all. If I had my way, I would take only private lessons where it's just me, Anna and Tessa to worry about.

But my dad, who was probably more traumatized than me about the whole school bullying incident, got it in his head that group lessons might be a chance for me to socialize. Which I get, in theory, except that I actually take lessons to learn how to be a better rider, not to make friends.

"It's that or nothing, Kira," he had said in that maddening way of his, "your choice."

Of course, that wasn't really a choice at all, which I pointed out several times, but since there was no way I was giving up riding Tessa, I had to settle with two group lessons a week and one private lesson. At least when I started taking dressage lessons with Elliot, I wouldn't have to ride with Isla as much.

"All right, everyone," Anna calls finally, "good job out there today. Kira, can you hang on a second? I'm just going to debrief Rebecca and then I'd like to talk to you."

She turns away without waiting for an answer. I head over to pick up my phone from where it's been propped up to record my lesson.

"Looks like you're in trouble, freak," Isla says in a low whisper, sidling up beside me. Her eyes glitter under the brim of her helmet and she twists her mouth into a hard smile, full of teeth. It's an expression she seems to save just for me. To the rest of the world, she acts charming and innocent, but I know that this is the real her.

"Not as much trouble as you were in attempting to ride that course," I say, not stopping Tessa when she shakes her head warningly at Hilty, making the bigger mare lurch away.

Isla makes a feral, growling noise under her breath. "It's not my fault this horse is useless."

She takes a quick look around to make sure Anna isn't

watching and then gives Hilty an unnecessary thump in the sides with her blunted spurs.

My heart catches as the mare grunts and jolts forward in surprise.

"Don't," I say, even though that's exactly the response Isla wants.

"She deserves it." Another thump and Hilty jerks her head up, eyes widening unhappily. "She's a waste of space and would be better off as dog food." One more thump.

"That is animal abuse," I say, my voice as steady as I can make it. "Stop it."

With effort, I keep the tremor out of my voice and my facial expression neutral, trying not to give away how deeply her actions are disturbing me. The bigger my reaction, the more she'll do it. I've known Isla for years.

Do not get upset, I tell myself, *just email Anna about it tonight and let her deal with it. Hilty isn't mortally injured; just unhappy.* I exhale slowly through my mouth and feel my heartbeat return to a more even pace.

My counsellor, Donna, and I have come up with a lot of strategies for dealing with weirdos like Isla and the girls who had bullied me at school. I used to go ballistic when anyone was mean to animals, or to other people for that matter, but I'd learned to squash down all that anger and react more constructively now. Most of the time.

"Oh, calm down," Isla says, rolling her eyes and jerking Hilty's head abruptly toward the barn. "I barely touched her. You're just too sensitive, freak. I bet you're going to run and tell Anna, aren't you?"

"I always tell Anna when somebody hurts the horses," I say as calmly as I can. "And blaming other people when you do something wrong is called gaslighting."

"Huh?" Isla squints over her shoulder at me.

"It's a big word. You might have to Google it." I look down

at Tessa's coppery neck and run my fingers through her short, silky mane, so glad that she didn't fall into the wrong hands. How awful would it be to have an owner like Isla?

Poor Hilty is a good horse, even though she's older and kind of lazy. She doesn't deserve to be treated like garbage, anyway. She'd been a successful show horse once. I'd bet money that she'd live up to her potential more if she had a half-decent rider.

"Thanks for waiting, Kira, this will just take a second," Anna says, smiling as she walks toward me and Tessa. She clearly hasn't noticed the latest incident with Isla. Sometimes I think she doesn't *want* to see.

I nod, drop my toes out of the stirrups and lean way over so I can loosen Tessa's girth, resigning myself to being late getting back to the barn.

I don't like small untruths like *just a second* and *in a moment*; they feel too much like lies to me. It will probably take at least five minutes for Anna to talk to me and then a minute to ride to the barn. In six minutes, someone else will have hogged both wash stalls and Tessa will have to wait longer for her bath.

But since Anna is nice, and has given me countless extra opportunities to ride, I stuff down my irritation.

Tessa's ears slowly pin back as our coach gets closer and her whole body tenses. This is not because Anna is a bad person. Tessa is just very clear about her personal space. She doesn't like people, or other horses, too close. That even includes me sometimes.

"Kira, the John Riddle clinic is coming up in two weeks and I know how disappointed you were about not being able to ride Tessa in it."

"Oh." I shift uncomfortably in the saddle, not liking to be reminded of the gigantic fight my dad and I had had when he'd told me that I wouldn't be able to ride with my favourite five-time Olympian. The one whose training videos I fell asleep watching almost every single night.

It was an invitation-only clinic which meant you had to be a good enough rider to be chosen, or be able to buy your way in somehow. I'd been beyond excited when Anna had told me that I was on the list.

So, *disappointment* did not accurately describe the crushing pain I'd felt when my dad had told me flat out that I wouldn't get to ride with the world-class rider I'd been obsessing over since I was like six years old. I hadn't exactly handled it well.

"Well," Anna goes on, "Marsha Townsend has broken her leg so she won't be able to ride in the clinic after all. She doesn't want to give up her spot, though; she wants John to see Flicker go since she's thinking of selling him. She's wondering if you might like to ride the horse for her."

I blink at her in surprise.

"Not Tessa?" I say automatically, because every wishful fantasy I've had of riding in this clinic has involved me soaring with Tessa over intricate combinations while John Riddle watches admiringly.

"No, not Tessa. I know that you love your horse, Kira. But this would be an amazing opportunity for you. I know how much you wanted to meet John. And, if you play your cards right, you might get to keep riding Flicker until he sells. And you said you wanted to spend more time at the barn this summer."

This is an understatement. I would spend all day, every day at the barn if I could. I've begged to be able to work here every summer since I first started riding at Three Sisters. But it's never happened. Anna says it's against the rules for boarders to also work there. That there is a firm line between staff and clients that should never be crossed. Which is pretty much the stupidest rule I've ever heard of.

"Yes, I do. Why me, though?" It's true that I'm a decent

enough rider, but there are plenty of people at Three Sisters with more experience. And Marsha isn't exactly my biggest fan.

"Well, to be honest, Kira, Flicker isn't the easiest horse to ride. He's quirky. And most of the riders capable of handling him already have their own rides for the clinic. And nobody else stepped forward. It was Marsha's idea to ask you."

"Really? I thought she hated me."

"No, of course not. She's just…eccentric. Anyway, she said you handled Flicker brilliantly last year. And she's watched you ride Tessa. Everyone knows how feisty this little redhead can be."

She reaches out to pet Tessa, thinks better of it, and wipes her hand on her breeches instead.

"This would be a great opportunity for you, Kira. All expenses paid. It's not the best timing, I know, what with me going away next week. But we'll figure it out. Flicker is a fast, strong horse but I think you can handle him. Darla says he's been going well lately and he's a hot and forward ride—just your type. Marsha said you had a way with him."

That was a bit of a stretch. I'd ridden Flicker exactly one time. And it was last year after he'd bucked Marsha off and went careening around the ring, bucking and squealing. I'd just happened to be the one to catch him. He'd run right up to me, all rolling eyes and snorting breath, and I'd just reached out and taken his reins.

Marsha had been too bruised to get back on and had asked me to do it since there wasn't anyone else around.

"Just pop up and walk him around for me, ducky," she'd said in her nearly incomprehensible accent. "Just so the cheeky bugger doesn't think he's won."

Ignoring the fact that she'd called me a duck, I'd led Flicker over to the mounting block without arguing. I knew it was dangerous. I knew that my dad, Anna, and anyone with half a brain would tell me not to get on that horse.

He'd gained quite the reputation since Marsha had bought him last fall. He'd once been a stallion so was brimming with attitude and energy. And, although he hadn't had that bad of a reputation when Marsha purchased him, he quickly descended into being a known bucker, dirty stopper and occasional biter.

But the only thing I felt at that moment was a burning desire to try him out. Even when he was being naughty, he was a magnificent horse. A well-built, glossy bay with a jet-black mane and tail and a wide blaze. He was a huge horse, but compact too. Not long and lanky like most of the Warmbloods I knew. He was all muscle with a thick, arching neck and a wide chest. And the way he carried himself, you could tell that he knew that he was special and should be admired.

His back had tensed the second I lowered myself gingerly onto the saddle, but I took my time and kept my seat as light as possible, letting my legs drape around him ever so gently without constricting. His sides shivered and twitched when I touched him with my calves and I felt him gather himself beneath me, power coiling upward until he seemed about two feet taller than he had the moment before.

It was terrifying and it was exhilarating. He didn't explode. Instead, he strode forward, his ears swivelling around, trying to figure out what I was going to do to him.

You're waiting for something bad to happen, I thought, *you're expecting a fight. Why is that?*

By the time we'd done a few circles at the top end of the ring, a little of the tension had ebbed out of his body and he'd started to mouth the bit gently, that testing, questioning beginning of a conversation.

"Hmmm," Marsha had said, "he likes you. Maybe let him trot out a little."

I felt the buck coming about five seconds before it hit. His mouth grew hard on the bit, his neck curled and I could feel his back dropping away from me before he plunged forward and twisted to the side. But I was ready and waiting for him; I sat deep, lifting his shoulder, and urging him onward so that that energy channeled him forward instead of exploding. His powerful hind legs propelled him into a canter, but I could feel that there was something a little off, a hitch where there should have been only smoothness.

"Hit him when he bucks," Marsha had yelled, but I'd ignored her. I didn't have a crop with me anyway, and anyone with half a brain could tell that he was sore somewhere.

I brought him down to a trot and then to a walk, hopping off while he was still moving. I ran a hand down his neck in appreciation.

"He's wonderful," I'd told Marsha truthfully, coming to a halt in front of where she was leaning against the fence. She'd had one hand clutching the rail and the other pressed over her ribs like they were sore.

"When he's not trying to kill his rider maybe. He's bad-natured through and through. I think that Clara sold me a lemon."

"He's not," I said, struggling to control my temper. "He's sore. That's why he tried to buck. I think it's his right shoulder. Maybe his saddle doesn't fit properly."

"Bah. I don't believe in making excuses for them."

"That's why you get bucked off. And it probably doesn't help that you bounce all over him like a sack of bricks. You should take some lessons on a school horse until you have control over your seat. He's too much for you."

Ignoring her sputters of rage, I'd stuffed the reins into her hands and walked away.

Marsha had complained loudly and bitterly to Anna about my rudeness and poor attitude afterward. She'd even tried to evict me from the barn for a while. So, it was extra strange that she'd ask for me to ride Flicker now.

"Kira? Are you listening?"

I shake my head and come back to the present moment to see Anna staring at me impatiently.

"Sorry. I was not. Could you please repeat what you said?" This is a phrase that my counsellor Donna gave me for those times when I zone out during conversations or when my brain is trying to multitask a dozen things at once. It's come in quite handy.

"I was asking if you think you'd like to try Flicker? This could be a great opportunity for you."

"I won't ride with Darla," I say quickly, feeling a spike of anxiety at even the thought of being coached by that barracuda from up the hill.

Three Sisters is actually a very large property with two barns. Ours, Barn B, is at the bottom of the hill near the big outdoor ring and the newly-built smaller dressage ring. We have lots of pasture and a network of trails that loop down the hillside.

Barn A sits at the top of the hill, overlooking everything below, and has its own fancy indoor arena attached to it. The big grass ring is up there too, which is one of my favourite places to jump on the rare times that I'm allowed to ride there. They also have a big network of trails that go all the way back down the other side of the mountain. But I haven't explored them very much. We sort of mostly stick to our own sides.

Each barn has a head trainer—Anna and Darla—but they are complete opposites in every way. Anna never says anything bad about Darla, but I don't think she likes her any more than I do.

Technically, everyone at Three Sisters is supposed to be one big happy family riding under the same banner. We share the rings and everyone is expected to cheer for all our riders loudly at shows, especially when people are watching. But everyone knows that Barn A is the one that matters. All the wealthiest clients keep their crazy-expensive horses up there and you have to agree to be in a full-time program of training and competitions to even be on the wait list to board there. Barn B riders who start having success at the rated shows or who are extra talented are encouraged to move up the hill as fast as possible.

Barn A is for the real winners and Barn B is for the rest of us.

The truth is that I wouldn't keep Tessa at Barn A even if you paid me a million dollars to do it. Despite the oversized stalls and prime access to the fancy indoor arena, the horses don't get as much turnout as ours do and you're expected to let the grooms get your horses ready for you instead of brushing and tacking up yourself. There are even grooms standing by to boost you into the saddle if you're feeling too feeble to climb up there yourself.

But worst of all is that Darla is a bristling, shouting psychopath who can be heard yelling and swearing at her students from all the way down the hill. Why people pay ridiculous amounts of money to ride with her is beyond me. Half the people in her lessons end up in tears.

"Yes, I already warned Marsha how you felt about Darla. She's agreed that you can ride Flicker with me."

"Oh, okay, I'll do it."

"You will?" Anna sounds surprised that I've agreed so easily. She usually has to do a lot more convincing before I'll agree to try something new. "You'll need to ask your dad."

"He won't mind."

"He'll have to sign a waiver giving permission; you're still under age."

"Yes. Tell Marsha I'll do it."

"I'm so happy about this, Kira. You're a talented rider, and you've worked wonders with Tessa. You deserve this opportunity more than anyone."

She reaches out quickly and squeezes my knee, smiling up at me before turning back to the barn.

I know that I'm a bit of a puzzle for Anna. Three Sisters isn't the type of barn to cater to casual, non-competitive riders, so she sometimes is at a loss of what to do with me. If I'd wanted to show, then she'd have known exactly which direction to push me in. She'd probably have convinced my dad to get me a second horse by now, a youngster or a high-quality lease that could take me higher than Tessa could.

But I didn't want any of that. I hated horse shows: the overwhelming noise, the chaos, the gross food truck smells, the riders taking out their nerves by snapping at their parents and their horses. No thank you.

I just wanted to be the best rider possible; a kind, effective-yet-brilliant rider like John Riddle. That was enough.

"Hope you don't mind that I'll be riding another horse, Tessa," I say as we make our way slowly back to the barn. "It's too good of an opportunity to pass up. You'll always be my best girl, though."

She snorts and shakes her head, only thinking of her bath and being turned out on pasture for lunch.

I untack Tessa quickly inside and then lead her back out into the sunshine for her post-workout bath.

"So, did you get in trouble?" Isla smirks at me from where she has predictably hogged the outdoor wash stall. She is spraying water in Hilty's general direction with one hand and scrolling on her phone with the other. Typical.

"No." I let Tessa tug me over to the grassy lawn while we wait our turn. "She just wanted to offer me a last-minute spot in the John Riddle clinic. That's all."

I say it casually like it's no big deal, but inside I'm grinning like crazy. The realization that I actually get to ride with my idol finally catches up with me and I'm suddenly brimming with excitement. I'd never let Isla see that, though. She is the killer of all joy.

"You are freaking kidding me." Isla shoves her phone in her pocket and tosses the hose aside, ignoring the spurting nozzle that spatters a wild column of water across Hilty's twitching side before hitting the ground with a clatter. "Why would *you* get a spot?"

I don't answer. Letting Isla seethe is always the best revenge. She has made it clear that she thinks she's too good to be riding at Barn B. She has all sorts of dreams of heading up the hill to ride at Barn A, which is where she feels she belongs. But the truth is that Isla is a terrible rider who does not deserve a sweet horse like Hilty, and there is no way her family could afford the board at Barn A anyway.

I've mentioned both those things to her in the past when she was moaning about what a winner she'd be if she was training with Darla, but she hadn't seemed to appreciate my logic.

She sends me a nasty glare and jerks a still-dripping Hilty from the wash bay, not even bothering to strip the excess water from the mare's coat.

"Come on, Tessa," I say, sighing a little.

I don't remember exactly when it was that Isla and I became enemies or when she started being so mean. We've both been riding at Three Sisters since we were little kids. And way back when we were very small, before my mom left even, we'd been friends. We'd even had playdates and things.

But somewhere around middle school things had changed abruptly and it was like she started becoming this awful person overnight. Even though she hid her worst side from Anna, she wasted no opportunity to make fun of me or do something nasty when she thought nobody was watching. She doesn't even seem to like the horses very much anymore. And she's outright mean to Hilty. I don't know why Isla bothers to keep coming to the barn at all.

As soon as Tessa is clean and mostly dry, I turn her back out on the pasture to join her friends.

Tessa doesn't love a lot of horses, but she goes out with a few friends that she gets along with really well. Her favourite group to hang out with are three small ponies from the school string. They're all older than her and seem to put her on her best behaviour for some reason.

"Have a good day," I say to her retreating back as she sets off at a rapid trot to join her little herd.

I spend the next hour carefully cleaning my tack and organizing my locker, trying to put off the moment when I have to go home as long as possible. Which, considering that I like to keep everything neat and tidy in the first place, doesn't take nearly long enough.

Finally, even I have to admit that there is nothing left to keep me here and I head out into the aisle with a sigh. I would spend every spare moment at the barn if I could. But the rule is that we have to leave once our ride is over. No hanging around once we are finished.

"Are you sure I can't go up to Barn A and say hello to Flicker?" I ask Anna wistfully as I pass her open office door. I'd already asked her once but I was hoping she might have changed her mind.

"Not until you're officially his rider," she says firmly. "Get your dad to sign the waiver tonight and then we can figure out a schedule."

"Okay. Are you sure there aren't any chores I can help you with?" I ask, feeling a little desperate.

Technically we're not supposed to help with manual labour around the barn, but sometimes, when there isn't anyone else around, Anna will give in and let me assist her with some project or another.

"Sorry, kiddo. Not this time. I wish we had some sales horses in right now for you to help with. Hopefully, this thing with Flicker will work out."

She smiles at me kindly, but it's clear that she has other things on her mind and would prefer that I just go home.

A couple of winters ago I had begged my way into helping Anna start some young prospects that had come in as a group. It had been at a low point in my life, and she had probably only agreed because she'd felt sorry for me, but it turned out that working with young and green horses was something I'd been good at.

I hadn't gotten paid for it or anything, but I'd learned more in that winter than I had during my whole life as a rider up until that point. It was so exciting and satisfying to see the horses learn and figure stuff out. Like solving a series of living puzzles. Most of them had turned out really well and sold for good money.

And the one that hadn't turned out to be a successful sales horse…well, that had been Tessa.

"All right, I guess I'll see you tomorrow," I say reluctantly.

"Great. Sorry I can't stay and chat, but I have a new groom coming for an interview in a few minutes."

She gives me a preoccupied smile and shoos me away, leaving me feeling deflated. *Lucky new groom. I don't know why Anna doesn't just hire me. I know all the horses. I'm a hard worker. I'm efficient and I'm always on time.*

I sigh and reluctantly pull out my phone to call the car service to come and collect me.

I love the quiet and tranquility of Three Sisters. It's a very calm and serene place most of the time, which is great for someone like me who hates loud noises and chaos. It's not like one of those barns where parents can just drop their kids off for the day so they can run around wild and unsupervised.

I'd been to places like that before and they were a bit of a nightmare. But, still, it would be nice if the rules at Three Sisters weren't quite so strict sometimes. It wasn't like I was hurting anyone by quietly hanging around.

Sighing again, I press the number for Blacklock, the car service my dad uses, and listen to the familiar ring. There's no point putting it off any longer. There is nothing else for me to do but head home.

Chapter 2

Lena

Gravel skids under my tires as I lean my weight against the handlebars, pushing the battered old bike up the endlessly steep hill.

I am grateful to have you, bike, but right now I kind of hate you, I think, stopping for a second to catch my breath and adjust the heavy backpack that is digging sharply into my shoulders.

I was lucky to find the bike at the second-hand store in the first place, but it's a bit of a lemon. Half the gears don't work properly and I'd given up trying to ride up the hill about five minutes ago. Although even a brand-new bike would have trouble with this climb. It is practically vertical; I'm not even halfway up and I'm already exhausted.

My breath comes out in short gasps and I feel the clean blue T-shirt I'd put on that afternoon dampening with sweat. Hopefully, the navy colour is dark enough to hide it.

I know that I'm going to look all hot and sweaty for my interview now but it's too late to turn back. I don't think I even have enough energy to turn around. It's easier just to keep trudging endlessly upward.

Come on, you can do this, I remind myself firmly. *You've got this.* But now I'm wondering if any stable could be worth all the effort. If I get the job then I will have to do this impossible climb every day in all sorts of weather.

It will toughen you up. Those words are my mother's and I push them firmly out of my head. That's her answer to any hardship she throws my way. No food in the house? *Toughen up.* The landlord going to evict us? *Tough.* Kids at school laughing at my shabby clothes? *Stop complaining, it will toughen you up.*

The driveway is thickly lined with tangled old-growth rainforest, the type you rarely see close to town. Just huge, ancient trees, ferns and darkness on all sides. The sun is at the wrong angle for them to cast any shade, though. It beats down on me without mercy.

Still, I find myself edging closer to the woods as I climb, drawn to the cool temperature and the silence. This terrain is nothing like the photos of the farm I'd seen on the internet and I'm beginning to wonder if I'm even at the right place. The small brass sign at the bottom of the hill had read Three Sisters Farm. But there was no sign of any picturesque orchards, rolling fields or shiny, expensive horses.

There is a sharp, cracking noise off to my right and I jump a little, peering between the huge ancient-looking tree trunks that are each draped with about five different types of moss. Nothing moves and, after a long hesitation, I push on.

The hill ends abruptly and I stop, gasping for air and looking around in surprise. Suddenly I am in a completely different world. The rainforest is gone and I am looking at exactly what I'd expected: a long flat driveway and miles of gently undulating pasture lined with white board fences.

The transition is so surprising that I stand rooted for a moment, getting my bearings.

And then I see them: acres of horses grazing peacefully in the distance. Even from here, I can see the healthy gleam of their coats and the ripple of their well-muscled flanks. My breathing slows and a feeling of peace washes over me like it inevitably does the second I'm around horses.

The climb is worth it, the long bus ride from our crappy run-down rental on the wrong side of town is worth it, any effort is worth it if I can just spend the rest of my life in a place like this.

From here I can see the long, gabled barn where I think I'm supposed to meet the trainer, Anna. I gulp, taking off my forgotten bike helmet and hanging it carefully over my handlebars. I rub at my forehead, trying to get rid of the sweaty red line from the helmet that I know is probably imprinted above my eyebrows. I smooth my hair back and make sure my braid is still in place. I hope I look as presentable as possible under the sweaty circumstances.

I can already tell that this is a much fancier barn than any of the places I've worked at before. It just oozes money and high-class expectations.

My gaze travels past the barn and I realize that the driveway winds between a few outbuildings and pastures before it travels steadily upward to where an even bigger barn, matching in shape and colour but three times the size of the other one, sits at the top of the hill.

Wow, two barns. And probably an indoor arena up there too. I gulp and make myself keep moving. I should have paid better attention when I was looking up the website. This does not look anything like the family-friendly eventing barn I'd spent the last three years working at.

White fences line the driveway and I study the rails for telltale clues of what the people who run this place might be like. Orderly, exacting; no peeling paint or fallen boards here. The grass around the posts has been whacked ruthlessly to the ground and there is not a weed in sight.

Closer to the barn I see a ring full of colourful jumps off to the right, and beside it is a smaller ring that I guess is for flat work. The place is deserted, though. I suppose nobody is desperate enough to brave the blazing sun besides me.

I pause in the open doorway of the beautiful barn and then wheel off to the side to stash my bicycle behind a wooden pillar, safely out of sight. It looks extra shabby in these surroundings, the frame dented and dusty with bits of gold paint peeling off in places.

I am a good groom, I tell myself fiercely. *I belong here, Gretchen has already talked to them and sent them my references. They're expecting me.*

I push my shoulders back and stride into the barn, ignoring the fact that my jeans have seen better days and my ancient paddock boots have a worn spot near the toe that is threatening to disintegrate at any moment.

You are my hardest worker, you are great with horses, and they all love you. You have a real future with them. Don't give up. I inwardly repeat all the words that my last boss, Gretchen, has told me over the years. She'd been a real mentor to me, more like a mom or a big sister than a boss. She'd broken down in tears when I'd told her that I was leaving. Even though I'd never told her much about my home life, I think she'd guessed that it wasn't that great. I knew she worried about me.

Cool air ripples over my skin the moment I step inside and my weary muscles relax automatically. I inhale deeply, hungry for those familiar smells that have come to mean *home* to me. And I know instantly that this is where I belong. The place where I can be myself.

My eyes adjust to the dim light and I see that I'm not alone. A girl is walking slowly down the aisle toward me, her gaze fixed on her phone.

"Hi," I say, warmly, plastering on my friendliest smile. "I'm here to see Anna."

The girl jolts as if I've startled her and then stops dead, staring at me as if she can't quite believe that I've dared to speak to her.

Something flickers in her eyes and I feel a knot of dread in my stomach. She has clearly already judged me and found me lacking.

Her green eyes skim me over from head to toe and stop abruptly at my feet. She is pretty, with an extra-pale face and dark, straight hair that falls to her shoulders in a shimmery wave. There is a smattering of freckles across her nose and cheeks, but her face itself is strangely expressionless.

"You must be the groom Anna is interviewing," she says without smiling or looking up. "Do you know you have a hole in your boot?"

I glance down, cursing inwardly to see that the long walk up the driveway has been too much for my end-of-life paddock boots. My white sock is starkly visible through the gap. And it's not white anymore; it's grey with driveway dust.

"Um, no I didn't," I say, gulping, my cheeks burning. I need this job. I need the money. I can't let her drive me away. "Thanks?"

The girl acts like she doesn't hear me. She is still staring at the wrecked leather as if it's the most offensive thing she's ever seen.

"Well, um, it was nice to meet you," I finally say lamely, trying to salvage any hope of coming across as a professional groom. *Always be the bigger person*, was Gretchen's mantra. *Always have a helpful attitude and a smile on your face.* "I should go find Anna."

"She's in her office. My horse is Tessa; she's sensitive and needs lots of turnout time. You should really fix that boot. I don't like things with holes."

Her eyes flick up to meet mine and there is a long, uncomfortable silence while we just stare at each other. And then she looks away and makes a slight fluttering motion with her hand before stuffing it hastily into her pocket.

"Um, okay. I'll get right on that." I'm beginning to wonder if she's quite all there. Maybe she's on prescription medications or something and it makes her act weird. One of Gretchen's adult clients was like that. Sometimes she'd be so out of it on sedatives that she could hardly stay in the saddle.

"Goodbye, Kira," a firm voice calls from the depths of the barn. "I'll see you tomorrow."

"Yeah, bye," the girl mutters, staring meaningfully at my boot before heading outside without a backward glance.

That was probably the weirdest conversation I've ever had, I think, watching her walk away.

"Sorry about that." The woman, who I'm guessing is Anna, gives me a warm smile. "She doesn't mean any harm, she's just…well, it's complicated. Now, you must be Lena, right? Gretchen has told me such good things about you."

"Nice to meet you." I turn on whatever lingering charm the wilting sunshine and the weird encounter with Kira hasn't destroyed. "Your farm is beautiful."

"Well, thank you. We do our best. One of the rules around here is that everything has its place. We like things neat and tidy." Her gaze drifts down to my boot and my mortification ratchets up another notch. I am so not going to get this job.

"Tidiness and attention to detail are important for both barns here at Three Sisters but maybe doubly so for the barn up the hill. We're a little more casual at this end, at Barn B, because this is where the beginners start their lessons and we have more children here. We try to cultivate more of a family atmosphere. Barn A is where the more serious, or at least more *particular* boarders are."

"Understood," I say, knowing what she means right away.

At Gretchen's barn, most of the riders had been nice, but every so often we'd get a boarder in who acted like they were royalty and like you were their servant or something.

"But our riders in Barn B are still used to a certain level of service. We do encourage them to brush and tack up their own horses for the most part, but there are a few clients who we make an exception for."

I wonder how many spoiled princesses like Kira there are here? I think. I can't imagine her doing anything like manual labour.

Anna motions me to follow her back outside into the blistering sunshine. I send up a silent prayer that she doesn't notice my bike until she's already hired me. *If* she's going to hire me.

"You can see how hot it gets here in the middle of the day, so we usually have our outdoor lessons in the mornings and late afternoons. Most of our clients can't tolerate bad weather.

"We have two large outdoor rings, one for each barn, and the indoor is attached to Barn A as well. We can use those too, of course, but boarders in the upper barn get priority. We've put in a small dressage ring here as well since there has been some interest in flat work and dressage lately."

She shrugs like she can't quite fathom it.

Sweat is rolling down my forehead now and I'm feeling a little faint. My stomach growls with hunger; the granola bar I had before I left home is long gone. But I nod politely and try to pay attention as she lists off the paddocks and pastures and talks about turnout time and grazing rotations.

"Our grooms don't have to clean the pastures or paddocks, but once in a while, you'll be asked to help the cleaners with the stalls. Our manure bins are out back here. They get dropped off every couple of months and then taken away when they're full."

"No manure pile?" I ask in surprise. Every place I've worked at has had a giant, smelly, nearly out-of-control pile tucked somewhere out behind the barns.

"No, we prefer to have it taken off the property regularly. Right, well, come on back inside and we'll talk about what your duties would be. You come with some good references; Gretchen said you were an integral part of the team at Pine Woods."

"Yes," I say, feeling more comfortable with this part of the program. "I've worked at two barns before but I loved Pine Woods the best. I learned so much from Gretchen. I would have stayed working there forever if we hadn't had to move so far away."

I stop talking abruptly, worried that I've said too much. I tend to babble when I'm nervous.

But Anna is still smiling at me warmly.

"Gretchen and I were old school friends and we grew up riding together. I trust her opinion quite a bit and she spoke very highly of you. She did mention that your family moved around a lot. Do you anticipate being in the area long?"

I nod and plaster a smile on my face. "Well, we used to get transferred a lot. My dad is in the military so we've had to move around quite a bit. He's stationed overseas right now so we should be here for quite a few years. He's in the Marines."

All lies. But I've been working on this same cover story since I was ten years old and it's pretty much flawless. I can answer almost any question a curious person wants to throw at me. I have a whole notebook filled with background information on this made-up man's life. It's so detailed that sometimes even *I* believe it.

"Oh." Her kind gaze is now a mixture of sympathy and understanding. Which is exactly why this cover story works so well.

People always root for the hard-working girl with a dad who is off serving his country. Not so much the girl whose family is on welfare, has had their utilities cut for the fifth time and whose father might easily be one of a dozen guys her mother partied with and then forgot about long ago. Who would trust *that* kid with their expensive horses and saddles that cost more than the price of a used car?

"Oh, that has to be rough. You must be proud of him, though," Anna says, right on cue.

"Oh, we are," I say earnestly. "We couldn't be any prouder."

During an hour-long tour of the property, Anna grills me about my experience and my goals while she introduces me to some of the horses and to the other stable hands who move around quietly as they work, hardly glancing at us at all.

I hope I'm making a good impression; Anna smiles the whole time, but it's hard to know what she actually thinks of me.

I already know that I'm in love with this place. It is so quiet and tranquil and the grounds are beautiful. And, best of all, the horses seem happy.

"We like to give them as much turnout time as possible," Anna says, leaning her arms on the top of the fence as we gaze out at a small herd of grazing horses.

A finely bred chestnut mare throws her head up to stare at us, chewing thoughtfully before ambling over to investigate what we're doing.

"Well, that's a change," Anna says as the mare lips gently at my fingers, searching for treats. "She doesn't like very many people."

"She's gorgeous," I whisper, running a hand softly down the mare's neck.

"This is Kira's horse, Tessa. She is quite the feisty girl, but Kira just adores her. They're a good match."

Lucky Kira, I think, dropping my fingers away from the

mare's silky coat with a sigh. I can't imagine having a creature like this to call my own.

We finally end up back at her office and I sway a little as I go through the doorway, the heat and the hunger finally catching up with me.

"Are you okay?" Anna asks, putting a hand on my shoulder to steady me.

"Sorry, yes. It's just the heat. And I was so excited about this interview that I forgot to eat. It was silly of me."

"Oh, you poor thing. Sit down. I have some bottled water right here, and help yourself to a muffin. We horse people have to keep up our strength."

I do my best not to lunge at the box of muffins she holds out to me. But the one I choose is so good that I can't help but close my eyes in relief. It is the best thing I've ever tasted.

"They're from a local bakery," she says, laughing. "One of the boarders brings them a few times a week. The raspberry is my favourite too."

I nod and try not to stuff the entire thing in my mouth at once. I hadn't even paused to think about what flavour it was. My stomach grumbles, wanting more, and I clasp my hands tightly together to keep from reaching for another one.

"Well, I think that concludes our tour." Anna smiles at me. "So, what do you think?"

"It's amazing," I say, "you have such a beautiful place. And the horses look fantastic."

This is the complete truth. Three Sisters is an impressive farm; the facilities are top notch and the horses all look happy and healthy. I can see myself working here. Despite the awful hill.

"Well, I think we should do a trial period then; say a month. It's minimum wage to start, but we'll do a review in three months' time and we can talk about a raise then. Or, of course, you can do a partial exchange for lessons instead if you like."

"No, thank you," I say, too quickly, "I'll just take the money."

She raises her eyebrows and I gulp.

"I mean. I really like taking care of horses more than I like riding. It's enough to just be around them."

And I need the money.

Anna's expression softens and I breathe a sigh of relief. In a different life maybe I could afford the luxury of taking lessons instead of a paycheque, but in this life, I need every last cent I can scrounge up. Minimum wage isn't going to get me far when there are bills and groceries to pay for.

Truthfully, I could make more money working in a restaurant or as a telemarketer or something. But I'd discovered the hard way that life without horses was the same as being without oxygen. Excruciating. Being around them was the only way to make the rest of my otherwise depressing existence bearable. Horses ground me, make me feel safe and like I have a purpose in life. I would make almost any sacrifice to be around them.

"I want this job," I say firmly. "I'm a hard worker and I won't let you down. I promise."

Anna's smile returns like magic.

"You can start tomorrow morning," she says warmly, reaching out to shake my hand. "But we need to fix those boots before you start. You probably won't have time to get to the tack store this afternoon to replace them, but I think I have a pair of paddock boots in the lost and found locker that someone left behind. Consider them a permanent loan."

I fly down that giant hill to the bus stop without hardly touching the brakes, the wind hot against my cheeks and a pair of hardly-used paddock boots sitting snugly in my backpack. My heart is thumping with excitement.

I have a place in the world again. A barn to call my own. It made the sadness and embarrassment of our latest move a little less painful. And a little burst of hope flares to life in my chest. Maybe I'll be able to survive this next year after all.

Humming under my breath, I coast toward home.

Chapter 3

Kira

I can hardly believe my luck. There's a traffic situation downtown, so it will be another hour until the car from the service can get to Three Sisters. Which is just fine with me. I find an out-of-the-way spot under a tree near Tessa's pasture and pull out my phone so I can watch the videos of my ride again.

But, for some reason, even though I usually love pulling apart my rides so I can keep improving, I don't seem to be able to concentrate.

My thoughts keep dragging back to that groom. It wasn't just the hole in her boot that had bothered me. And it hadn't been only that she was getting interviewed for a dream job that should have been *mine* under different circumstances.

It was like there was something not quite *right* about her. I knew I'd only met the girl for less than a minute, but I'd had the weirdest impression that she was hiding something. That she was a fake who was just *playing* the part of a groom, not a real one.

It was a weird thing to think, I knew that, but I'd also had my fair share of dealing with fakers in the last few years so I felt like I had a pretty good eye for them by this point.

The girls in my last school had been completely awful, manipulative witches. They'd basically made my existence a living hell until my dad finally pulled me out of school because I was so miserable.

It had been bad enough being bullied by people my age, but the worst part was that nobody in charge at school had believed me. Not the teachers, not the principal, not even the school counsellor who was supposed to be there to protect students. They all just thought I was exaggerating or making things up to get attention.

Every single one of those girls had been so good at lying that they'd convinced the entire school that I was nuts and that they were completely innocent. And the other kids who'd witnessed things had been too scared to speak up and defend me even if they'd wanted to. Which, quite honestly, they probably hadn't.

It had been a year-long nightmare which had pretty much destroyed my confidence and self-esteem. Only the barn and my house had felt safe for a long time.

So, it bothered me that this so-called groom looked an awful lot like those girls had. I knew exactly the type. They seemed perfect on the outside; all wide-eyed and innocent like they could do no wrong. People would probably believe whatever came out of her mouth no matter what she said. She even had waist-length blond hair that she'd tied back into a thick braid. I was one hundred percent certain that nobody who looked that pretty could be trusted.

And anyone who resembled a Disney princess did not just show up here out of the blue to be a groom. There was definitely something sketchy about her. The hole in her boot had been the last straw.

I'd almost told Anna not to hire her right there on the spot, but I'd restrained myself. I would write a carefully worded email tonight telling her about all my suspicions. I had to tell her about Isla hurting Hilty, again, anyway. I might as well do it all in one email.

Feeling better, I lean up against my backpack and try to concentrate on my video again.

The shade protects me from the worst of the sun but even so, the ground around me shimmers with heat. Summer has only just begun, but already it feels like August. Lately, all anyone talks about is the drought and the climate crisis and how we might run out of water one day. My dad is obsessed with it. Before he'd become a corporate lawyer with a big office, he'd wanted to go into environmental law. He used to have all these side projects where he gave free legal advice to activist groups and things, but he doesn't have time for that these days. So he makes up for it by regularly boring me with climate disaster statistics instead.

I sigh and put my phone away again, feeling too restless to concentrate.

I'll go see if Flicker's outside. Anna had said I couldn't visit him yet, but nobody would notice if I just happened to walk past his pasture. Especially if I followed the back fence line that led behind the fields. It would only take me a couple of minutes. I could be easily there and back before the car service showed up.

I scramble to my feet and hike along the wooden fence until I come to the corner of Tessa's pasture and then turn to head upwards toward the top fields.

Tessa looks up as I walk past and lets out a low, warning nicker as if she's guessed that maybe I'm up to something.

"It's fine, Tessa," I call to her softly, "just going for a walk."

The grass is longer back here; it hasn't been mowed as carefully as the rest of the property. And the tall blades swoosh against the knees of my breeches.

I hum happily under my breath, feeling freer than I have in a while.

The ground gets a bit uneven as I climb and I have to walk carefully, sometimes holding onto the fence so I don't twist an ankle or something. But finally, I am at the top.

Now, which one would Flicker be in? I have no idea how much turnout he gets, if any, or where he'd be kept.

The pasture next to me has three horses in it, but I can't make out their features because they are dressed head to tail in colourful fly sheets with hoods that go right up to their ears.

After studying them, I'm pretty sure none of them is Flicker, so I keep making my way further along.

He's not in the second field either. But when I get close to the third field I have to stop suddenly and hide behind a tree because I realize that I am not alone.

The boy hasn't noticed me. He's sitting on the grass, with his elbows resting on the second rung of the fence facing the field. And there in front of him is the dark bay horse I'm looking for.

What on earth? I press my hands against the rough bark of the tree, hardly breathing in my effort to stay as still as possible.

Flicker is grazing just a few feet from the fence, one ear turned sideways so he can listen to the boy. He's dressed in a similar fly sheet to the others but it doesn't go up his wide neck. His neatly pulled mane is dark and silky against his bay coat and suddenly I wish I was the one down there, that I could groom him and make friends with him.

As I watch, the boy reaches down and rolls something into the field. Flicker makes an eager nickering noise and pounces on the apple, drooling juice and apple bits onto the grass as he crunches.

That's Oliver, I realize suddenly. *Josh Prescott's step-brother.* Josh is one of the best riders at Barn A and he and his horse Hectic Electric have won all sorts of prestigious competitions. Everyone wants to ride like him, and all the girls want to be around him, although he hardly seems to notice. I've never really seen the attraction. He hardly ever speaks to anyone or smiles. Although he does seem to love that horse.

Oliver is nothing like Josh. He is one of those smiling, easy-going guys who is always surrounded by a crowd of friends. Up until a couple of years ago, he'd kept his horse Bluebell up at Barn A and he'd also gone to the same school as me once, the one where I'd been bullied. We'd run in completely different crowds, though. I would bet money that he didn't even know I existed, not at school and not at Three Sisters.

Bluebell is a big, elegant gray hunter who has won Oliver nearly every championship on the West Coast. Although it was my private opinion that it was Bluebell who was responsible for their successful career, not her rider. Oliver gave the impression that he just sort of sat there and let her make the decisions.

Anyway, they'd both disappeared to some sort of exchange school the year before and I'd had no idea that either of them had even returned to Three Sisters.

From inside my backpack comes the muffled beeping of my phone and I freeze, wondering if Oliver will hear it. But he's lost in his own world and doesn't look up so I turn and head as quickly as I can down the hill, fishing my phone out so I can see the message.

As I suspected, it's Regan from the car service telling me he's five minutes away, so I pick up speed until I make it back to the barn, wheezing a little for air.

There is no sign of Anna or the suspicious groom and I wonder how the interview went. Hopefully, Anna won't decide until I've had a chance to talk to her.

"How was Tessa today?" Regan asks, grinning in the

rearview mirror as I slide onto the polished leather seats. This car is always immaculately clean and smells pleasantly like mild citrus, like it's just been spritzed with fresh oranges.

My dad always has to work long hours, sometimes even on weekends, so we've been using Blacklock to drive me around to school and riding lessons since I was a little kid.

Even though Blacklock has lots of other drivers, it's almost always Regan who comes for me and we've developed a good friendship over the years. He's one of those people who you feel like you can tell anything to.

"Great, fast as always," I say. "And guess what? I was offered a spot in the John Riddle clinic after all. It's paid for and everything."

"See, I told you things would work out. How did it happen?"

"Marsha broke her leg." I shrug. "I'm not sure how. But her horse, Flicker, needs a rider so she asked me to do it."

"Congratulations."

I don't mind that Regan doesn't know anything about horses and asks the same questions every time he picks me up. He's a very calm, reassuring type of person and always makes you feel like you're his best client. He remembers the smallest details you tell him, too.

"How are the models going?" he asks now, easing the car down the steep back entrance to Three Sisters. There is another entrance, on the other side of Barn A, but this one is closer to my house.

"Good. I finished the one for the competition last night. The appaloosa."

"The one with the spots, right? Does it have a chance?"

"Yes, a good one. It looks pretty amazing."

"I bet. Show me the ribbon once you win."

"I will."

We smile at each other and I marvel at how easy it is to get along with him.

Regan is old enough to be a grandfather, but his grown-up kids don't live around here and he only gets to see them once a year or so. I think he only drives for Blacklock so he can get out of the house and talk to people.

We've just made it to the bottom of the driveway when a splash of gold on the right catches my eye.

"That's her," I say out loud as the girl on the bike cruises down the road. I'd recognize that fluttering Rapunzel braid anywhere.

"A friend of yours?" Regan asks, and I don't miss the hopeful note in his voice. He's as bad as my dad sometimes about the friend thing, although much less pushy.

"Definitely not. I just met her once. She applied for a job at the barn but I don't think Anna should hire her; she looks suspicious. Regan, do you think we could try following her? I'd like to see what she's up to."

Regan makes a choking noise that sounds almost like a laugh.

"That will cost you extra," he says, trying to sound serious. "And it would look pretty dubious if we followed her bicycle with the car. A tad stalkerish."

"Well, maybe we could circle the block a few times. I want to see what she's up to so I have proof that Anna shouldn't hire her."

"I'm not sure what sort of proof you're looking for here. Why don't you like her?"

"I know it sounds silly. But I just don't trust the look of her. She's too pretty. Plus, she had a hole in her boot."

Regan's smile drops away and he drives right past the girl without slowing down. Clearly, he is terrible at stealth missions.

He meets my gaze in the rearview mirror but all the fun has gone out of his expression.

"It's a big world out there, kiddo," he says to me solemnly. "And there are a lot of people living very different lives than the one you have. I'm not sure if you realize how lucky you are."

I blink at him, startled by the almost disappointed look on his face.

"I know I'm lucky to have Tessa," I say slowly, wondering exactly what I've said to ruin the mood. People are funny sometimes, and usually, the last thing you think would bother them is the one that has insulted them the most somehow.

"Yes, and don't forget you have a big house and a dad who loves you like crazy, and food on the table. And you can replace your boots whenever you like. Not everyone has those luxuries."

I look out the window, wishing he'd stop lecturing. I know that there are poor people in the world; I am not completely oblivious to current events, as much as I'd like to be. That wasn't why I'd been judging the girl at all. It was because…because.

"See you tomorrow," Regan says suddenly, turning to look at me over his shoulder, and I glance up, surprised to find that we've already made it through the main gate of Sunrise Estates, the private subdivision where my dad and I live. I didn't realize how long I'd been lost in thought.

Regan's smile is back in place but I see a bit of hesitation lingering around his eyes. As if maybe he didn't like me quite as much as he usually did.

"Bye, thank you," I say, sliding off the seat into the bright sunshine.

I stare at my house and then glance back at Regan, who is already pulling away.

He probably thinks I'm lucky to live here. But I would much rather live in an old house in the country with land enough for Tessa to graze. And where you could have a dog and the neighbours wouldn't constantly be judging each other.

Every house in our subdivision looks nearly the same, and they are set close together with just some hedges and shrubbery separating them.

There are vibrant green front lawns that the landscapers keep mowed to exactly two inches tall. And all the houses have matching front doors and flower boxes with the same red geraniums planted in them.

There are all sorts of rules too. You have to have your house painted a specific colour and your car has to stay in the garage, not in the driveway. You're not even allowed to fence in your back or front lawn at all, so there isn't a safe space where a dog could run free. You can't let your cats outside either, if you're lucky enough to have them.

The tiny backyard looks right out onto the golf course. Which is okay for my dad who loves golf but not so thrilling for me. Every time I look at the perfectly manicured rolling hills, I imagine horses grazing on them. So much good pasture space is wasted so people can hit a little ball around. It's tragic.

I hear someone's front door click open nearby and quickly pick up speed until I'm safely inside the house.

Mrs. Harris, who lives a few doors down, is newly divorced and has a thing for my dad. She's always trying to find an excuse to talk to me and get invited inside. One day she just stood there and rang the doorbell over and over while I hid in my room with my headphones on and watched her through the security cameras. She's nothing if not persistent.

I lock the door carefully behind me, just in case, hang up my backpack and head to the kitchen to assemble a snack of chips and dip.

Balancing the plate carefully, I head upstairs to the sanctuary of my room.

As much as I dislike the neighbourhood, and the boring

exterior of my house, there is something nice and welcoming about the *inside* of it.

There's a big kitchen and living room on the main floor, plus the big den, my dad's bedroom and a few guest rooms. The basement has a media room with a big screen that comes out of the wall, theatre seating and even a little popcorn machine. There is also a pool table down there and shuffle-board, not that either of us uses it much.

There is a small bar and the place my dad calls his wine lair, which may sound exciting and like it could contain vampires but is just a boring old temperature-controlled room for wine.

But the upstairs of the house is the best part, because it's all mine. I'm not sure what the builder had originally meant the upper floor to be, because it was just one giant open room. My mom had used it as a gym and a yoga studio when I was little. But when she left, it didn't get used for anything at all for years and years.

When I was fourteen, and my model horse collection was beginning to overflow from my old room on the main floor, my dad had suggested that I take over the big unused space for myself. He'd let me pick out the paint colours on the walls and decorate the whole thing however I'd liked.

It had been a pretty life-changing move, actually, and had given me a lot of space to evolve my interests.

At one end I have my bedroom area with bed and dressers and the bathroom. There are a few of those Japanese screens for privacy if I want it, but I rarely use them because I hardly have any guests.

In the middle of the room, there are bookshelves filled with my epic collection of actual, retro videos. I have a refurbished DVD player and even an authentic VHS machine from the nineties that actually works. My collection is mostly riding and horse training videos, but I also have old-school anime there, as well as some Disney and Pixar I've gathered over the years. Mostly classic stuff I've hunted down on eBay.

Next to that, I have a giant table for working on the complicated puzzles I like to buy, and I've framed my favourites and displayed them on the wall opposite. The rest of the walls are filled with framed photos of me and Tessa and also posters of some of my favourite riders and horses.

John Riddle's oversized poster is right there in the middle in the place of honour. The picture is of him leaping off a nearly vertical bank with his stellar horse, Pictionary, both of them spattered in mud and turf. John has a fist raised in victory because he knows right there that they've won the Nation's Cup. It's one of my favourite photos and I stare at it often as I'm falling asleep at night.

And, lastly, at the far end of the room is my small workshop where I repair, customize and paint my model horses.

It had started as a small collection. I'd get one every Christmas or on my birthday. But then they came out with the kits where you can paint your own model horses and I was instantly hooked. I hadn't been very good at it at first. It had been more about glopping as much colour on them as possible rather than aiming for accurate detail. But gradually that had changed and my skills had improved. Eventually, years later, I'd won my first online model horse exhibition.

Now I win pretty consistently and, not to brag, but I'm known as a bit of an expert in the model horse fandom.

My dad is tolerant of this hobby, although he doesn't like me spending all those hours alone in my room working on projects. He thinks I spend too much time obsessing over getting each model perfect. But he just doesn't understand how much time and attention goes into creating even the simplest of hair-coat patterns. Each piece can take me months to get right. Imagine trying to get every small spot and swirl of an appaloosa down perfectly.

He also doesn't love me spending all that time online, talking to other model horse enthusiasts from around the world. For a smart guy, he has weird ideas about the internet and automatically assumes that everyone I talk to is a potential criminal out to take my money or kidnap me to sell on the dark web.

And he doesn't agree with me that internet friends are just as valid as in-person friends.

The truth is that he just wants me to be interested in something other than horses, even model horses, for once. He thinks I'm overly obsessed with them, that it's my autistic brain that makes me hyperfocus on them, but that's not the case at all. I just like them best, that's all. Why would I want to focus on anything else?

Anyway, it's not like he'll stop me from doing what I like or anything, but you can tell he's just dying for me to take up a new hobby like golf or tropical fish.

I glance over at my newest model horse project, already primed and waiting for its first layer of paint, and sigh.

It will have to wait for today. If I'm planning to ride Flicker in that clinic, then I'm going to have to do a bit of convincing with my dad. And he likes nothing better than a carefully outlined proposal.

I look at the clock. I have four hours to get everything perfect before he gets home. Time to get to work.

Chapter 4

Lena

The bus slides to a stop with a hiss of air brakes a few blocks down from my new house.

"Thank you," I tell the driver, "I'll just get my bike."

Our rental is right on the outskirts of downtown and, luckily, buses come by about every fifteen minutes. It's not the type of neighbourhood where everyone owns a car and the stops are usually packed with people.

The best thing about these buses, though, is that they all have a rack on the front where riders can stash their bicycles. There is only room for two bikes at a time, but so far there has always been at least one vacant spot for me.

The first thing I did when we moved here to the Island was to use my meager savings from my last job to get the bike and a bus pass. That is the ticket to freedom around here. The buses stop a five-minute ride away from the barn, and they go right downtown and to the beach, the inner harbour and the library.

Spending too much time at home when my mom, or

Natalia as she likes to be called, is around isn't always the healthiest choice. So, I have spent many hours just riding around exploring and figuring out the layout of the city.

Tourists might learn the way to museums and the wharf and China Town, but I know the way to the food bank, the thrift store and the library. Also to the kiosk in the mall where I go to pay for my monthly cell phone plan since I don't have a credit card.

I should set myself up as a tour guide for poor people.

I cycle slowly home, trying to put off the moment as long as possible. If I hadn't been so tired from climbing that unexpected hill to Three Sisters, I would have spent a few more hours cycling around town to pass the time. But the exhaustion and the hunger have caught up with me and I can feel all my limbs shaking.

The squat, wood-board houses that line the street are leftovers from a time when this area had been a factory town and they all share the same worn-out, sagging look. There are no shady front porches or gardens here. Just patchy, burnt lawns and narrow concrete paths leading up to a set of steps that end in identical screen doors. Some of the houses have bags of garbage sitting outside that haven't made it to the curb or cars parked on the dried-up lawns.

A dozen doors down from my new house is a yard where the entire front lawn is filled with half-broken cars up on blocks, all in various stages of being taken apart or being put back together.

I keep my eyes averted as I ride slowly by. The tenants are probably car thieves or drug dealers or something, and the safest thing to do is just mind my own business and pretend I don't see anything.

Something metal clatters to the ground right next to me and I jolt, jerking the handlebars and making the tires wobble precariously.

"Oh, did I scare you?"

A boy rolls out from under the car, grinning up at me from under a messy fringe of brown hair. The first thing I notice is that he's not wearing a shirt, and the second thing I notice is that he has these startling blue eyes that stand out against his tan. Smears of black grease cover his bare arms in streaks.

I hadn't even realized that I'd rolled to a stop. And that I'm staring. I look away abruptly, cheeks stinging with embarrassment.

"Sorry," I say quickly, even though there's nothing for me to apologize for.

"Hey, you're new around here, right? I'm...."

I pretend not to hear him. Standing up so I can push the pedals hard, I bike toward my house as fast as possible.

This is not the sort of neighbourhood where I want to make friends. Trust the wrong people and you end up just like my older brother, Garret: an addict with a criminal record who mostly lives on the street in downtown Vancouver. I am so not going down that path.

The houses just get more depressing as I ride along. Some don't even have curtains; they have blankets or flags tacked up to cover the windows instead.

Two children are listlessly kicking a ball back and forth on one of the front lawns, looking hot, bored and unhappy. There is a small, wooded park at the end of the street with a rickety playground, but I've already guessed that it's where the local drug dealers hang out because everyone else seems to avoid it.

My new house is just as run-down as the rest of them. It had been painted green once but most of the colour has peeled away, leaving just the worn exposed wood in spots.

Right, I fish my keys slowly out from my backpack. *Home sweet home.*

· · ·

I shoulder the door open and haul my bike inside behind me. This probably isn't the type of neighbourhood where you can leave your things lying outside on the lawn unless you want them stolen, not even for an hour.

There is no sign of Natalia or her latest boyfriend, Todd, which could mean anything. Maybe they're out on another furniture-gathering trip, or maybe she's moved into his apartment by now. At our old place, with her last boyfriend, she would often be gone for weeks at a time. I was used to fending for myself.

I look around the barren living room and sigh. This is our twenty-second rental house that I can remember and, as depressing as it is, it is not the worst place I've lived in.

When we were little, my brother Garret and I would lie together in the dark and make a game of reciting all the places we'd lived in, ticking them off on our fingers one by one. The falling-down house by the river, the apartment over the biker bar, the cute little cabin Natalia had accidentally set on fire when she'd forgotten to turn off the stove. It seemed important not to forget, somehow. Like the houses were pieces of us, knitting our lives together.

Back then, I loved moving to new places. There was something magical about a fresh start; anything felt possible somehow. And Natalia was always happiest when she had something new to occupy her. New boyfriends, new houses, new lives.

And, in the beginning, some of the rentals had been good, big rambling old farmhouses with more rooms than we could ever need and floorboards that creaked and old blackened steel wood stoves that belched smoke in the air whenever you tried to light them.

Those were fun days with Garret and I exploring all the hidden nooks and crannies and choosing our rooms and peeling back the layers of crumbling wallpaper to see what other patterns lay underneath. And we'd explore the woods and make up games, me always pretending to have a horse and Garret to be some sort of pirate.

But in the winter, the houses would be cold and damp, especially when our electricity would be cut off because Natalia forgot to pay the bills for months on end. We'd often run out of firewood for the finicky old stoves. And our thrift store winter coats were always too thin so we'd be constantly sick with colds.

The novelty of our midnight moves had long worn off by the time Garret was sixteen and so, instead of coming with us one time, he'd simply packed his few belongings in his backpack, smashed my piggy bank open so he could raid it for my meager life savings, and left without looking back. Without taking me with him.

This place is no rambling farmhouse. Inside there are just two bedrooms, separated in the middle by the only bathroom, a living room with a small window that overlooks the street, and then a kitchen and dining room combo.

The kitchen floor is covered with cracking yellow linoleum and the so-called dining room has brown carpet with suspicious-looking stains on it.

Mom's new boyfriend had found us a battered wooden dining room table from somewhere that came with three chairs. And we had a bookshelf where Mom, I mean Natalia, had already piled all of the ratty old hardcover books she'd insisted on bringing with her. She'd been carting them around since before I was born. Which irritated me every time I saw them since I had only been able to bring a handful of my own things. Bringing those stupid books had meant that we'd had to leave behind important things like food from our fridge and the toaster.

"But these are *heirlooms*," Natalia had told me once when I'd complained. "I'm keeping them so I can hand them down to you. And you can give them to your own kids someday. By then they'll be worth a lot of money. You'll see."

I would have preferred the food and the toaster. There was no way I was *ever* having kids of my own, and anyone could tell that those books were worth about ten cents each on a good day. But I didn't tell Natalia that. Arguing with her only led to violence.

I roll my bike down the hall and wheel it into my room, leaning it up underneath the window sill as I turn to survey the nearly empty space.

There is just the air mattress on the floor that Todd has loaned me and an old desk lamp set beside it. That's it.

My limited clothing supply hangs in the closet on the few old wire hangers that had been left behind by the last tenants. My old riding helmet and two second-hand pairs of breeches are placed neatly on the narrow shelf above.

The room is small and painted a pale yellow that is actually kind of pleasant. It isn't the worst room I've ever had, that's for sure. The carpet isn't too bad and the window looks over the fence into the neighbour's backyard behind us. It doesn't open, unfortunately, because somebody in the past had painted it shut, but it's still nice to have a view.

The people behind us have a tree and a small garden. If I squint hard, I can almost pretend that the lone maple and the tomato patch belong to us.

Sighing, I set down my backpack and pad toward the kitchen to find something to eat. Todd had brought us all pizza last night and I'm hoping there might be a slice or two left.

I'm in luck. There is one piece left in the box and I inhale it greedily while I stand in front of the open fridge, my stomach rumbling. There is nothing else in there besides a jar of mustard. And even I'm not desperate enough to eat that.

Back in my room, I unzip my backpack and set my things out in a row beside the desk lamp. It's an unpacking ritual I always do when I come home, wherever home might be, and I find it comforting somehow.

First is my last letter from Garret from the day he stole my life savings and left for good. I've read and re-read it so many times that the envelope is soft like silk and disintegrating at the corners.

The hurt I felt when he left has faded until it's like an old bruise, only sore when I press on it, and I set the letter automatically to the side without reading it for the millionth time.

Next is a braided piece of black mane from my favourite horse at Gretchen's. He was her big show jumper, Critter, who I'd taken care of almost every day for the past two years. He was a towering bay who stood nearly eighteen hands, all rippling muscle. He'd looked intimidating but inside he was the biggest sweetheart, at least to me.

"He's like butter in your hands," Gretchen would say, watching him follow after me like a puppy. She'd even scheduled his vet and farrier appointments for when I could be there because he'd stand so well for me when he wouldn't for anyone else.

I had no reason to explain why this was. It wasn't like I was an exceptionally gifted horse person or anything. I just really loved everything about them. And I think Critter sensed that I was someone who was always on his side and who would try my best to make him happy. I knew when his blanket wasn't sitting quite right or when he needed a day off or wanted to go for a gallop. And he'd responded to that by becoming my best friend.

I press the braid up to my face and inhale, trying to capture that last lingering bit of Critter's essence before setting it down next to the letter.

I prop my phone up against the wall right next to the bed, ready to grab it just in case there is an emergency and I need to dial 911. This is something that I have to do to make myself feel safe. Otherwise, I would never be able to sleep in strange houses alone at night.

"Hello, Jax," I say, pulling out the battered plastic horse that has been with me since I was a little kid. I am well aware that it is silly to be carrying around a child's toy with me everywhere at my age, and even sillier to be having conversations with it when I'm on my own. But Jax is the only thing that I have left that reminds me of happier times when Garret and I were young. And I can't leave him behind when I leave the house if I ever want to see him again.

I'd used to have a little collection of plastic and porcelain horses, mostly presents from Garret, but over the years they'd become broken, lost, or fallen victims to Natalia's vindictive rages.

Jax is the only one who has made it this far. He's a little battered and is missing an ear and one front leg. But he's become like a symbol of hope to me. Like, if somehow he can survive against the odds, then so can I.

"We're fine, Jax," I say. "I got a new job and in two weeks I'll get my first paycheck. Maybe things will be different this time."

They probably won't be different. Natalia has followed the same pattern as long as I've known her. Eventually, the new shine will wear off Todd and our new town and our new house and she'll find a way to wreck it. Todd will be lucky if he lasts the rest of the summer before she dumps him.

There is a rattling sound at the front door and I jolt upright, reaching automatically for my phone before I hear Natalia's familiar voice yelling for me to open up.

She's probably lost her key again.

I hurry to the front door, throw back the multiple locks and the deadbolt and pull it open.

"What took you so long?" Natalia snaps, raising her eyebrows.

"Sorry, I just got home. I got the job."

If I expected her to be excited for me after all this time, I was about to be disappointed.

"Oh." A few different emotions flicker across her face, too fast for me to decipher but, as Todd comes up beside her, she settles on a slightly insincere smile.

"You're just an industrious little worker-bee, aren't you?" she says, her eyes glittering. "You're a shining poster child for capitalists everywhere."

I struggle not to roll my eyes. Natalia does not believe in money, or in working for a living. It's hard to tell what she believes in actually, but it definitely isn't me.

"Well, anyway," she goes on when I don't say anything. "It's a good thing you're home because just look what we found in town."

She waves in the direction of Todd's battered old truck where a dark, wooden dresser is perched in the box.

"It was just sitting there at the flea market," she says, clasping her hands under her chin and opening her eyes wide. "Todd spotted it first and we just knew it belonged here." She reaches out and wraps her fingers around Todd's arm possessively. "I think it's an antique. It's old anyway. I bet it's worth lots of money. A diamond in the rough."

Uh-huh. I try not to look too skeptical as I glance over at the heavy piece of furniture. It looks kind of like junk to me.

"Don't just stand there, Lena. Help get it inside. You don't expect Todd to do it all himself, do you?"

She doesn't offer to help with the lifting, but she does a stellar job of directing us as we heave the oversized thing off the truck and somehow carry it into the house.

When we get to the living room, I have to put my end down and take a break. Todd looks much worse off than me; he's red-faced and sweaty and is making an alarming wheezing sound when he breathes.

"Almost there," Natalia says encouragingly. "Keep going."

I don't think either of us wants to lift it again so we drag it across the carpet instead, the legs making a dry, rasping sound as it moves slowly across the floor toward Natalia's bedroom.

"Be careful, don't wreck the finish." Natalia hovers behind us anxiously as if this was some prized possession instead of a battered junkyard item full of dents and scratches.

We push it up against the wall next to the secondhand bed that Todd has found for her somewhere.

"Hmmm." Natalia stands in the doorway with her arms crossed. She frowns, tilting her head to the side and tapping one finger against her chin. Her long bleached-blond hair hangs around her face and shoulders in ropy, windblown tendrils as if she were the one who'd just done all the work, not us. "I don't know if I like the look of that now. It was better when it was outside in natural light. It looks so dark in here. I wonder if it should go back in the living room instead."

Todd and I exchange a long look over the back of the dresser, and I see defiance flashing behind the surface of his usually mild expression.

Don't do it, I want to warn him. *Don't argue with her or she will dump you so fast you won't even see it coming.*

Poor guy, he is already on his way out and he doesn't even know it yet. Natalia only likes people who follow her directions.

"Well, how about we have a snack and think about it," he says diplomatically after an inward struggle. "I know I need a break after all that lifting. I think I strained something in my back."

"Lifting is good for you," Natalia says, waving a hand dismissively, "it builds muscle." She pauses and runs her gaze over his thin chest and tall, lean frame, arching an eyebrow just enough to show him that she might not think much of what she sees. "Which you could definitely use more of."

Despite my vow not to get attached, I can't help but feel

sorry for him. He's clearly more of an intellectual type rather than an athlete. And if a person has any sort of insecurities about their body at all, then Natalia will ferret them out and use them mercilessly.

He gulps and a blush rises up his neck, staining his pale cheeks. I can see it even through his scruffy beard.

"So, I could eat," I say to break the tension. "But I don't think there's any food in the fridge."

Natalia turns her glittering gaze on me and frowns. "Well, the two of *us* already had lunch in town. Todd took me to this adorable little bistro in a converted warehouse: Chez La Vie. It's too bad you couldn't have joined us. But he was nice enough to bring back some donuts from a local artisan bakery. And, since you were helpful, you may have one."

"Okay, but we could use some actual groceries." I know right away that I have pushed the envelope just a smidge too far. I wouldn't have even brought it up, but my stomach is grumbling with hunger. That single piece of pizza barely made a dent.

Her smile freezes in place and her eyebrows raise even higher. If we'd been alone she would probably have slapped me for saying something like that. But with Todd there she tosses her head back and breaks into jangly laughter.

"Lena, you're like a little old woman sometimes. You're always so serious. So boring and practical. Maybe some sugary donuts will sweeten you up a little."

My stomach growls and I sigh and give in. I don't like sweet things very much. But donuts are better than starving.

"I could drive you for groceries," Todd says, looking concerned. "I don't mind."

Natalia turns her brittle smile on him.

"Oh, don't worry about her, babe, she's good at fending for herself. Maybe her rich horse friends will feed her."

Todd frowns again but doesn't argue and, grabbing two of the least obnoxious donuts, I retreat to my room.

An hour later, I hear the front door slam and Todd's truck start back up. I'm alone again.

Poor Todd. He seems like a decent enough guy and I hate to think about how Natalia is using him.

I know it's disrespectful to think badly of your own mother, but the way Natalia treats her boyfriends is something that has always bothered me.

The thing is that Natalia is beautiful. I mean like movie-star, top-model, possibly-an-alien beautiful. And she knows exactly how to use those looks to her advantage. I've even seen her practicing different facial expressions in the mirror so she can figure out which ones to use on her latest victims. She would have made a terrific movie actress but instead, she uses her powers for pure evil.

Well, maybe not evil exactly. But she loves to manipulate other people into doing things for her even when she doesn't have to. It's practically a sport for her.

"Why do something yourself when you can make other people do it for you?" she'd always say.

She hasn't worked an actual job in all the years I've known her; when she's not on social assistance, she uses a never-ending series of boyfriends to pay her rent, buy food and clothes, and take her places.

The worst thing is that she always picks nice, kind guys as her targets too. It's not like they're even creepy or mean or anything; it would be easier to stomach if they were. It's like she specifically seeks out the meekest people to prey on.

I'd made a vow when I was a little kid that I would never, ever treat people that way. I would never use other people to get what I wanted in life. I was going to work hard and make my way on my own. And, someday soon, I was going to leave my life with Natalia far behind me.

I look up and stare at my reflection in the mirrored closet door reluctantly.

The awful thing is that I think I'm starting to look like her. I can feel it in the way people react to me. That strange double-take people do when something about my appearance draws them in like moths to a flame. Or repels them completely. There is no neutral reaction to me anymore; people seem to either love or hate me at first sight. Just like I've watched them do with Natalia all my life.

That strange girl, Kira, at the barn today was a perfect example. I could see the automatic dislike and mistrust on her face, even though she didn't know anything about me at all. She'd taken one look at me and already decided that I didn't belong there. That there was something wrong with me. It had made me feel ill.

Anna liked you, I remind myself. *And she's the one who counts. You're there for the horses, not to make friends.*

Life would just be so much simpler if there were only horses to worry about and no people. Horses didn't judge you by what you looked like or if you were too poor to afford new boots. They only cared that you were kind and that you took care of them properly.

For some reason, I think about the neighbour boy who'd been working under the car as I'd biked past him. That flash of interest in his eyes when he'd looked at me had made me want to get as far away from him as possible. I didn't like that he'd noticed me at all. It would be too easy for my plans to go off track if I lost focus. If I was going to escape this place next year then I couldn't let anything distract me.

"Guess it's just you and me, Jax," I say, looking down at his vacant, plastic stare with a sigh.

Making sure my phone is safely within arm's reach, I settle in for a long night.

Chapter 5

Kira

Surprisingly, my dad is not as thrilled about the clinic as I thought he'd be.

He comes home, looking exhausted, about an hour before dinner so I wait until he's changed out of his work clothes and poured his glass of wine before I approach him with my proposal.

I've done my best to make it as detailed as possible, outlining the benefits of participating in this clinic in the most convincing words I know. But still, his eyes don't exactly light up when he flips through the carefully prepared binder.

"I don't know, Kira." He sighs heavily, rubbing a hand across his eyes. He's been looking more tired than usual lately. And kind of sad. I hope it's work problems and not because he's worried about me again. No matter how little of a hassle I try to be, he always ends up worrying. It's like it's hardwired into him or something.

"What's not to know?" I point to the two columns on the page in front of him where I've written the pros and cons. "There are literally no cons. I'd get to ride with an Olympic-level rider for free."

"Do we know anything about this horse? Is he safe for you to ride? Will there be anything extra you need for this clinic? I just…"

He breaks off and I sit down beside him on the couch, not sure what to say. I don't know why he's making such a big deal out of this. It's a free horse to ride. End of story.

"Well…" I pause. Traditionally everyone gets new outfits, saddle pads and fly bonnets for the big clinics so that they and their horses look matchy-matchy and professional. At our barn, it sometimes gets to be a bit of a competition to see who can outdo each other. Some of the girls even buy their horses new boots and bridles. But I keep my stuff clean and tidy as a rule. I could get away with not having new things. And finding saddle pads and boots for Flicker would be Marsha's problem, not mine.

"No," I say firmly. "Nothing. And Anna said that Flicker is my type of horse."

I swallow hard, feeling a little guilty about leaving out the other things I know about Flicker. That he's quirky, that he has a buck and a dirty stop, and that some people at the barn would rather miss the John Riddle clinic altogether rather than ride him.

"Well, I guess it's okay then. If Anna thinks he's safe."

He doesn't look entirely happy when I hand him the waiver to sign, though. And I wonder if he's thinking about the fight we'd had when he'd first told me that I couldn't ride Tessa in the clinic.

Dad and I get along great most of the time, even though he has worried about me nonstop since I was small. He had to raise me by himself after Mom left and I think he's done a pretty good job, even when things were at their most challenging.

We both had to work so hard to understand each other when I was little. Being an autistic kid with a neurotypical parent is challenging at the best of times; he just doesn't think the same way I do. But we made it through somehow. I don't think I could love anyone more even though our communication styles are pretty much opposite.

He's always been supportive of my riding. I mean, he still thinks it's a phase I'll grow out of eventually and he definitely doesn't believe I could ever make a living being a professional trainer, but he let me have Tessa. And he pays for her board and all my lessons. Which is pretty amazing.

So, when he'd said *no* to me riding Tessa in the John Riddle clinic, completely out of the blue, it was like my brain couldn't even comprehend it. And then it had sort of exploded and I'd had a complete, ridiculous meltdown worthy of a four-year-old.

To be fair, I've been a John Riddle fan since before I started riding, since I was practically an infant. I've obsessed over his videos for as long as I can remember and he is always pretty much perfect. He's been a member of the Canadian Equestrian Team for years and has been to the Olympics five times. He is exactly the type of rider I want to be. He is brave and kind and never hauls on his horses' mouths or kicks them like a barbarian. He also rarely pulls a jump and he is fast, fast, fast. Like I said: perfect.

So, when my dad dropped the bombshell that I wasn't going to ride with my idol, it was like this wall of red-hot anger had slammed into me from out of nowhere. It was like one of those out-of-body experiences where I could see myself flying around the house screaming and breaking things but I felt detached from it somehow. Like it was happening to someone else and not me.

I'd left a trail of disaster in my wake. I'd even yanked my bedroom door open so hard that the handle drove a hole right through the drywall.

I'd felt so sick and ashamed about the whole thing afterward that I ran to the bathroom and threw up. Worst of all was the disappointed look on my dad's face when I'd come to apologize. He'd looked so sad and lost. As if *he* was the one to blame for all this and not me.

Once I'd stopped crying, my dad had sat me beside him on the couch with a pad and paper between us. At the top, he'd written his salary, which looked like a big, healthy number to me. And then he listed off all the bills like electricity, our housekeeper Grace's salary, HOA fees and taxes on our house, groceries, insurance, the car, etc. And finally, he listed off Tessa's board and my lessons, which come to nearly fifteen hundred dollars a month. Then there were my therapy sessions with Donna and my private school fees. All huge numbers which made my head ache and my palms begin to sweat.

Even someone who wasn't a math genius could see that a very large portion of his income was going directly to *me*. Something I'd never even realized before.

Dad had always said things like "oh well, it's only money" every time he had to pay a bill, so how was I supposed to know that we were operating on a very thin margin? And that maybe he could barely afford to cover his golf membership every year. Something he sort of needed to have for networking with clients and stress relief and things.

Anyway, the short answer was that the John Riddle clinic cost over a thousand dollars for the week, which was probably still a good deal when you take into account that he was a real Olympian and everything, but it was still too much for us to afford.

"Kira, are you listening to me?" Dad's words bring me abruptly back to the present and I shake my head to clear it, glad that I'm here and not back on that awful day.

"Huh, no, sorry. I was thinking of something else."

He smiles at me tiredly.

"That's what I suspected. I asked what's for dinner?"

"Um." I sniff the air and try not to gag. "Some sort of pasta, I guess. Something with garlic."

"I'm supposing that answer means that you haven't been helping Grace prepare the food?"

"I was doing up the proposal for my clinic," I protest.

"We have a deal. You know the rules."

"Yeah, yeah." I sigh. "I guess I'll go make the damn… darn…salad."

"Good choice. And Kira—"

He breaks off and I turn back to look at him.

"Yes?"

"I know you love Tessa and that the barn is your happy place. But let's not go any deeper into the horse thing, okay? It's a great hobby but you don't want it to take over your entire life. It's time to start thinking a bit more about your future. Broaden your interests."

I open my mouth to argue and then shut it abruptly, not willing to risk my spot in the clinic over an old argument we'd had countless times before.

"Okay, I'll think about it," I say, in the sincerest voice I can muster.

I shuffle to the kitchen, trying not to retch at the smell of all that cooking. Dealing with food, and learning how to cook it properly, is one of my challenges this year. My counsellor Donna says that if I want to go off on my own one day, I'll have to figure out a diet that consists of more than white bread and peanut butter.

She's right, I know that, and logically I understand that a

person's body cannot survive on white bread, French fries and un-sauced pasta alone, but my relationship with food is more complicated than that.

When I was younger, I had no words to explain how much the textures and tastes of things freaked me out and overwhelmed me. I mean, most people can just bite into a grape and not even think about it. But for me, a grape comes with about a billion sensations that threaten to shut me down. The colours of the skin, the way it smells, that disturbing hole where the stem used to be, the contrast between the firm, almost bitter, outer layer and gushy, overly sweet insides. And heaven forbid if there were seeds. It was just too much. And that was pretty much the same with every single thing I'd eat. It was like a billion overwhelming sensations with every bite. Only bland, colourless foods with specific textures gave me some sort of relief.

Of course, it got better when I was older and could articulate what I was feeling. And it was better after Mom left and nobody was standing over me with a dripping spatula screaming at me to just bloody well eat my food before she shoved it down my throat.

And it helped once I had a bunch of allergy panels done. Because it turned out that some of the foods that I hated most were things I was actually allergic to. It was literally making me sick to eat them. Now that we have a list of things that won't make me ill, I'm trying to be a bit more adventurous.

"Oh, there you are. Just in time to make the salad," Grace says, leaning her face right over the pot of sauce and inhaling the aroma deeply.

I pretend not to notice. Grace is a nice, grandmotherly type of lady, but I wish she wouldn't put her face so close to the food. It's hard enough for me to eat sauce at all without also imagining all her germs sticking to the tomatoes.

"Sorry I'm late," I say quickly as she looks up at me with a smile.

"That's all right, honey. Do you need any help chopping things?"

I grit my teeth, both at the food-based term of endearment and at the offer to help me assemble some vegetables and store-bought dressing in a bowl. I'm not completely incompetent. Grace still acts like I'm five years old sometimes.

"No, thank you," I say with a sigh.

Chopping things used to be a bit of a challenge for me, as were many things requiring fine motor control. When I first started riding, I could never close my fingers properly on the reins. No matter how hard I tried, I would either drop them or they would just slide through my fingers until I was holding them at the buckle.

It took years of struggle to make my body do what I wanted it to do. It wasn't until I started videoing my rides that I had my biggest breakthrough and started to advance in leaps in bounds. I don't have a natural *feel* like some riders do but, once I've seen a video or a picture of myself riding, then I can usually make the corrections I need. It also works for me to watch videos of great riders. I can often carry those images with me and use them on my own rides. I have a library of images built up in my head that I can use when I need to figure out how to navigate a tricky course or fix a problem. It might not be a conventional way to learn, but it works for me.

"And how did your proposal go?" Grace asks, tilting her head slightly so she can keep half an eye on me so I don't stab myself and bleed out into the lettuce.

"Good, Dad said I could ride in the clinic."

"Well, I'm glad. You deserve it. I know you're happiest when you're at the barn."

Grace understands the way I feel about horses, even if she

doesn't like them herself. And she's one of the few people who didn't laugh when I said I wanted to be a trainer.

It almost makes up for the fact that she's breathing over the sauce again. Almost.

Chapter 6

Lena

When morning comes, Natalia and Todd still haven't returned.

I scarf down two stale donuts for breakfast along with a cup of milk-less instant coffee. It's the worst meal ever, but I know I won't be able to face that hill and a full day of work without at least something on board. Maybe, if I'm lucky, Anna will give me another one of those muffins.

The food bank is only open a few days a week and I've already spent nearly everything in my wallet paying for my phone plan and getting a bus pass, which I kind of needed more than food. Without the bus pass, I can't get to work, so I didn't have much of a choice.

The hill isn't nearly so bad without the blazing heat. I make it almost halfway up this time before I have to get off and push.

Once I'm at the top, I pedal slowly down the driveway, the cool morning air brushing my face and the smell of green grass, horses and hay all mingling together make me almost giddy with happiness.

It's always this way, though; the moment I step on a farm it's like I leave my old worried self behind, relax, and become someone new.

I stash my bike around the side of the barn, close to the metal manure bins at the back where the clients are unlikely to see it, and head into the aisle.

"Good morning," Anna calls as soon as she catches sight of me. "You're a few minutes early. I like that."

"I'm excited to be here," I say, which isn't a lie. But me being early is due to the bus schedule. The next bus would get me here far too late, so it's either show up early or hide in the woods for twenty minutes to kill some time.

"Perfect. Well, you're just in time to help feed. Our head groom, Tonya, is running a little late today, so we're on our own for another few minutes or so. The cleaners will show up in about an hour. I've already given the horses their hay, so you can come to the feed room to see their schedule and get a feel for the way things work around here."

I follow her dutifully to the feed room and hover in the doorway, taking in the neat rows of buckets on the floor and the custom-designed plastic feed tubs that line the walls. The whole room is immaculate. Not a speck of dust or loose bit of grain in sight, which is amazing.

I mean, Gretchen's barn was fantastic, but the feed and tack rooms were always a flurry of chaos and general disorder. The place was swept twice a day but there were so many kids spilling things, muddy dogs barging in and out stealing feed from the buckets, and horses dribbling their breakfast into the aisle that things stayed pretty messy. Here everything is silent and serene. And spookily tidy.

A whiteboard on the far side of the room lists off the horses by name, stall number and description, and there are paragraphs of complicated feeding instructions beside each of them.

I can feel my eyebrows rising incredulously into my hairline. These horses are being fed things I've never even heard of. And so *much* of it. Each one must cost a fortune to feed.

Beside the whiteboard is a whole shelving unit just for supplements, oils, prescriptions and homeopathic preparations.

"It looks overwhelming but you'll get used to it," Anna says, catching my expression. "Most of the owners like to add their own supplements. It's all vet-approved, of course."

"Right." It isn't my place to question it, especially on my first day of work.

"Today I'll mix the feeds and you can deliver them to the correct horses. We'll do the school horses first while you get the hang of it."

I take the buckets from her, two at a time, and hurry back down the aisle to find who they belong to.

The horses' names are stenciled on little wooden squares on each door, thankfully. I greet them all softly, marveling at how well-mannered and beautiful they are. They are some of the prettiest school horses I've ever seen.

Gretchen had fabulous schoolmasters but for the most part, they'd been older, grizzled and a little more banged up than the other boarders. But these animals are fine-boned with huge, intelligent eyes and wide jowls. They are all dressed in immaculate plaid sheets and some have their tails wrapped up in tail bags.

Some of them nicker softly when I slide back their doors, but they all step back politely and wait for me to dump feed in their buckets, pausing until I step away before they move in to eat.

"Wow," I say when I get back to the feed room after my fifth trip, "they're all so well-mannered."

Anna smiles at me warmly. "All the horses that are

employed here are very well bred and are chosen for their temperaments as well as their movement. Our clients expect to have good experiences when they come to ride."

"Okay." I try not to sound too surprised. Gretchen's horses had been mostly seasoned campaigners who taught their riders to ask correctly or suffer the consequences. It had been more about learning the hard way rather than having good experiences.

"Some of the clients' horses are a little quirkier," Anna goes on. "But they fall into line soon enough. We have a top-notch feeding, turnout and exercise routine here to ensure that they receive the utmost care. We also expect our staff to handle them firmly but kindly. Gretchen said you were very good at handling her more difficult horses."

"They weren't really difficult," I say, feeling a little defensive on behalf of my old friends. I clear my throat, modifying my tone to one that sounds more like a good employee's. I'd made up my mind that I was going to hold on to this job no matter what. "I mean, that was nice of her to say so. I loved her horses. Her big jumper Critter was my favourite."

Anna arches an eyebrow. "Oh, I've heard all sorts of stories about him. I seem to remember Gretchen telling me about him dragging a previous groom halfway across the show grounds at a gallop just because he felt like it."

"He could be a little, uh, strong-willed when he wanted to be," I say, fighting back a smile. "But not once you were friends with him."

I break off, suddenly wondering who is handling him now. Does he miss me? Does he wonder where I disappeared to and when I am coming back? It is enough to bring a painful lump into my throat and I have to look away.

"Well, we don't get too many like that here. We focus mainly on our hunters, although there are a fair number of jumpers as well. Most of our horses are model citizens but once in a while, we get one in that needs a special touch. I'll be sure to send them your way when that happens."

She smiles and winks to show me that she's teasing.

After everyone is fed, Anna takes me to her office and shows me her multicoloured schedule plastered on yet another whiteboard. This one takes over an entire office wall.

"This is where the magic happens," she says with a laugh. "It's how I keep track of lessons, farrier, vet appointments and ride times. And our show schedule, of course. But it's also how I keep track of each horse and rider's progress. Everyone is on a particular program. The horses do not get ridden in the ring or jumped every day. Sometimes they just get lunged or they go for a conditioning ride around the property. And some days they just get turned out to decompress. It's all here on the chart, so if you're ever confused about what is happening, or wonder where you're supposed to be, you just have to come in here and consult it."

"Wow," I say, staring at the giant chart in awe. It looks incredibly complicated.

"You won't understand it all right away. We use our own blend of shorthand here, but I expect you'll get used to it soon enough. Everyone does."

She looks at me expectantly so I nod and smile like I know what I'm doing.

I do my best to focus as Anna goes over the chart from top to bottom, hoping that I will remember at least some of it.

The rest of the morning passes in a whirlwind. The head groom, Tonya, a tall girl with her curly hair wrestled into a ponytail, comes rushing in, apologizing to Anna profusely for being late. She barely says hello to me before putting me to work. Not that I mind.

In no time she has me getting the school ponies out and helping the deluge of small riders that appear out of nowhere to brush and tack up. I have no time to be nervous or wonder if I'm up to the job and soon I fall into the familiar routine.

A dark-haired, older girl named Samantha is Anna's assistant instructor. She's the one who handles the younger kids, the beginners and the remedial riders. She seems nice enough and the kids all like her, as do the ponies who nicker when they see her, eager to get the peppermints she keeps in her pockets.

The kids are all nice too but they are nothing like the loud, enthusiastic children that had been at Gretchen's barn. They are all polite and conscientious about caring for their ponies properly, but there is none of the laughing, shouting and running around that I am used to.

Nobody hangs around once their lessons are over either. I was used to an army of barn kids spending the entire day, helping out and watching lessons. But these kids just quietly thank Samantha for their lessons, put away their ponies and disappear.

It is a bit of a culture shock. I find myself trying to keep my voice down and not laugh too loud. Not that anyone has told me that's what I'm supposed to do, but it just kind of feels like I'm in a library or a museum or something.

After Samantha is done teaching the younger kids, Anna's students begin to arrive. Most of the morning lessons are for groups of three to four riders, but I notice that Kira is down on the board for a private lesson on Tessa at noon.

I cross my fingers, hoping that I will be able to avoid her. So far none of the older girls had needed, or wanted, any help getting their horses ready. And they'd all been polite.

As the morning moves along, I begin to relax a little, feeling more at home with the job and with the people. So far, I haven't made any huge mistakes or had anyone yell at me.

Hopefully, I can keep it that way.

Chapter 7

Kira

*W*ednesday morning, I have a meeting set up with my counsellor Donna, before I go to the barn. And, though I usually love my sessions with her, I almost contemplate cancelling. All I want to do is get to Three Sisters and make sure that everything is still all right with me riding Flicker in the clinic. I'd sent Anna an email late last night to tell her that my dad had signed the waiver. And I'd told her about Isla's latest incident and my doubts about the groom. But, so far, she hadn't responded.

Donna's building is downtown, right by the inner harbour, with a view that looks over the water. Even from the waiting room, you can watch the float planes taking off and teams of rowers making their way up and down the gorge and out toward the ocean. It is very soothing. But then everything in her office is set up that way.

Having Donna take me on as a client was the only good thing to come out of being bullied in my last school. Meeting her for the first time had felt like I'd been tossed a life preserver in a stormy sea and towed to shore.

Donna is nothing like the old counsellors I've had in the past. She's autistic too, for one thing, and is also completely brilliant. She's written four books and has spearheaded lots of cutting-edge research projects on the way the brain works. She's just fascinated by the way people think. And she also happens to be a great counsellor.

Donna was the first therapist to say flat out that there was nothing wrong with me, that my brain was unique and interesting and that I was under no obligation to change myself in order to fit in with so-called *normal* society.

It had been kind of a revelation and I'd left my first session practically crying with relief that finally, somebody not only understood me but actually thought I was valuable.

Since then, I've been going to see her once a week. Every visit is different. Sometimes we talk about difficulties I'm running into or we just talk about horses or the research work she's doing.

It was Donna who told me about Temple Grandin, who is this animal behaviourist who also happens to be autistic too. Dr. Grandin is an expert on the way animals think and see the world, and reading her books had made me approach horse training much differently.

Donna also has some really interesting theories as to why some brains are so-called "typical" and some are not. She thinks that autistic, or neurodivergent, brains developed at the same time as neurotypical, or so-called regular, brains because prehistoric tribes needed both types of people in the group to survive.

Like a person who could see intricate patterns or be hyper-sensitive to changes in noise and light and temperature would be able to sense when danger was coming more quickly than a neurotypical person. But a neurotypical person would have a strong social desire that makes working together in a tribe easier.

In the beginning, everyone got along, but Donna says that when the world became industrialized, neurodiverse skills weren't valued much anymore. In fact they were kind of shunned. Not only that but the noisy, smelly, fast-moving world was overwhelming and painful to people like me.

Anyway, that's just a few of the things that make her different from other counsellors I've had in the past. She is always interesting and always supportive. And, although she's happy to help me develop skills so I can fit in with other people if I *want* to, she's also fine if I just prefer to be myself and not have to mask, or fake, who I am. Which is pretty refreshing.

"Come in, Kira," she says happily, ushering me into her office. It's a beautiful place, painted in soft greys and with that same view of the harbour. There is no annoying fluorescent lighting or computers buzzing. Everything is serene and made so that her clients can relax and let their guard down. It's like a sanctuary here.

I don't need any prompting to talk to Donna. I tell her all about my week, my excitement to ride Flicker and about the newest incident with Isla. And then I tell her about the groom with the boots.

"Hmm," she says when I get to that part. She's not the type to come right out and tell me when I'm maybe not being entirely fair, but I've come to know what her sighs and raised eyebrows mean.

"You think I'm wrong about this girl?" I ask, frowning out the window at a rowboat struggling its way through the water.

"Not necessarily. I'm not going to tell you to ignore your instincts. I know you've been through a lot at school and it's probably hard to trust people anymore. It's not a bad thing to want to protect yourself."

"Definitely. I won't make that mistake again."

"There's no harm in being selective on who you let into your life. But, you might want to give her a bit of a trial period before making a final judgement. So far the things you've mentioned are mostly about her appearance: the boots and the fact that she's pretty. Those might not be things she can help."

"Hmmm." I tap my fingers against my knees. "Maybe. But I still get the feeling that she's hiding something. That she's a fake."

"You could very well be right about that. I suppose only time will tell. But, she also could have been nervous at her job interview and not acting quite like her normal self. You might want to give her time to settle in. Now, how are the cooking lessons with Grace going?"

The rest of the hour passes quickly after that and soon I'm back in the car and headed to the barn.

Donna, as usual, has given me a lot to ponder, but right now all my thoughts have turned toward the horses.

Wednesdays are my favourites because it's the day I get a private lesson instead of having to ride with Isla.

"Did you get my message? My dad says it's okay that I ride Flicker," I call to Anna breathlessly as soon as I hurry into the barn. But my good mood drops when I see that *girl*, that fake groom, hovering a few paces behind Anna.

I skid to a stop, suddenly remembering the email I'd sent to Anna last night and feeling the smallest stab of guilt. What if Donna was right and the girl was just nervous? She looks nervous now, her eyes wide as she stares at me like a deer in headlights.

I glance down at her feet and am relieved to see that she's taken my advice and found herself some new boots anyway. So that's something.

I send her the tiniest of half-smiles and she answers with a surprised grin of her own, the type that lights up her whole face. Which makes me feel even more guilty for sending that email.

"Kira, that's great." Anna beams at me. "It's going to be such an exciting chance for you. I was almost certain he'd say yes so I made up a schedule with Marsha yesterday. Oh, this is our new groom, Lena. Lena, Kira has been riding here since she was small and she knows this place inside and out. You two are just about the same age actually, only a few months apart. Feel free to ask her if you have any questions. She knows all the horses and our routine."

"Hello," the girl says quietly, "it's nice to meet you."

I nod, not quite knowing what to say. The truth is that I still don't trust her, no matter what Donna says. Instead of answering, I pivot around to go get Tessa.

"Kira, wait," Anna calls. "Sorry, there's been a change of plans. Marsha would like you to ride Flicker in your lesson today so she can see how you two do together."

At the words *change of plans* my whole body tenses up and my throat closes painfully.

"But, this is Tessa's lesson," I say automatically, "it's on the schedule."

The new girl, Lena, raises her eyebrows at me as if I've said something bizarre and I feel a rumble of anger rising in me.

Anna exhales slowly. "Sorry, I should have called you last night to give you a heads-up. I know that it's usually Tessa's lesson, but Marsha is being very generous in giving this opportunity to you. She's paying for your lessons up until the clinic too, remember, so you might have to be a little flexible even if it's difficult."

"Okay." I swallow hard, pushing back the anxiety that is flapping its sharp wings in my chest. Adapting to sudden changes is one of the hardest things for me to deal with. It makes me feel suddenly unanchored or off-balance, like my world has tilted and anything terrible can happen.

"You can have a free ride on Tessa too, of course," Anna says, looking at me hopefully. "And we'll make up your lesson another time. Think of it this way: now you get to spend longer at the barn."

"Right." The tension in my shoulders loosens a little. I will go on a trail ride after my lesson. Tessa loves exploring the woods. I can spend as much time as I like out there.

"Great, now do you want to go up to Barn A and collect Flicker or should we have a groom bring him down?"

"I'll get him," I say quickly. I haven't even seen him up close since last year. The more time spent getting to know him, the better.

"All right, I'll be at the ring when you're ready."

▭

I trot up the hill as quickly as I can and then pause outside of the magnificent entrance to Barn A. Despite the fact that I'd never want to board here, I have to admit that it is beautiful and grand.

Everything about it is huge. The aisles are extra wide, the stalls are double the size of the ones in Anna's barn, and everything is spotlessly clean; even the stall bars are polished.

I gulp, feeling another flare of anxiety. It's a little like walking into a new school on day one when you don't know anyone or where anything is.

But then I see Flicker standing in the aisle and everything else is forgotten. This is why I'm here: for him. He is already fully groomed and partially tacked up, his hooves gleaming with polish and not a hair out of place. But, for all that, he doesn't look as magnificent as he did the last time I rode him. He seems smaller somehow and his eyes don't have that bold, proud look that they used to have.

I step up to him slowly, holding out my hand for him to sniff, but he raises his nose slightly, looking over my head so he can stare past me down the aisle like I'm not even there.

"Hey there," I say softly, noticing other slight changes in the way he carries himself. The proud arch of his neck is nearly gone; the muscling is on the underside of his neck now instead of the top and his shoulders look narrower. I step back, frowning at the slight dip in his spine behind the saddle and the hollow spots on his haunches. It's not like he's skinny or anything, his sides are well padded, but it's like the whole shape of his body has changed.

A smiling groom appears suddenly beside him as if she's materialized out of thin air.

"You must be Kira," she says excitedly in a sing-song voice. "I'll just get him bridled up for you if you're ready."

She stares at me expectantly and I realize after too long of a pause that she's waiting for some sort of response.

"Okay, thank you," I say finally and she beams at me, immediately lifting a complicated bundle of leather from a hook on the wall.

"Wait, what is that?" I ask in confusion. "Is that actually his bridle?"

I've never seen such an odd setup in my life. From what I can see, the bit is actually two bits welded together, one lying sort of on top of the other. Each piece is made of twisted metal and three rings are joining them together at each end. The noseband isn't like anything I've seen before either. It is made of a thick piece of hard, black plastic and then has long shanks attached to a separate pair of reins. Two metal curb straps run underneath his jaw, one for the bit and another one set higher up that I can't see the point of. A yellow elastic tube is attached to each rein and it runs up through the bit along the cheek pieces, running over his poll.

Still more straps run down between his front legs and attach to the girth. I can't tell if it's part of a martingale or something else. It's hard to see where everything attaches.

"Oh, I know this looks complicated," the groom says, laughing, "but it really does the trick for him, Darla designed it herself."

"But what is it all for?" I ask, completely bewildered. Most of the horses at Barn B just wear plain snaffles, like Tessa, or light pelhams. I'd used martingales, of course, and even draw reins. But this…contraption is like nothing I've ever seen before.

"All you need to know is that it slows him down and makes him rideable," she says, smiling at me earnestly, her dark pony-tail bobbing up and down. "And it doesn't hurt him unless he plays up. Have you used a double bridle before?"

"No." I shake my head back and forth slowly. At least Flicker doesn't seem to care that his entire face is crisscrossed with various straps. He is still looking off in the distance like he doesn't even know we're there.

"Well, don't worry, it's not hard once you get the hang of it. This isn't a true double bridle anyway. The two bits in his mouth are fused together so that's just one rein to worry about. The second rein goes to the hackamore; that puts pressure on his nose if he's not listening to the bit. And this part here runs over his poll and attaches to the top rein to give you more leverage, and this part here runs up from his girth, through the lower bit and attaches to this rein to help him keep his head down. Like a modified German martingale. See?"

She gives me a reassuring pat on the arm, probably sensing just how over my head I might be right now.

"You'll be fine. It looks more complicated than it is. Just ride like you always do and it will all make sense. Okay?"

"Okay," I say weakly as she shoves the reins into my hand.

"He's a good boy once you get to know him. I'm sure the two of you will get along. Do you need help leading him down to the ring?"

"Um, no thank you."

"Well, have a great ride then. I have to get my next horse ready." She bustles away, her ponytail bobbing.

"Right, Flicker, I guess it's just you and me," I say, giving him a pat on the neck that he doesn't respond to. He follows me politely enough though, and as we step outside into the sunshine, I feel a little better.

There is a light breeze on my face and I inhale the fresh smell of newly cut grass. Gradually, I relax and just enjoy the sound of Flicker's hooves crunching down the gravel driveway beside me.

When I get to the ring it's not just Anna there. Marsha is standing beside her at the fence, with one leg in a cast and a crutch under each arm. She's leaning toward Anna, speaking so rapidly in her thick accent that I can't understand her even though she's certainly loud enough. And, on the other side of her is Oliver.

What on earth is he doing here? I think in irritation. *This is my lesson.*

He doesn't even look at me. He's focused totally on Flicker, his wide mouth pulled down into a frown.

I look away quickly before memories of my last school overwhelm me and distract me from my lesson. Oliver had never bullied me himself, but it had been some of his so-called friends who had been my worst tormenters. Honestly, he probably doesn't even remember that we'd gone to school together. We might as well exist in completely different universes.

"There's my boy," Marsha bellows suddenly, making both

Anna and Oliver jolt in alarm, "there's that handsome lad. Come say hello, love-bug. Come see your mama."

Flicker doesn't acknowledge her at all; instead he stares off in the opposite direction, watching the horses out on the pasture with what I imagine is a look of longing in his large eyes. A soft nicker rumbles in his throat.

"It's okay," I whisper to him. "We've got this."

I look up and see that Oliver's blue-eyed gaze has switched to me, and he's frowning even deeper. But before I can start freaking out over that, Flicker shifts beside me, bumping his nose on my arm softly and I turn all my attention on him.

Forcing myself to focus, I lead Flicker over to where Marsha is shouting some story to Anna at the top of her lungs. I don't know why Marsha thinks that everyone around her is deaf, but she seems to only have one voice level and that is full shout.

"And then the dirty bugger dropped his shoulder and dumped me in the corner. He's a rogue, that one. You have to watch him every second."

"Why am I just learning all this now?" Anna looks angry. "Darla assured me that he would be safe for Kira to ride."

"Oh, he is. He's safe as houses. Most of the time. Just don't let your guard down for a second."

"Great." Anna rubs a hand across her forehead. "Kira, I'm not sure this is the best idea."

I almost agree with her. Flicker seems like a different horse than the one I rode last year. But there is also something about him that makes me want to give him a chance. A real trainer can't just ride the horses they like, after all; they have to take all of them unless there's a good reason not to. Also, Flicker is my only way of riding in the John Riddle clinic.

"I'll be careful," I tell Anna firmly. "Let's just flat him and see how he goes."

Anna makes a face but nods reluctantly, and I lead him

over to the mounting block quickly before she can change her mind.

She follows me and puts a firm hand on the reins while I get on.

"What on earth have they put on his face?" she asks, raising her eyebrows at the contraption on his head.

"I have no idea; I was hoping you would know. The groom said that Darla had it custom-made. She assured me that Flicker liked it and told me to just ride him like normal, whatever that means."

"Great." Anna sighs heavily again. "All right, let's get this over with. Your father is going to kill me if anything happens to you."

"It won't," I say with more confidence than I feel.

Marsha's calfskin saddle is buttery soft when I climb aboard and I sink into it about an inch, marvelling at how anything can be that comfortable. My own tack is nice but this is something extra.

"Just take it slowly, Kira. And if I see things getting out of hand then I'm going to tell you to get off. And you're going to listen to me for once. Understand?"

"Yes, I promise."

"All right, let's not worry about the bridle too much. You have soft, following hands so you're not going to hurt him. Just keep a light, even contact for now and we'll see how he goes."

Anna adjusts my stirrups and checks my girth, all things she would never do if this were just a regular lesson. For some reason, this particular situation is making her extra nervous.

"Got him?" she says, looking a little white-faced.

"Yep, I've got him."

Holding the double reins feels weird, but it's not as awful as I was expecting. I take a soft contact and wait for Flicker to move out into the rambling walk that I remembered from last year.

But, instead of striding out, he takes these little, hesitant mincing steps forward as if he's afraid to move any faster.

"Ask him to move out more, Kira," Anna says and I give him a little nudge, which he ignores.

I ask again and then bump my legs lightly against his sides. And instantly, like a spark of electricity has been lit under him, he becomes a different horse.

His ears flash back at me for a second and then his stride opens up until his head is bobbing with the rhythm and his entire body sways from side to side. It is a huge walk. It catches me off guard for a second; it feels like I'm riding an elephant in the jungle.

Anna walks with me, keeping pace and watching me with her arms crossed over her chest.

I look away from her pinched expression, because her nerves are a bit contagious, and concentrate on Flicker instead.

"Good boy," I say softly.

I take a deep breath, running over a mental list of all the things I want to accomplish in this lesson. I want to get to know Flicker better, I want him to relax and enjoy himself and also not kill me.

"All right, buddy," I whisper, "that's not very much to ask. We can do this."

The big horse flicks another ear back at me briefly. I adjust myself a little deeper in the saddle, draping my legs softly around him, trying to get a feel of his stride.

I massage the reins gently with my fingers, trying to start a polite conversation with him, but there is no answer. Instead of mouthing the bit or responding to my question, he suddenly ducks his head right in, arching his neck until his chin nearly touches his chest and I have to shorten the reins abruptly so I can feel him again. His free-moving walk compresses until he's mincing along.

"Trot him out!" Marsha bellows from the rail. "He doesn't

need to spend all that time lollygagging around. Get him moving."

I glance over at Anna, not sure what to do about him ducking his head in like that.

"Leg before hand, Kira. See if you can ask him to stretch down." Anna frowns. "Don't trot until you're ready."

But Flicker is not interested in stretching down. He keeps his nose tucked so tightly against his chest that I can hear his breathing getting raspy, like his airways are being cut off. I've never encountered anything like it before.

"Trot on," I say gently, asking him to move forward. He doesn't hesitate, he steps up obediently into a trot, but it's not the powerful, free-flowing gait I remember from last year. This trot is compressed and choppy and he is still carrying his head in that funny tucked position, like he's afraid to go anywhere near the bit.

"Easy, Flicker," I say in a crooning voice. "You can relax and stretch down." I let the reins out as much as I dare as we weave around the jumps. And it seems to take forever but gradually he stretches his nose down and his stride opens up a little. Finally, he snorts and heaves a little sigh, and I can feel some of the tension easing out of him.

"Nice, Kira," Anna calls. "Just stay right there with him."

"Good boy," I whisper, scratching my fingers against the top of his withers.

And suddenly he finds his second gear and his whole way of moving changes again. It's like he's suddenly been plugged in and I can feel the power and energy running through him.

I can't help but grin; I can see how riding a horse like this could get addicting.

"Let's see a canter," Marsha shouts as we're passing by, making both Flicker and I jump a little. I really wish somebody would shut that woman up.

Despite myself, I feel a shiver of nerves run up my spine at the thought of cantering Flicker. He's been perfectly well-behaved so far, if a little strange, but I'm under no illusions that he won't try something cheeky at any second. I've seen him launch Marsha into the air from a standstill.

Still, I can't jump if I don't canter, so I shift my seat bone back and ask him to step up.

For a second, his ears flatten and he surges forward, rocking me in the saddle. But, when my hands close protectively on the reins, he shuts down instantly, ducking his head in that weird way again and compressing his steps so that he's nearly cantering in place like a carousel horse. It is the weirdest thing I've ever felt.

"Good job containing him," Anna says reassuringly from the center of the circle we're on. "Just keep him there for now. We can ask him to stretch out once he settles."

"I give him a good crack on the rump when he does that," Marsha says loudly. "He just needs to know that it's time to get to work. Lazy sod."

Ignoring her completely, I keep my breathing soft and even, trying to make my whole body as loose as possible so that Flicker can relax. But there is zero response. It's like he's on auto-pilot and nothing I do gets him to untuck his nose from his chest.

"You're a good boy," I whisper, finally bringing him down to a walk. "We'll figure this out."

"Do a few more transitions from walk to canter, Kira, and then we'll try him over a couple of low jumps."

We canter a few more times in both directions but I don't get that stretchy, relaxed feeling out of him again. Flicker is eerily obedient but there is no back and forth communication between us at all. He listens to my instructions like he is a robot but that's it.

"Just a few small jumps," Anna says, "and then that's enough for him. We want to end on a good note. Let's just trot that vertical there and see how he reacts. If he's good, then carry on down the line for the next two jumps. Let him take his time; no rushing. If you don't like the way he feels then just circle and ask again."

I move Flicker in a large circle, trying to get him to stretch and relax again, but when it's obvious that's not going to happen, I point him at the first little jump. But, the second Flicker realizes that I want him to jump, his entire body changes.

His sides go rock hard and his neck is suddenly damp with sweat. I can feel his heart jackhammering away. He leaps into a canter and tosses out the smallest of bucks. It doesn't unseat me, and I can't tell if he's anxious or just excited. Either way, he's barely listening to me at all.

"Slowly, slowly. Easy, Flicker," Anna says. "Circle him, Kira, and get him focused again."

There is no mincing, rocking-horse canter now. He is full of adrenaline and barely in control. I take a firmer hold on the reins and instantly that snorting, dragon of a horse disappears again like I've flipped a switch. It's a bit spooky, actually. All the energy leaches out of him, his nose tucks into his chest again and, though he's still cantering, he barely moves forward at all.

"Huh, well that's different," Anna says, tilting her head as she studies him. "There's no middle ground with him, is there? Okay, well, let's try that jump again. Keep him exactly like that."

But when he's facing the jump again, Flicker suddenly jerks his nose in the air, ripping the reins painfully through my fingers, and takes off before I can even blink. I don't even have time to react before he's at the little vertical. But he's come at it so fast that he arrives deep and has to scramble over it. He bucks on the other side and charges down the line, as if he is trying to get the whole thing over with as fast as possible.

"Kira," Anna bellows, "get control over him right now.

He's not Tessa. You can't let him do that. Take charge or get off him."

I can tell by her voice that she is scared. I'm a little intimidated too, to tell the truth. And she's right this time. Flicker is completely telling me off.

As much as I hate getting handsy with this ridiculous bit, I need to get on top of this situation before something bad happens.

"Whoa, Flicker," I say firmly and take a hold of the reins, sitting back in the saddle.

He tosses his nose in the air, and I'm not sure if he's just frustrated or if the bit has hurt him. He jerks his nose again, nearly pulling me forward out of the saddle, but he still doesn't slow down.

"No, that's enough." I turn him in a circle, using my body and my reins to make it smaller and smaller. I sit deep and massage the reins, first one and then the other, hoping for some sort of response. But there is nothing. With an angry grunt, he surges forward again, towing me along, and kicks his left leg into the air, cracking it against a jump standard.

That's it. I pull the inside rein hard, using all my body weight against him, until he skids to a sudden stop, puffing and blowing from all the excitement. And, just like that, all the fight is gone again. He tucks his nose in again, his whole body trembling.

Feeling a little shaky myself, I reach down and pat his sweaty neck. I am known for having light and kind hands; that's the only type of communication that will work with Tessa, but there are some moments on horseback when you just need to get your point across. However you can.

"Good job," Anna says quietly, and I look up to see that her face is white and her eyes are huge. We must have really scared her. "Do you want to get off?"

"No." I shake my head. "I think he's fine now. I'll let him catch his breath and then try again."

After a few moments, I move him into a walk. His ears are swivelling around but at least he's listening to me. I move him back into a trot and then a canter. He is scarily obedient, back to being a robot rather than a fire-breathing dragon.

We drop back down to a trot and I point him at the vertical again, saying "whoa" firmly the second his ears flash forward. I half-halt the second he speeds up and he keeps from rushing until we're a half-stride away. He shoots over it but he doesn't buck on the other side this time.

I let him canter a circle, drop down to a trot and finally a walk.

"Good boy." I pet him on both sides of his neck and shower the praise on him.

"Good job, Kira," Anna says, sounding as relieved as I feel, "that's enough for him for today. He can walk on a loose rein."

I've already let the reins out to the buckle but he hasn't changed his head position at all. He just keeps walking along mechanically like a wind-up horse.

"Do you think he's okay?" I ask Anna. "I didn't hurt him, did I?"

"No, you did what you had to do to get him to slow down. But this behaviour of his is pretty odd. I'll need to talk to Marsha and Darla about him. It's a little concerning."

I look over at the rail, remembering for the first time that I have an audience. But Marsha is looking down at her phone, not even paying attention to us and Oliver is gone.

To my surprise, I find his absence strangely disappointing.

Chapter 8

Kira

"Can I ride him up to the barn?" I ask Anna hopefully. Flicker is so tired now that I can't imagine him causing any trouble.

"If you feel comfortable," Anna says. "Just stay alert in case he acts up. I'm going to talk to Marsha. You and I can debrief about your ride later. We need to decide what our next step is."

"I want to keep riding him," I say quickly. Because, despite his tantrum and his weird quirks, I'm already hooked on this horse. I can never resist a puzzle or a mystery. And I can't resist a chance to help a horse who is obviously a little lost right now.

Flicker doesn't untuck his nose until we are halfway up the hill and then he gives a huge sigh and sort of shakes himself like a dog. It's like he's just woken up from sleepwalking or something. He looks around with interest like he's surprised to find himself outside of the ring.

"Good to have you back, Flicker," I tell him. "I'm sorry I

pulled on your mouth. But you weren't listening at all. Why did you take off on me like that?"

He marches on, not interested in sharing any of his secrets with me.

Near the top of the hill, I catch sight of a trio of riders heading toward me and I groan inwardly under my breath.

Isabelle Carlisle, daughter of the farm owner, and her aggressive little sister, Alice, are two of the three sisters that give Three Sisters Farm its name. They all keep their many horses at Barn A, of course.

Some people love them, or claim to love them, but all three sisters have a reputation for being unpredictable and a little scary. Isabelle is my age but that's where the similarities end.

Unlike her other two sisters, she only has one horse, a lovely grey named Shamus, and last summer she caused a bit of a scandal when she switched completely from jumping to dressage. Which is how Three Sisters got the new dressage ring in the first place. She just asked for it to be built and there it was.

Her little sister Alice is a complete terror. She just says whatever she likes, hurting feelings left and right, and has an awful temper. I've seen her yell at parents, coaches and even small children when they get in her way. She's ten times worse than Isla, and that's saying something.

They're getting closer now and I don't know where to look. I settle on smiling vaguely in their general direction and steer Flicker to the edge of the wide driveway to avoid them.

"Hello," a kind voice says as they all stop in front of me, practically blocking the way. "Did you have a good ride?"

I look up, startled, caught off guard by the friendliness of the question. I recognize the speaker right away as the neighbour girl who rides the draft horses. Right now, she's mounted on one of Alice's ponies, a leggy grey with a sculpted face and finely pricked ears.

"Yes, it was good, thank you," I say nervously, my words barely audible. My hands are suddenly slick against the reins. The girls all stare at me, waiting for me to say more, and I gulp, trying to figure out the easiest way to escape. It's funny how riding a tricky horse like Flicker doesn't scare me but facing this trio of possibly hostile girls terrifies the pants off me.

"It's amazing that horse can function at all with that thing on his face," Alice says sharply, glaring at Flicker's bit.

"Um, yeah, it's Marsha's bit," I say, clearing my throat. "I usually ride in a snaffle."

Alice swivels her angry gaze my way, looking me up and down slowly as if I'm a weird specimen under a microscope. She gives off the same hostile vibe as the mean girls at school had. There is something volatile and unpredictable about her.

"Stop being so cranky. It's not like it's her fault, Alice," Isabelle says, rolling her eyes. "Darla designed it and Marsha has pretty much ruined poor Flicker by now anyway. Clara would lose her mind if she saw him now. She'd literally die."

I remember suddenly that Flicker once belonged to Clara Carlisle, the oldest sister, the one who'd been sent away last year. There were so many rumours about the terrible things Clara had been caught doing that it was hard to know what was truth and what was just a story. She'd been a great rider, though. I remembered that.

"Did he buck you off?" Alice demands, still looking at me like I'm dirt. She blinks suddenly, then puts a hand up near her helmet as if she's blocking the sun from her eyes. Which is weird because the spot we're standing in is slightly shady.

"No," I say slowly. I wish they'd all just move along. Flicker shifts a little underneath me as if he can tell how anxious I am.

"Well, that's a first. But don't get too confident. Flicker gets everyone off eventually."

"Come on Alice, she's a good rider." The draft horse girl smiles at me again, her gaze calm and reassuring. "I've seen her on that spicy chestnut mare. Anyway, we should get going. Nice to meet you."

She nudges the pony she's riding along, sends me one last smile and, thankfully, leads the others away.

I sag in the saddle, feeling like I've safely navigated a minefield. Or hostile negotiations with an unpredictable species. Humans are the absolute worst.

But, as soon as they're a safe distance away, I can't help but swivel around in the saddle and stare after them. I would never want to hang out with Isabelle or Alice, but a pulse of envy washes over me as I see how easy they are with one another. Casually talking and laughing, already forgetting that I exist. I wonder what it would be like to have a bunch of friends like that. It's been a long time since I've been a part of a group.

I'm so lost in thought that I don't look up until we arrive at the barn. Flicker has marched himself right up to the outdoor wash bay and is standing there, waiting not-so-patiently for me to get off so he can get back to the business of being a horse.

"Hello, you must be Kira," a friendly voice says, and I look down to see a guy with kind brown eyes staring up at me. It takes me a second to recognize him. It's Ben, the barn manager for Barn A. And he also happens to be the brother of the dressage coach, Elliot.

"You can hop off; I'll take him from here."

"Okay," I say, sighing with disappointment. I had hoped to spend some time hanging out with Flicker, just getting to know him better. That was how I'd won over Tessa when she'd first arrived.

"He's pretty hot still," I add, stalling for time. "I could walk him around the driveway again to cool him out more."

"Nah, don't worry about it. He'll feel better after a good bath."

He's staring at me, waiting for me to get off, so I have no

choice but to kick my feet out of the stirrups and hop lightly to the ground.

I step back and watch as he quickly untacks Flicker, unhooking the extra straps that run through the girth with practiced ease and unbuckling the complicated bridle from the gelding's head, replacing it with a soft leather halter.

My gaze zeroes in on the foamy area on the edge of Flicker's mouth and I freeze. There is a large grey, hairless patch that looks like an old scar at the corner of his mouth. For a second I panic, thinking I've hurt him during my ride today, but it's an old mark, a scar or callus, that must have happened a long time ago. It still looks awful, though.

When Ben turns away to switch on the water tap, I reach up and snag the bridle off the hook, taking it over to the next wash bay, which is empty. I hang the thing up and study it carefully, trying to figure out how the whole contraption works. Why are there two bits and what on earth is the strap that goes over his poll for?

"Do you need help with anything?" Ben is there, staring at me kindly, and I wonder how long I've been standing there puzzling out the bridle. Sometimes, when I'm really concentrating, I can easily lose track of time.

"Can you tell me how this all works?" I ask, feeling a little embarrassed. I mean, I'd just ridden the horse for an hour, I should have had some sort of idea of what I was doing.

"Sure, no problem. Let me just get this guy set up under the lights. Then I can show you. I'm Ben, by the way."

"I know. You're Elliot's brother."

"That's right. Have you ridden with her yet?"

"Yes, just once. She was very helpful with my mare Tessa. I'm going to take more lessons when Anna is away showing."

I watch as Flicker saunters inside to stand under the lamps that will dry his coat properly. They also have some sort of healing, infra-red properties that are supposed to improve performance or something.

"Don't feel bad if you haven't seen one of these before," Ben says, appearing beside me again. "Marsha had it custom made for Flicker and then Darla added even more modifications. It's definitely one of a kind."

"Good," I can't help myself from saying.

Ben smiles and shakes his head. "Anyway, you can see that the mouthpiece is like a stronger version of an elevator bit. This is the curb strap underneath."

I nod. I haven't seen many elevator bits but I understand the concept. It puts pressure on both the poll as well as the mouth of the horse. But I'd never heard of a bit that had two mouthpieces like that.

"He used to just blow through any contact Marsha had," Ben is saying. "He kept running away with her and it was getting dangerous. One of them was going to get hurt."

"Okay," I say dubiously, thinking that maybe Marsha should have just learned to ride better. But, miraculously, I don't say this out loud.

"The noseband piece with the shanks is just a mechanical hackamore. That puts pressure on his nose rather than his mouth. It has its own curb strap up here, see?"

"Right, so what's the weird poll strap for?"

"It keeps him from lifting his head too high to evade the bit. And then the German martingale helps to keep his head tucked and in a frame. It's all set up to give the rider maximum control."

Something in the flat tone of his voice makes me look over at him.

"It's like a nutcracker," I say finally, feeling a little sick. "No matter what he does, he can't get away from it."

"Well," Ben says slowly, "the individual pieces are not so

bad on their own, as long as they're used tactfully and with the horse's best interests in mind."

He breaks off and I wonder if he thinks any of this is for Flicker's sake. It all seems to be about controlling him so that Marsha won't get killed, not about teaching him anything. Maybe with a different rider Flicker might not even need all this junk on him.

"Thank you for telling me all this," I say finally.

"No problem." He smiles at me kindly. "I always appreciate when a rider is interested in understanding how things work. And someone who puts the welfare of the horses first."

Ben looks at me meaningfully and I can't help but think that he's trying to tell me something.

But I don't get to find out because the next thing I know he's saying goodbye, scooping up Marsha's tack and disappearing back into the barn.

The afternoon sun is climbing as I thoughtfully make my way down the hill toward Barn B. I'm wondering what John Riddle will say when I show up for the clinic riding Flicker in that contraption.

John Riddle has a reputation for being able to successfully pilot his horses around with minimal gear. Sometimes it looks like he's directing them with his mind or something because his aids are invisible. I've watched videos where he's jumping big courses using only a rope around his horse's neck. I hope he doesn't kick me out of this clinic.

The barn is quiet when I get back; all the horses and riders are already hiding away from the heat of the day. Despite the heat, I love riding at this time because there are hardly any people around. Sometimes it's like I have the whole place to myself.

There is no sign of Anna or Marsha so I swig down a bottle of water and go to find Tessa.

She's in the far corner of her field. But when she sees me at the gate, she throws up her head dramatically, lets out a piercing neigh and charges toward me. I'd like to think that it's her undying loyalty and not the carrots in my pockets that has her running so fast in my direction.

When you're not riding her, Tessa looks, and acts, like a horse from the movies. She is strikingly beautiful, for one thing. She has a coppery coat and a blaze and four white socks that come up past her knees. Picture perfect.

Her good looks are why Anna first took her on as a prospect even though the mare had a reputation for being a bit scary to ride. She'd been a racehorse once and then somebody had bought her off the track to give her a new career. But it had been a bad match and by the time we got her, Tessa had become both angry and unpredictable.

Tessa might be built like a model hunter, but in her head, she is a jumper through and through. More like a steeplechaser maybe. All she wants to do, from the second you put your foot in the stirrup, is gallop and jump. She only thinks forward, forward, forward.

She is honestly the best horse I've ever ridden, but not everyone likes her. She has lots of opinions and she doesn't like being told what to do unless you ask her in just the right way. She's spicy and sensitive and she used to have these complete meltdowns whenever things didn't go her way.

But, from the first moment that I met Tessa, I knew that she was the horse for me. And I think that she knew it too. She never pins her ears at me or acts snarky. And she probably looks forward to our rides almost as much as I do.

Tessa had turned out to be a terrible resale prospect so, when we discovered that the mare and I were actually a good match, Anna decided to cut her losses and practically give the horse to me.

It is a good deal for all of us. Anna gets all the board and lesson money from my dad once a month, I get the world's best horse to call my own, and Tessa doesn't end up being shipped for meat or made into glue. Win-win-win.

I slip the halter over her head and organize her silky forelock so that it's lying perfectly flat against her broad forehead. One of the many things I like about Tessa is that, despite being a large animal who likes to roll in the dirt, she always looks clean and tidy. It's like her coppery coat just repels dirt and mud somehow and she sparkles with good health.

She walks beside me happily, her head swinging from side to side as she strides along. I drape an arm over her neck and run my fingers through the fine strands of her neatly-trimmed mane, just enjoying the warmth and companionship from her.

The barn is nearly empty as I brush and tack up. Lunch has been fed to all the horses and the aisle is freshly swept. This is the time of day I like best. That quiet lull when the morning riding is over and the horses are having their afternoon siesta.

A few grooms are having lunch in the feed room and I can hear them talking quietly, faint laughter drifting down the aisle.

I sigh happily as I slip Tessa's gear carefully into place and buckle her leather boots onto each leg.

Tessa opens her mouth obligingly for the soft snaffle and I think again about the grey, hairless callus at the edge of Flicker's mouth.

"Come on, girl," I say to her softly and she clops down the aisle, practically pulling me toward the ring.

Anna's lessons are over and there is nobody in sight. Tessa starts to head automatically toward the main ring with the jumps and, for a second, I'm tempted. But, it's one of the barn rules that we're not allowed to jump without supervision, even if we're good riders.

"Sorry, Tessa," I say, leading her into the smaller dressage ring. "No jumping today."

I head over to the mounting block, a feeling of joy washing over me. Just having the whole ring to myself so I can quietly work on things without anyone interfering is almost as satis-fying as jumping. Almost.

Tessa strides out boldly the second I'm in the saddle and I feel her whole body alive with electricity.

I nudge my feet into the stirrups and let her move into a trot right away.

Ideally, a rider should give every horse some walking time at the start of a ride to warm up their muscles before moving on to faster work. But Tessa is not interested in anything slow. Every fiber of her being wants to go. It's easier to just let her warm up in her own way rather than fight with her.

I post along with her quietly, waiting for her to settle so I can let her find her balance, and gradually, she stops thinking like a racehorse. Her rhythm slows and her body softens as we do a series of figure eights and serpentines, flowing lines and circles.

I don't have a lot of fancy words to describe the way riding Tessa feels to me. How when she hits her groove, it's like we're flowing through the air together, almost flying and the whole world just seems right. Time slows and it's like it's just her and me in the center of the whole universe. Anna calls it riding in the zone. Donna calls it a transcending moment. But, whatever it is, it feels great.

Tessa snorts softly, caught up in the spell of movement just like me, and I gently flex her to the inside, seeing if I can ask her to stretch her poll.

We cruise around happily like that for a while before I start working on the harder stuff. Some things, like jumping and going forward, are always easy for Tessa. What's more difficult for her is to slow down and work on the more collected, fiddly things.

Leg yields should be an easy exercise but for some reason Tessa hates them. She always wants to lead with her shoulders, and every time I shift my leg back to push her haunches over she just wants to canter. I have done lots of reading on how to fix this, but Tessa doesn't seem to care what I try. She just does what she wants anyway. This is one of the reasons I'm looking forward to having Elliot's help this summer.

After a few half-successful attempts, I give up and let her canter on. I've learned that there is no point in drilling her until she gets frustrated. It's better just to move on to something else and then try again later.

Tessa's canter is light and springy and, for just a second, I close my eyes so I can enjoy the feeling of flying. So, I am not prepared at all when she does a sudden violent spook at the gate that nearly unseats me.

"Sorry," a voice calls out and, once I've calmed Tessa down, I turn to see the draft-horse-girl mounted on Alice's haywire pony, Jiggs, just outside the ring. She's doing her best to make the pony stand still while she unlatches the gate but the animal is practically shaking in place, eyes wide and white-rimmed.

"I thought you both saw me," the girl says, patting Jiggs' neck as he scoots through the open gate. "I'm Fina, by the way."

The pony prances and gnaws the bit nervously the whole time, never relaxing once.

"Kira." It comes out stiff and unfriendly because my heart is still beating hard from the spook. I'd come close to falling off, which is rare, and it has shaken me a little.

"Sorry for startling her," Fina says, moving Jiggs into a wide, prancing circle around me. "Your mare is beautiful and you ride her so well. She can't be an easy horse."

"Are they supposed to be easy?" I ask curiously. Riding has never come naturally to me. I've always had to fight hard for every skill I've gained.

"Well, I just mean that some horses are much more forgiving of our mistakes. My girl Beatrice puts up with so much. And, she looks out for her rider. If I was about to fall off she'd do her best to keep me in place. Not like Jiggs here. He'd just dump me and run."

She laughs and I can't help but join in. That's exactly what Jiggs would do. Probably what any pony belonging to Alice would do if they were smart.

I look down at Tessa's glossy neck, trying to imagine her saving me on purpose if I was falling. I can't quite picture it.

Jiggs scuttles sideways and the girl, Fina, laughs again, not bothered by his shenanigans.

While she's focused on him, I take a second to study her surreptitiously. Although I have seen her dressed in normal breeches and polo shirts before, she just as frequently wears brightly coloured leggings or these tasseled, knit shawls, or soft leather boots that look more like moccasins than actual riding boots.

I've never seen anyone just wear whatever they want like that and it's both horrifying and intriguing.

Today she's wearing suede-looking boots with cream breeches and a purple beaded T-shirt with a picture of an upside-down sloth on it.

I realize suddenly that she's stopped Jiggs and is watching me curiously, probably wondering why I'm just staring at her silently like a creeper.

"Why aren't you riding your draft horse?" I blurt out because that's the first thing I think of that sounds somewhat normal. "Jiggs is Alice's pony."

Fina looks a little startled at my abrupt question. "Beatrice is going to have a foal," she says finally, "so she gets to lounge in the pasture for now. I'm just helping Alice out this week with a few rides since she hasn't been feeling well lately."

"Oh," I say, wondering how you could tell a healthy Alice from a sick one. She always looks cranky to me.

"I usually ride up at the indoor when it's this hot out, but Darla's there right now. And she's kind of scary."

She grins at me when I start to laugh.

"Terrifying," I agree. "I'd never ride with her."

"No, me neither. Elliot and Anna are so much better."

"So, when is your foal arriving?"

Fina's whole face lights up with excitement. "Not until late July or early August. She was bred late so she's going to have a summer baby. I can't wait. She's going to be such a good mom."

Her excitement is contagious and I have a sudden desire to see the foal too. I've never even seen a baby horse before.

"Do you think maybe I could come to see it when it's born?" I am surprised to find myself asking.

"Yes, of course. That would be great. Actually, I'm sort of looking for extra hands to help me exercise our horses too. My brother has a job on campus this summer and Isabelle can't come over as much now that she's doing her internship."

"You are?" For some reason, in all the time that I'd been begging to work at Three Sisters, it had never occurred to me that I might be able to ride somewhere *else* instead. But then I think about my dad's warning when he'd agreed to let me ride in the clinic.

"I doubt my dad would let me," I say with a sigh. "But I'll ask him. He's all about me finding new hobbies."

"Ew, like what?" she asks, crinkling her eyebrows.

"Good question. Um, maybe golf? Competitive ping-pong? Ceramics? Just anything but horses."

She snorts with laughter and then stops abruptly when Jiggs skitters sideways.

"Well, let me know. You can ride over to our place from here, actually; our farm is right next door. You don't have to ride on the road or anything; there's a shortcut between the properties. It's easy. I'm sure Anna would say it was okay. And, er, I guess your dad."

Fina gives me a bit of a pitying look and I wonder if she bothers to ask anyone before she goes off on adventures. She can't be much older than me but she seems pretty independent. She doesn't look like the type who needs permission.

I chew on the inside of my cheek, something I do when there are too many thoughts flying around inside my head.

"Well, I'd better get this guy working before he melts down," Fina says, laughing as Jiggs snorts and scuttles sideways again. "I've never met such a scaredy-cat pony before."

She trots off without saying another word and I decide that I've had enough human interactions for one day. I have a sudden, desperate desire to be alone.

"Let's go on a trail ride, girl," I whisper, running my hand down Tessa's silky neck and turning her eager nose toward the woods. "Just the two of us."

Chapter 9

Lena

ell, one thing is sure, that girl can ride. Although I'm not sure that horse is exactly sound. I edge back toward the barn as soon as it's clear that Kira's lesson with Flicker is nearly over.

I've been secretly watching the lesson from under the shade of a nearby tree, hoovering down my tiny supply of food where nobody can see me.

I was lucky enough that I'd had anything to eat at all. One of the riders had brought another box of muffins from the bakery for everyone and I managed to sneak two when nobody was looking. And I'd also snagged a carrot from the horses' treat shelf which I'd eaten quickly and guiltily, not sure that it didn't count as stealing.

Tonya had told me that I could eat anywhere on my break, but I'm not quite sure if I'm allowed to be out here watching the riders or if the grooms are supposed to stay hidden somewhere. It's hard to tell what the rules are here.

A boy my age is leaning against the fence watching the lesson and as soon as I move, he catches sight of me. I freeze as he straightens up and moves my way, eyes locking onto me speculatively.

I groan, turning abruptly back toward the barn. I don't know who he is but the last thing I want to do is draw unwanted attention on my first day. Maybe I'd made a mistake eating out here after all.

"Hey, wait up." The guy catches up to me easily as I near the barn and falls into place at my elbow, not even having to hurry on his long legs to match my pace. I send him a sidelong glance, doing my best to mask my irritation with a polite smile. I know the drill: be polite and professional, and don't mix your work life with your personal life.

"Do you work here?" He blinks at me owlishly and rubs a hand across his face.

"Um, yes?" I look down at my brand-new polo shirt with the Three Sisters logo emblazoned on the front. It's pretty obvious that I work here.

"Great, I'm Oliver. Can you give me a tour? I just want to see how the other half lives."

I stare at him, not sure what he means by "other half." Grooms, girls, or just poor people in general?

"Uh, it's my first day so..." But he's already walking away, peering up and down the aisle like he's assessing prime real estate.

"The stalls are smaller," he mutters, "but there's more turnout. And less yelling."

I watch him in fascination, hoping that I'm allowed to just let strangers walk in here, not that I'd know how to stop him. I'm not sure if he's a potential boarder or a student or an undercover health inspector.

He doesn't even notice me watching as he walks slowly down

the aisle, staring into the stalls, so I take the opportunity to check him out. He's good-looking in a thin, bookish sort of way and he has bright green eyes. He's dressed in breeches and tall boots but his T-shirt has some sort of retro Star Wars design on it.

I look away quickly, just in case he thinks I'm staring at him for the wrong reasons. He's cute and all but he's not my type. Not that I'm allowing myself to even *have* a type until I'm free to move away from home.

For some reason, my thoughts flick back to the neighbour boy I'd seen working on his car yesterday, but I push them firmly away. No complications.

"This is my first day," I say again, trailing behind him, "so I'm not sure where everything is yet. But I can grab one of the other grooms if you need a hand finding something."

"What?" He glances up, looking startled to find me still standing there. "Oh, right, no thanks. I just wanted to look around. I keep my horse up at Barn A but she's ready for a lighter workload now. I don't want to keep competing with her full-time. So, do you like working here so far? How do you find the atmosphere? Do the horses seem happy to you?"

"Ah." I step back, unprepared for all the questions. "I'm still learning my way around. But yes, the horses seem happy. And the people have all been nice so far."

Most of them, I add silently, thinking of Kira.

"Good to know. Well, thanks for your help. I'll be in touch if I need anything else."

Without giving me a chance to answer, he turns on his heel and walks toward the exit, whistling, not looking back.

"Who was that?" Tonya pokes her head out of the feed room and raises her eyebrows at me. From behind her, I can see two of the other grooms sitting on folding chairs, listening eagerly.

"I have no idea," I say, shaking my head. "Some guy

named Oliver? He said he's looking to partly retire his horse. Maybe he's looking to board here."

"Oooh, *that* Oliver," she says. "I heard he was thinking of stepping Bluebell down. That will cause some drama around here if he decides to board with us."

She smiles like drama is something she's looking forward to.

I don't see Kira again until much later when she brings Tessa in after a trail ride.

I'm busy helping Samantha get some of the school ponies tidied up before they go away for their show next week. They already all have full body clips but their bridle paths need to be cleaned up and their fetlocks and their ear hair touched up. Just a general overall tidy.

Unlike Gretchen's sometimes feisty horses, all these ponies stand rock-solid while I zing the tiny clippers over them. I think they've just gone to so many shows over the years that they no longer care.

Over in the next grooming stall, I can hear Kira murmuring softly to Tessa as she fusses over her and I smile despite my general dislike of the girl.

No matter how rude she'd been to me earlier, she sure likes her horses. I'd been very impressed at how she'd handled Flicker. He seemed pretty emotionally damaged to me and I thought she'd been very tactful on how she'd ridden him. He couldn't be an easy horse to manage.

I drift off in my own thoughts and don't look up again from the pony I am working on until the sound of clopping hooves brings me back to the present.

When I glance up, I see Kira leading Tessa back out toward the pasture and two girls are standing side by side in the aisle near me, staring after her.

I blink in surprise at the expression on the face of the girl nearest to me. Her eyes blaze with pure hatred as she glares at Kira's retreating back and there is a cruel twist to her mouth.

"Kira's horse is so fancy," the other girl says wistfully, oblivious to her friend's simmering rage. "If she showed her, they would definitely clean up."

"That mare's a freak, Rebecca," the angry girl says sharply, making her friend jump in alarm, "just like her rider. Kira's not as talented as everyone believes. She's just Anna's pet, that's why everyone thinks she's so good."

"You don't think Kira's a good rider?" Rebecca turns toward her friend with an incredulous look.

"Oh, she's all right, I guess. At least here at home. But take her to a show and she falls to pieces. She says she's autistic or something, but I think she's just making it up to get attention. Plus, have you noticed how skinny she is? I heard that she has some sort of eating disorder. I knew a girl who went to her last school and she said that Kira was a complete nut case. They had to kick her out because she threatened a bunch of girls."

"I think those must just be rumours," Rebecca says quietly.

"No, that's the reason why Anna treats Kira like she's made of glass or something; she's afraid she'll go ballistic and hurt someone. Nobody can do anything to upset her precious student. It's so gross."

"Hmmm." Rebecca changes the subject abruptly. "I can't wait to show Rio. It's so fun to teach a green horse the ropes, isn't it? It's all new and exciting to them."

"If you say so. I just wish Hilty wasn't such a dog. I need a better horse. I told my dad we should sell her."

"Oh, Isla, don't say that. Hilty is so sweet. Anna says…"

"I don't care." Isla shoots a hard look at her friend. "She thinks Hilty is a good schoolmaster or something but I don't need a babysitter anymore. I need something that can really jump and that looks flashy. Hilty is only holding me back."

They disappear into the tack room and I slowly finish off the pony I'm working on, my mind mulling over the conversation.

"There, don't you look pretty," I tell the pony, who I think is named Daisy. I slip her summer sheet on and lead her back out to her pasture.

It has been a long, overwhelming day and my whole body feels heavy with exhaustion. I can't help thinking about what the two girls had said about Kira. I was guessing that most of it was just gossip; she didn't exactly seem like the violent type who'd get kicked out of school for fighting. But I wondered about the showing thing. Why would someone that talented and with such a nice horse not want to show off? It didn't make any sense.

And yet, maybe it was the same way I didn't really care if I rode or not. I just wanted to be around horses, to take care of them and be surrounded by them. The riding part hardly mattered as long as I could spend my life with them. I wonder if Kira felt something similar.

That Isla is something else, though, I think with a little shiver. The look on her face had been a little unhinged. I will have to do my best to avoid her as much as possible.

Turning the pony loose, I stretch out my aching back and head back to the barn to start the next one.

Chapter 10

Kira

The next week is probably one of the most interesting I've ever spent.

The day after our first ride, Marsha announces that Flicker is being put up for sale. Luckily I am to have the ride on him until after the clinic and right up until he sells.

"I'm already looking at new horses," Marsha bellows loudly in my direction. "This time I'll be buying something without so much—personality. Maybe I'll pick a mare this time."

I stare at her in alarm, thinking about all the sensitive mares out there about to be subjected to Marsha's stellar personality.

Still, I am grateful to be able to ride her horse. The whole week, Flicker continues to be unpredictable and difficult; he sure doesn't go easy on me, that's for sure. Even though I am trying my hardest to make friends with him.

As focused as I try to be for all my rides, there is always that moment, usually right when I point him at his first jump, where he either explodes in a bucking fit or takes off. And it isn't like we're asking too much of him or that he is in pain or anything either.

His tack has been professionally fitted to him and Marsha tells us she's already had the vet, a massage therapist and a chiropractor out to see him too.

"There's nothing wrong with that horse," she tells us firmly, "I've given him plenty of chances. And I've spent way too much money on him. He's just spoiled. The sooner he moves on to a new home the better."

I am lucky she'd decided not to list him for sale until after the clinic. I have a feeling that she is hoping John Riddle will take one look at him and convince one of his upper-level friends to buy Flicker. Though I have my doubts that's ever going to happen. I am just crossing my fingers that I'll be able to control the horse well enough that I won't be kicked out of the clinic on the first day.

Anna and I keep his workouts easy and try to end on a positive note each time no matter how weird he is being.

"With our tight timeline, we're not going to risk pushing him," Anna says. "We just want you two to get to know each other and be working as a team by then."

We would need a little luck for that to happen. I still can't stop him without resorting to being heavy on the reins. But I am getting better at reading his moods; more and more often I can catch him ahead of time and redirect his energy before he can do anything too naughty.

As much as I wish I could take that stupid bridle contraption off of him before the clinic, it looks like I am stuck with it until I can figure him out a little better.

Marsha doesn't show up for any of my lessons after the first two. But, twice I'd caught sight of that groom, Lena, watching us. And nearly every day Oliver drops in, leaning against the fence to stare for a few minutes. He always disappears before my lesson is over, though, so I still have no idea why he is so interested in Flicker.

Each night I sit down and study the videos of my lessons, poring over them for clues on how I can give Flicker a better ride. I knew it would take time. And that I probably wasn't going to be able to work any miracles before the clinic.

Despite the setbacks, our rides do improve a tiny bit every day and I find that I look forward to my time with him almost as much as I do my rides with Tessa.

I have to cram in as many lessons as possible with Anna because in a few days she will be off to the mainland for the week-long spring show. She'll be back in time to give me one last lesson before the clinic but, for this upcoming week, I'm going to be Elliot's problem.

As the weekend draws near, the whole barn is buzzing with excitement. Everyone bustles around acting busy, the trailers get packed and then repacked, fights break out, there are tears, and people make up. Horses lose shoes or hurt themselves in silly ways. And I just try to avoid it all.

This is exactly the sort of chaotic environment that makes me avoid showing like the plague. I can hardly wait for them all to leave so the barn can be peaceful again.

And then on Friday morning, I suddenly get my wish. The whole place is practically empty, like a carnival that had packed up its tents in the night and fled to the next town.

All I can hear is the chirping of birds and the soft rustle of the horses in their stalls finishing breakfast.

The air is fresh and cool; there will be no more mid-day rides for me this week. My lessons with Elliot are all scheduled for first thing in the morning. First up will be Flicker and then Tessa; it's going to be a flat-work boot camp for all of us.

Flicker is already tacked up when I get to Barn A. An unfamiliar dark-haired groom is waiting with him outside right next to the mounting block, eager to boost me on board.

"I've got it, thanks," I say, avoiding her help by quickly springing aboard. I nudge my toes hastily into the stirrups before she can place my feet in them for me. This barn takes full service to a whole new level.

"Do you need me to give you a lead down to the ring?" she asks, holding a lead rope in one hand as if she's about to clip it to his bit and drag me to the ring like a little kid.

"No, I'm good." I nudge Flicker away before she can come any closer. "See you."

Flicker seems to be in a mellow mood, although I know that can be deceptive, and he strolls with me happily to the ring, his head swaying with every step.

"Hi, Kira," Elliot calls out enthusiastically as I ride Flicker into the ring. "Nice to see you again. Are you ready for a week of fun?"

"I am," I say, pushing down my nerves. I know I have nothing to worry about with Elliot, but I can't help but be a bit anxious anyway. It's just the way I'm built.

"Me too. So this big guy is Flicker, yes? I heard he has a bit of a reputation. Ben said his owner finds him kind of hard to handle."

"Yeah," I say, looking around quickly to make sure that Marsha isn't hovering nearby to overhear. Thankfully we are alone. "She's afraid of him. She can't stop him and he bucks her off."

"Oh, dear." Elliot studies me as I circle Flicker around her. "How is he with you, though?"

"Different. I mean, sometimes he feels amazing and then other times he has these huge tantrums. He also does this strange thing where he ducks his head to his chest whenever he wants to avoid contact or not move forward."

"Well, that bit is pretty intense," she says, narrowing her eyes at it. "I'd probably avoid contact with it too."

"I know, I know," I say. "But he can get strong really fast. He'll go from ducking in to suddenly grabbing the bit with his teeth and tearing off. And he will barely ever relax and stretch down. I can't figure out how to get him to do that."

"He sounds like a complicated project. Does he like to jump?" She tilts her head, studying him as he walks. For once he's not doing that weird mincing walk that he usually starts our rides with; he is striding right out, flicking an ear now and then uncertainly in Elliot's direction.

"I think so. At least he's good at it. He usually tries to bolt toward the jumps rather than away from them. I think he just wants to do things his way."

"Okay, well, we'll see if we can figure that out. He seems to be stretching down now for you. What happens if you pick up the contact?"

I shorten my reins, but I'm a little nervous so it's too abrupt for Flicker and he immediately ducks his nose in right to his chest.

"I'm not doing that to him," I say quickly, holding the reins at the buckle to show her that Flicker is the one pulling his nose in so tightly all by himself.

"Oh, boy, that's an interesting habit," Elliot says, eyeing the horse with a frown. "Let's see if we can get him to stretch down again. Leave the reins for now and let's just get him loosened up. Do some serpentines and some circles; no straight lines. Don't use your hands to bend or turn him, just your seat."

The next forty-five minutes leave me exhausted and puffing with effort but sort of triumphant too. I have never worked so hard in my life to get a horse to do something so simple as stretch his nose down. But, finally we manage to do some wide trotting serpentines and figure eights with him stretched out, relaxed, with his poll low and his back rounded. It is such a small thing but it feels like a complete miracle once we've accomplished it. And Flicker hasn't offered to take off or buck even once.

I glance up, noticing that Oliver has appeared out of nowhere. He is leaning his elbows on the gate, studying us quietly.

"Let's end it there on a good note," Elliot calls. "Pat him and tell him he's a good boy."

We haven't even cantered but I feel as limp as a noodle. He is the complete opposite of riding the quick and responsive Tessa. It felt like I was pushing his big body through molasses sometimes. My legs are actually shaking with effort.

"Do you need a break before your next lesson?" Elliot asks, looking at me in concern.

I must look as overheated and shaky as I feel.

"No, it's okay. I'll just ride him up to the barn and then I'll grab some water while I'm getting Tessa tacked up," I say. But I break off when I see Oliver opening the gate and walking toward us.

"Hi," he says, smiling like we are old friends. "I've come to lend you a hand. I can take him up to the big barn for you. Lena already has Tessa in the cross-ties."

I stare at him in complete astonishment which is quickly replaced by simmering anger.

"What?" I say sharply. "I didn't ask for your help, and Lena shouldn't be touching my horse without permission. Tessa doesn't like other people."

"Um, she's a groom and that's her job?" Oliver says, looking at me like I'm completely crazy. "I'm just trying to help. You're supposed to say thank you."

"Why would I thank you for butting in where you don't belong?"

We glare at each other until Elliot clears her throat.

"Maybe you should let him take Flicker up to the barn for you, Kira. It would save a lot of time. Then you'd have a chance to grab some water and a quick snack. You're probably hungry after all that work."

I stare at her suspiciously, wondering if she's actually suggesting that I'm hangry. Then my stomach rumbles and I sigh heavily, reining in my temper with effort.

"Fine," I say through gritted teeth, jumping to the ground. "Whatever." I shove Flicker's reins into Oliver's hands and stomp off toward the barn to make sure Tessa isn't being manhandled.

Elliot is right that I need water and a chance to catch my breath. And maybe a snack. The lesson had been harder than I'd expected.

Tessa is indeed in the cross-ties when I get inside and her fly sheet has been taken off and folded neatly over her stall door.

"I didn't brush her," Lena says quickly, stepping away from the horse before I can snap at her. She gulps, looking at me nervously. "Oliver said I should bring her in for you but I thought you'd want to groom her yourself. I know you enjoy that part."

"Um, okay," I say, surprised that she even knows that much about me. I glance at Tessa who is just standing there, looking half-asleep and completely relaxed. "I'm just going to grab a quick water and then I'll be right back."

The barn is full of people now, and most of them are little kids. Someone has turned the radio to a classic rock station and cranked up the volume, something Anna never allows, and the aisle is filled with riders tacking up their horses. All laughing and chatting more loudly than usual.

Although I usually hate lots of noise, the festive-but-relaxed feeling in the air is kind of nice. There is no tension and everyone seems so happy.

Everyone but Isla, that is. She stomps by me with Hilty's tack, a sulky frown on her face. I guess she's still grumpy that she hadn't been allowed to go to the show.

"Get out of my way," she says rudely, jerking her elbow out at the last minute so it bangs my arm.

Lena stiffens and frowns after Isla, muttering under her breath as she goes to help one of the younger kids do up her pony's girth.

I'd been so busy the last week that I hadn't had time to think about my dislike of Lena. I had to admit that for a fake groom she was doing a great job with the horses. She was very patient with them and I hadn't yet seen her say an unkind word or act harshly to them.

I feel a small twinge of guilt. There is a tiny chance that Donna had been right and that maybe I'd been overly harsh judging this girl.

I head straight for the mini-fridge to grab some water and a power bar. As soon as I guzzle it down, I step back out into the aisle.

There is Tessa gently nuzzling Lena's cheek like they are old friends, and a little more of my mistrust toward the new groom thaws. Tessa does not like very many people, which gives her a bit of a reputation at the barn of being temperamental and hard to deal with. So, if she's actually deciding to like someone here, then I am definitely not getting in the way of that.

I send Lena a tentative smile, which only seems to startle her, and then quickly get to work. Tessa is already pretty clean so I just do a polish and pick her feet before tacking her up.

"Come on, princess," I say as I lead her out of the barn. "Let's get to boot camp."

· · ·

My ride with Tessa is easier in some ways and harder in others. And one of those hard things, unfortunately, is that Isla is also having a lesson at the same time.

Samantha has a class of four crowded in the ring beside us so there is plenty of time for Isla to hover near the rail and hiss nasty things at me as I pass by. She's like some sort of ventriloquist, able to make me clearly hear her insults while she keeps her lips completely still and stares off innocently in the other direction.

"Useless freak," she whispers. "Nobody likes you. You can't even ride."

I try not to let her bother or distract me but after a while, the steady drip of insults gets to be too much and I just avoid that side of the ring as much as I can.

Oliver is back too, leaning over the fence and watching me, although he looks more friendly and less judgemental than Isla.

I make my way through the lesson somehow, and Elliot comes over beaming, telling me what a wonderful mare Tessa is and what a great job we're doing together.

"She's your perfect match, Kira," she says. "Let me know if you ever want to take her out to a dressage show. I think she'd do well."

"We don't show," I say quickly before she can get too carried away. I had thought everyone at Three Sisters knew about my aversion to showing by now.

Elliot's eyes flicker in surprise. "Fair enough. Well, you could always try a virtual show too if you want to get a judge's feedback. Lots of people are doing that now."

"Like online?" I have never heard of such a thing.

"Sure. We'd just film your test and send it in. No pressure. Anyway, it's something to think about. I have to get ready for my next lesson, but I'll see you tomorrow."

I nod, already mulling over what she'd said. While I have no interest in showing just to get ribbons, I do really like feedback. And I'm not against winning things either as long as I don't have to subject myself to crowds of people.

"That was a good ride, Kira," Oliver says, meeting us at the gate.

"Thanks." I'm already feeling kind of bad at the way I'd snapped at him earlier. Sure, he shouldn't have done anything with Tessa without asking me first, but he'd been trying to help.

"Oliver!" I jolt as Isla's high-pitched voice carries across from the other ring. "Over here! I want to talk to you about the party."

Oliver makes a groaning sound and shakes his head. "I'd better get over there or she's going squawk louder."

I can't hold back my snort of laughter.

"You're not dating her, are you?"

"No way. Her family knows mine, sort of, and there's a fundraiser tonight that I couldn't get out of. I have to wear an actual suit if you can believe it."

"Sounds awful."

"Oh, it will be. And Isla has it in her head that we'll be going together."

"Well, have fun with that." I glance over to see that Isla has now parked Hilty right at the edge of the ring and is sending me death glares, completely ignoring that Samantha is calling, trying to get her attention.

"So, I'll see you tomorrow," Oliver says, turning away and jogging over to the other ring before I can answer.

I stare after him, wondering why he has suddenly appeared in my life on a daily basis, and it isn't until I realize that Isla is still glaring at me that I finally look away.

Chapter 11

Lena

My first week at Three Sisters is exhausting but wonderful too. I already love Anna and the horses and I feel reasonably confident that I am not going to be fired any time soon.

Every night I flop onto my slowly-deflating air mattress and fall asleep almost instantly. Between the biking and the barn work, and all the stress of life with Natalia, I am existing in a state of exhaustion nearly all the time.

But, when Monday comes and I have to face my first day off, I am forced to take the fact that there are zero groceries in the house, seriously. There is a whole other week before I get paid, so there will be no trips to the grocery store until then. If I want to eat then I will have to brave the food bank instead.

Natalia has always been awful with money. She just never seems to care enough to figure out how it works. If it's there in her bank account, then she will spend it without any thought to the future.

At least I don't have to worry about the rent these days.

Our grumpy, beer-guzzling landlord was one of the rare people not the least bit charmed by Natalia and he insisted on setting up rent payments directly through the bank. So, the second her monthly welfare cheque comes in, the rent portion automatically goes right to him.

It had pissed Natalia off big-time but it had been a huge relief for me. At least it took my constant worry about being evicted down a notch.

We were just lucky that Todd had loaned her the money for the damage deposit. I mean, he *called* it a loan, so I don't think he yet realizes that there's no way he's getting the money back. Ever.

Natalia's cheque covers the rent and basic utilities but it's not always enough for food. So that's where the food bank comes in.

It is not a place I want to go to. I do not like being poor and desperate and I always feel mortified whenever I first step inside. There is also that lingering terror that someone I know is going to catch me shopping there. Or that strangers on the street are judging me as some sort of inferior drain on society.

Once, when I was about nine or ten and had been tagging along with Natalia, a man in a business suit had glared at us both as he'd passed the lineup. He'd looked us both up and down like we were garbage.

"Talk about intergenerational poverty," he'd said loudly to a posh-looking guy beside him. "No wonder this country is going downhill."

And that's when Natalia had started screaming at them, calling them capitalist pigs, and chased them down the street with a can of pepper spray. Everyone had stared at us, and that encounter had stayed with me ever since like a bad stain.

I hadn't understood exactly the definition of the words but the tone had been clear. And googling the phrase at the library later had confirmed it. They'd meant that Natalia was a drain on society, a parasite, and I was going to grow up to be exactly like her. That I was stuck in a cycle of being poor and struggling for the rest of my life. And that my kids, if I had kids, would be too.

It had really affected me at the time and made me depressed and anxious for weeks.

Still, if I want to work with the horses then I need to eat, so it's just another unpleasant chore that needs to be done.

The biggest problem is that I can't afford a taxi and I can only carry so much on a bicycle. I'll have to be smart about it and only pick things that aren't too heavy.

The food bank is right downtown in a fairly nice area that looks safe enough. Some cities have them in the worst part of town and there are drug dealers and sketchy-looking people hanging outside the door, but this place looks just like a regular shop front.

I take a deep breath and a quick glance around to make sure nobody is watching me before pushing my bike inside. There is a proper bike rack outside, but I don't have a bike lock yet and I can't risk it getting stolen; it's my only way to the barn.

"Good morning," the older lady behind the counter calls loudly, making me jump. I usually like to get in and get out without attracting too much notice.

"Um, hi," I say quietly, gulping a little.

"I'm Carla, I'm a new volunteer here." She says each word loudly and slowly as if I'm hard of hearing or something. "Welcome."

"Okay, thanks." I can feel my cheeks starting to burn. Some food banks just let you go in, get a bag of food and get out. But others want to get a whole bunch of information from you and try to sign you up for programs or something. I have the feeling that this might be the second type.

"Have you been here before?" She peers down at me through her glasses and reaches for a clipboard and pen.

"Uh, no." I sigh.

"No problem. I'm here to help. Just write your name down here and then sign in. We don't need any more than that."

"Okay." I hover my pen over the paper, wondering whether to use my real name or not. Finally I decide not to. Who knows where this sort of information ends up.

"All right," she peers down at the paper. "Kira, is it?"

"Yes," I lie. "That's right."

"You can just set your bike here and I'll take you on the tour."

Reluctantly I lean my bike up against the wall and follow her through a door into a big warehouse beyond.

"Bags are here," she says, pointing to a bin of wadded, used plastic bags. "And here are the food charts. We do advise that you get something from all the food groups. I can show you how if you like. I'm an expert shopper."

"Um, that's okay, I can do it myself," I say, and her hopeful expression falls.

"Well, all right then. Dry goods are there; we don't have a lot of dairy today but it's in the fridge section here. One milk per customer."

I tune her out as I trail down the aisles, already calculating what I can carry on my bike. I know that if I plan it perfectly, I can balance four bags off my handlebars. Normally, I'd be able to use my backpack for more food, but right now it's full of my worldly possessions and, since I don't have any locks for my bedroom door yet either, I can't risk leaving it behind for Natalia to find. Still, if I'm careful, then I should be able to get us enough food to last the week.

"Three loaves of bread per customer is the maximum," Carla warns me with a smile. "Now, I'll leave you to it."

It's a relief to have her gone. I wander back to the bin full of bags and root through until I find some that look strong and don't have any holes.

Bread first, I think, stuffing three into a bag. There is still a bit of room in there so I find some toothpaste, which I've been out of for days, two rolls of individually wrapped toilet paper and a pack of sanitary pads. I'm not due any time soon but you can never have too many. Running out and not being able to afford more is a complete, embarrassing nightmare that I never want to live through again.

Cereal is next and I pick the healthiest type I can find, which in this case is oatmeal. Natalia likes the sugary cereal for kids and she won't touch anything that looks boring. Since Todd seems to be happy feeding her from restaurants and his own kitchen, I will load up on all the healthy stuff I can. Because, once she dumps him and starts eating at home again, Natalia will lose her mind if the food she likes isn't in the house. This is my chance to get the healthy, cheap stuff while I'm still not on her radar.

I eye up the peanut butter, wondering if I could get away with bringing the big jar home or just to stick with the small one. I can only carry so many heavy things. From experience, I know that if I get the big jar then I probably can't get the milk. Or any fruit.

Sighing, I pick the small one and then grab some boxes of quick mac and cheese and a small tub of margarine. Then I add a small bag of sugar and packets of those instant mashed potatoes. There is spaghetti there but the sauce is in those big glass jars and there is no way I'll be able to maneuver them home.

I move to the dairy section, but right before I get there I see those big bags of dry powdered milk on the shelf. It's the type that you mix up with water to make a sort of skimmed milk. It doesn't exactly taste like milk but, if you water it down a lot, it lasts forever.

Perfect, I think. And, there are actually slices of processed cheese in the fridge too. This is like the best food bank I've ever been to. Not believing my luck, I spontaneously grab a head of lettuce. I can make myself sandwiches to last me the entire week now. It's a complete luxury.

"Did you find everything?" Carla at the desk asks, peering down into my bags.

Before I can say anything, she swoops around the counter.

"Oh, my dear, this won't do. You don't have any fruit. Or juice."

"Um, I know. But I can't carry…."

She's already gone, and I can hear her rummaging around in the warehouse.

I quickly start to tie my bags to the handlebars, hoping I can get away before she comes back.

But I'm not fast enough and there she is, trundling in with two extra bulging bags.

One is full of oranges and potatoes and the other has a giant jar of spaghetti sauce, noodles and a tetra pack of juice. I can tell just by looking at them that they weigh a ton. The sharp edges of the tetra pack are already poking small holes through the thin plastic.

"Here," she says triumphantly. "Take these too."

"I really can't…"

"Nonsense." She shoves both bags into my hand and ushers me out the door before I can say another word.

And that's when I realize why the place was so empty. I must have snuck in there before official opening hours because there is a line of people staring at me as I come outside. The woman at the front of the line raises her eyebrows at my bulging food bags and I feel my cheeks flush.

"Come on in, everyone," Carla says in her loud, sing-song voice. "We're open for business."

I slink away, wondering if I'm imagining the dark looks people are sending me. I think of the powdered milk and the cheese tucked away in my bag. They'd been the only ones on the shelf.

I hurry away as fast as I can, the plastic handles of the extra bags cutting into my hand. I'm going to need to stop and shuffle things around before the bags break, but right now I just want to put some distance between me and that place. Away from the shame of needing to be there.

The further I go, the better I feel and the giddy joy of being in possession of so many groceries takes away some of my embarrassment. Being able to feed myself until payday is the biggest relief. I still can't believe that I found cheese.

I am halfway to the bus stop when the first bag in my hand splits wide open and the jar of spaghetti sauce shatters in the middle of the street. And that's when the second bag breaks. Potatoes rolling everywhere.

The people around me scatter and someone gives a startled yelp as a red-smeared grapefruit rolls directly in her path.

"Watch it," a man growls at me as he dodges out of the way.

"I didn't do it on purpose," I snap, but he just gives me a glare and strides away.

I stare down at the groceries on the sidewalk, my cheeks burning in mortification. Nobody offers to help.

Everything is covered in goo and glass and I don't know whether to just leave the whole mess behind and make my escape or if I should attempt to pick it all up.

Finally, my need to get food outweighs my embarrassment and I lean my bike up against a lamp post with a sigh.

A truck, desperately in need of a muffler, idles up beside me and I hear the window whir down. But I don't look up, concentrating instead on picking up the least damaged groceries to stuff into the bags on my bike.

"Hey, new girl."

I spin around warily and blink at the truck—if you can even call it a truck—rumbling away beside me.

I don't know what brand it had been originally, but the thing has been modified to look like something out of an apocalyptic movie. The hood is missing, so you can look right in at the engine and inner workings. And there are old nuts, bolts, and various car-bits welded artistically here and there. The whole thing is covered in a rusty patina instead of paint but you can tell that it was done on purpose, rather than through neglect. Welded at the very front, like a figurehead, is a large metal rat wearing a top hat and a monocle.

The truck rumbles and shudders loudly as it idles, and grey smoke belches from the exhaust.

I drag my gaze away from the oversized rat and see my neighbour, the boy who'd been working on the car last week, grinning out at me from the back seat. The rest of the windows are blacked out and I can't see the driver.

"Need a ride?"

I blink, wondering if I'm dreaming all this, and then shake my head.

"No thanks. I've got it handled."

That's a lie, but there is no way I'm getting in the rat truck with strangers. That's exactly how people end up dead or missing.

"Are you sure? I promise not to bite."

I keep my eyes fixed on the mess in front of me, willing the truck to go away, willing all these people to stop *staring* at me. I'm going to have to leave some of these groceries. There is no way I'll be able to carry them all. Tears sting my eyes and I wipe them away impatiently.

"Here."

The boy kneels beside me with a plastic bag in his hand. Before I can argue, he deftly sorts through the glass and plucks my groceries out one by one.

"Come on. We'll take you home, I promise. We'll put your bike in the back."

He's not grinning anymore; his expression is serious but kind.

I hesitate and then decide to risk it, hoping I'm not making a mistake.

"Fine, okay, thanks."

He slides the bags off the bike handles and puts them in the back seat before carefully lifting my bike into the truck bed. Even though it's a heavy bike, he lifts it with little effort, hoisting it over the side in one smooth motion.

"I'm Ethen and this is my brother, Owen," he says, ushering me into the back seat of the truck. There isn't a lot of space but I shift over as far as I can to the opposite side, my fingers touching the handle so I can make a quick getaway if I need to.

"Lena," I say automatically, and then blink in alarm as I catch sight of the man driving. He's so big that he hardly fits in the seat and he's covered in tattoos, even on his neck. When he turns to smile at me, I can see that some of his front teeth are covered in a grill of silver. It is not reassuring.

A second man is sitting in the passenger seat, but nobody introduces him and he doesn't say a word. He doesn't even turn around to look at me, just taps his fingers against his knees and stares out the window.

"Sooo, you're Ethen's new girlfriend, are you?" Owen says, laughing so deeply that his whole body shakes.

"No," I say quickly, feeling my cheeks flush with heat.

"Come on, she's lived here like a day," Ethen says, rolling his eyes at me in a way that makes me smile despite my embarrassment. "Not even I work that fast. Just ignore him, Lena. He's all talk."

I kind of doubt that. Owen and his silent friend look like complete gangsters. I'm pretty sure I'll be lucky to make it home alive.

"So, how are you liking the neighbourhood?" Ethen asks as the truck lurches forward with an alarming belch of smoke.

I think he must be joking but, when I turn to say something sarcastic, he looks dead serious.

"Um, it's all right," I say cautiously.

"I know it doesn't look like much, but there are decent people there," he says. "People who look out for one another. It's a good community."

I raise my eyebrows skeptically and he laughs.

"You don't believe me, but just wait until you've been there a while. You'll see."

"Okay." I'm not about to argue with someone who's doing me a favour. Or tell him that we won't be sticking around long. We'll probably be gone by winter.

"You just moved here with your folks?" Owen asks in his rumbling voice, looking at me in the rear-view mirror.

"Er, yes." I start to unfold my standard lie, about my dad in the military and my stay-at-home mom, but then change my mind. What harm would it do to tell these people the truth? I don't want them in my life and there is no way they have any connection with Anna and Three Sisters. And, honestly, I was getting pretty sick of telling that story.

"It's just me and my mom," I say finally. "She's usually busy with her new boyfriend. I don't even know who my dad is."

I slap a hand over my mouth involuntarily. I hadn't planned at all to say that last part. It had just slipped out.

There is a short silence and then Owen nods and turns up the radio.

Despite my misgivings, we arrive home in record time and nobody has murdered me.

"Thanks again," I say as I slide out of the car.

"Any time, neighbour." Owen grins at me in the rear-view mirror. The nameless friend bobs his head slightly but doesn't turn to look at me.

"You don't have to help," I tell Ethen quickly. "I can do it."

"I don't mind." He's already pulled my bike out of the truck bed and picked up two bags of groceries. There is no way to get rid of him without being extra rude.

"We don't have any furniture or anything yet," I say, my cheeks stinging with heat. I hope that Natalia isn't home. She can be at her most embarrassing when other people are around.

"Don't worry," Ethen says, propping my bike up against the wall and helping me carry the rest of the groceries to the kitchen.

I send him a few sidelong glances but if he notices the ratty carpet in the living room or the cracks in the kitchen linoleum, he doesn't show it.

"Thank you for helping me," I say, relaxing a little. He's turning out to maybe not be such a bad guy.

"Any time. I mean that. You should come over and see my house too."

Instantly I'm on guard again, and he must see the change come over me because he takes a step backward and sends me an easy smile.

"I have a younger sister and another brother besides Owen. And we have some of our cousins living with us for the summer. You should see how crowded our place is. And loud; nobody ever shuts up."

I have to laugh at that image.

"Aw, I miss having a brother," I say before I can stop myself. But it's the truth. Even though he stole all my money and left me to fend off Natalia by myself, I still loved him a lot. He had been my whole world when we were little.

Ethen stares at me kindly, waiting for me to go on. But I've said enough. I'm not interested in making friends in this place. I don't want to get attached to anyone.

"I have to get ready for work now," I lie, looking at my watch. It's the only excuse I can think of to get him to leave. "I'm going to be late."

"Sure, no problem. Maybe I'll see you around."

"Maybe. Bye." I follow him to the front door and shut it tightly behind him before he can say anything else.

For a second, I feel a pang of loneliness but I push the feeling away resolutely.

It is too tempting to have someone like Ethen around to make life easier for me. I could see it in his eyes that he is one of those kind, helpful guys who want to save people. Just like Natalia's boyfriends do for her.

But I can't do it. I won't be that person. I am going to make my own way through life without anyone helping me. I am going to do it all myself without using other people. I made a vow to myself and I am sticking to it.

I turn around to face the bags of groceries on the counter with a feeling of giddy excitement. For this week at least, I am going to live nearly like a normal person. I have food, a roof over my head, and a job with horses. Who could ask for anything more?

Chapter 12

Kira

$\mathcal{I}$ make it halfway through a week of morning dressage lessons before I finally beg Elliot to switch my ride times back to the afternoons.

Yes, I know it's hot and gross by then, but the mornings are just much too chaotic for me.

Too many little kids, noise and drama. And too much of Isla hissing mean things at me whenever she has a chance. Samantha has this booming voice when she teaches in the ring next to ours and by mid-week, I can feel a stress migraine coming on. I know, from experience, that I have to change things up for my own good.

I don't tell Elliot why I need to switch my times. I hate explaining myself to people, even though I'm pretty sure Elliot is not the type to think I'm high-maintenance or weird. Luckily, she just agrees without asking too many questions. Actually, I think I helped her out because she had a lot of people asking her for lessons, and everybody but myself seems to want the mornings.

Unfortunately, we'd forgotten to let the grooms at Barn A know about the switch. Which is how I find myself getting to brush and tack up Flicker by myself for the first time since I started riding him.

Flicker hasn't been turned out; he is still in his stall, keeping himself occupied by searching for bits of fallen hay in his shavings. He is dressed from nose to tail in a blue hooded spandex cover that goes right over his head nearly to his nose. There are holes in the material for his eyes and ears, and he gives me a disinterested glance before going back to searching for hay.

"Hey, buddy," I say to him softly, slipping inside his stall. As soon as I shut the door, he wheels around, turning his butt to me and puts his head into the far corner.

I freeze, wondering if he's about to try and kick me, but after a minute I realize that he's not attacking me; he's trying to hide.

"You're a pretty big guy to hide, Flicker," I say to him softly. "It's okay, we're just going to take it slow today. You like your lessons with Elliot, don't you? We'll have fun."

He drops his nose to the ground with a sigh and lips at the shavings but he doesn't turn around.

"That's a boy, let's just put your halter on and we'll give you a good brushing."

He doesn't object when I slide up next to his shoulder and carefully put his halter on, just lets out a deep sigh and then drags along behind me as if he is being led to his execution rather than the cross-ties.

"What's up with you, buddy?" I ask, not understanding what his problem is. Tessa loves getting groomed and being ridden, the same as most of the horses in Barn B do, so I'm not sure why Flicker doesn't feel the same way. But clearly, he is not thrilled for some reason.

He does relax a little as I brush him, his eyes half-closing with what I hope is contentment as I run the curry comb under his mane and down his neck.

I run my hands over him, frowning at the bulgy spot in his back behind where the saddle goes. Surely that isn't normal. None of the horses down at our barn have anything like that. But Marsha had said that he'd been vetted sound by the vet and the chiropractor. He even gets massages.

I groom him carefully and then go and find his tack, wondering if I'll be able to get the weird bridle fitted properly by myself.

I'd always arrived at the barn to find Flicker fully brushed and with his saddle in place, so I'd never gotten to see his tacking-up performance before. He starts shifting around when I approach with the saddle pad, then tosses his head and starts to paw the ground with one front foot as I settle it carefully on his back.

"No, stop that," I say firmly, "this is no big deal, you've done this before."

But Flicker doesn't listen. As soon as I lift the saddle, he pins his ears and whips around as if he were going to bite me. The cross-ties prevent him from getting too close but I hear the snap of his teeth dangerously near to my skin.

"Flicker!" I say, shocked that he'd tried to hurt me. "That's so bad."

He lowers his head sulkily, ears drooping. But when I reach to do up the girth he kicks one hind leg up toward me, narrowly missing my knee cap.

"Wow, you are a disaster," I tell him. "Why are you being so bad?"

I get the girth done up loosely on the lower holes and instantly all the weird behaviour stops. But he now has that strange far-off expression on his face again as he stares down the aisle toward the fields outside, as if he's imagining himself anywhere but here.

He doesn't argue as I slip the ridiculous bridle over his head and attempt to do up the straps; in fact, he acts like he doesn't notice me at all. He just opens his mouth robotically for the bit.

"You are the weirdest animal," I tell him. "I honestly don't get you. It's like you change into a different horse every minute."

I wonder if horses can have multiple personality disorders or anything. This is something I'll have to look up when I get home.

I hesitate when I go to put the weird over-the-poll strap on and clip up the German martingale. There's nobody around; this might be my only chance to drop some of this extra gear and see how he does. I've been thinking that both these pieces of equipment are what make him duck his head into his chest the most. I can't get away with changing his actual bit, but maybe eliminating these contraptions would help him to understand that I'm supposed to be his partner, not his tormenter.

I waffle for a second, torn between possibly getting in trouble and doing what's right for Flicker, and then finally make a decision. I pull off the martingale before I can change my mind, hang it and the other strap quickly back in the tack room, and lead the horse toward the mounting block just outside the barn.

I've been riding him down the hill to my lessons all week and he's been really good, better than in the ring. I have the feeling that he would love to get out and try some trail riding if we had the chance.

I can't feel any difference in him with the lack of gear as we ride slowly down the hill; he seems like the same horse so far.

There is nobody around when I get to the ring. Samantha's

morning lessons are done and all the riders are long gone. I still have fifteen minutes until my lesson with Elliot so, for a few minutes anyway, I get to spend some alone time with Flicker for the very first time.

It's hot, like usual, but not unbearable and I inhale deeply, feeling happy that I have all this space to myself.

Someday, when I'm older, I'll have a farm of my own, I think dreamily, *just a small one where I can play with horses all day and nobody will bother me.*

I do feel a little bit like a young trainer now, schooling my own project horse in the ring, making decisions about his tack and his care without anyone else bossing me around.

I move Flicker up into a trot, smiling at the way his powerful legs cut across the ground, weaving us between the jumps while I bend, stretch and supple him in a series of serpentines, arcs and circles.

Flicker pushes a little into the bit, testing the contact, and his ears swivel around suddenly as if he's trying to figure something out.

"Good boy," I say soothingly, "you're doing great."

He leans a little more heavily and I play with the bit, squeezing with my legs at the same time, asking him to move forward but also to rock his weight back to his haunches so he's not dragging on his forehand.

He pushes just a tiny bit harder and then, at the upper corner when I slide my leg back to ask for a canter, he plunges forward with a muttered squeal of triumph, grabs the bit hard in his teeth and takes off, bucking and farting across the ring.

There is a moment of panic when I realize that I can't stop him at all. My hands are useless on the reins; it's like pulling on a wall of concrete. I am completely helpless up there, being tossed around like a rag doll.

But then logic kicks in. I'm in an enclosed ring so he has

nowhere to go. All I have to do is stay on and try not to run into anything. Eventually, he will tire himself out.

I sit up and take a steady feel on the reins but I don't try and stop him. Instead, I look where I want to go and concentrate on making his wild circle smaller and smaller until he slows just a little on his own.

He snorts and tosses his head as if disappointed that I'm not fighting with him. I ignore that, focusing on seeing if I can get him to bend a little, to make his circle even smaller. Finally, he flicks an ear back at me, listening to me for just a second. His gallop is down to a powerful canter now and I'm feeling more confident that this might all work out. He isn't trying to hurt me, and he's not doing that weird mincing canter that he'd been offering me all week.

I let myself relax just a little, a part of me actually enjoying this wild ride; it's like flying. And that's when he sees his opportunity. He yanks his head down abruptly and takes off in a series of bucks. I manage to sit the first two, but then my body is slipping sideways and the next thing I know, I'm flying through the air. The ground comes up way too fast and I hit it with a mighty crunch that shakes every bone in my body.

For a minute I just lie there, dimly aware of Flicker's galloping hooves zooming around nearby. I wonder if he is about to run me over on purpose. But they slow down next to me, dirt and sand spattering my face, and I feel warm breath skittering across my cheek. Then there is a snort and I'm covered in a fine, wet spray.

"Thanks," I say weakly, reaching up to push his whiskery muzzle away and wipe my face. "I don't think I need any more help from you. You've done enough."

He snorts again and gives me a nudge on the shoulder as if he's wondering what on earth I'm doing down there. As if he'd had nothing to do with it at all.

"Oh my gosh, Kira, are you okay?"

Two faces loom over me—three if you count Flicker—and I have to blink a few times until they become clear.

"Just lie still." Lena peers down at me anxiously. "Don't move until we make sure nothing is broken."

"That was some buck," Oliver says, looking more excited than worried. "I can't believe you stayed on as long as you did."

"Thanks." I pull myself slowly into a sitting position, waving off Lena's outstretched hand. I am pretty sure nothing is broken but I am sore all over. There are going to be bruises tomorrow.

I narrow my eyes toward where Flicker has wandered over to graze innocently at the edge of the ring, his reins trailing in the dirt beside him. He looks unharmed and unrepentant.

"I'll catch him," Oliver says, rising to his feet. "Are you going to get back on?"

I hesitate and then nod.

"Here, let me help you up." Lena has my elbow and is pulling me upright before I can protest.

"Thanks," I say, stepping away from her as soon as I'm on my feet. "I can't believe he did that."

"Yeah, that was dirty. And he looked so great before that too, better than I've ever seen him go."

I raise an eyebrow. I hadn't known that Lena had been watching my lessons with Flicker.

"Sorry, I like to watch people ride," she says quickly, maybe guessing why I'd given her that look. "I learn a lot that way. And you're a great rider. He's a difficult horse. I wonder if he's sore somewhere and that's why he acts out."

"I wonder that too, sometimes," I admit. "But he moves fine. And he's been vetted, had his saddle fitted and had chiropractic adjustments. Everyone says he's fine. I thought he'd make this miraculous transformation when I took some of his gear off, but I just made it worse. I assumed he only needed all that stuff because Marsha's incapable."

"Oh, she's incapable," Oliver says, leading Flicker up beside us. "But Flicker is just really smart, strong, and he kind of likes chaos. Even Clara found him challenging and she was a brilliant rider."

"So, what did she ride him in?"

"Not this." He waves toward the bit angrily. "I'm sorry you got bucked off but I think you're on the right track with getting rid of some of that crap he's wearing. You just might have to do it more slowly. Lena agrees, don't you?"

"Um, yes?" Lena says, looking startled that she's been singled out. "I'd better get back to the barn. I just wanted to make sure you're okay."

"Thanks. I am." I hesitate. "I don't mind if you stay. I'm not sure how bad he'll be when I get back on so I wouldn't mind someone watching."

"Don't worry, we'll be your ground crew," Oliver says, leading Flicker over to the mounting block and holding the bridle firmly while I crawl back on. Normally, it would be annoying to have someone hold my horse for me, but right now I can't help but appreciate it.

I settle gingerly into the saddle and pick up the reins.

This time Flicker acts like a model citizen. A happy one. He marches along, neck arched and gently mouthing the bit. He feels much more responsive than he usually does, but he's also sharper and more alert. I definitely will not let my guard down with him again.

"Well, look at this guy," Elliot says as she moves at a trot toward the ring. "He's having a good day. Sorry I'm late."

Her gaze narrows in on my right side and I glance down to see that I am still covered with a layer of sand.

"He was feeling a little frisky," Oliver says, grinning at her disarmingly.

"I see that. You okay, Kira?"

"Yeah." I nod. "I'm fine." I don't mention how sore I am. I'm just hoping that none of this gets back to Anna, Marsha or my dad.

"Is he listening to you?"

"Kind of. Sometimes." I shrug. "Until he doesn't."

"All right, well then, let's work on some new things today. We'll keep the pace slow and focus on getting his brain to work. That's what smart horses like most, to have something to challenge their brains. If you don't give them something to work on all the time then they'll start making up their own games, like how to bolt and buck off the human."

I gulp and glance over at her, relieved to see that she's smiling.

Nothing else dramatic happens in the next forty-five minutes. We pretty much stick with walking, with just little bits of trot thrown in. We work on haunches-in and shoulder in, turns on the forehand, leg-yields and collecting and extending him at both the walk and trot. Neither Flicker nor I have done a lot of this in the past so we're not exactly brilliant at it. But, those few moments where we actually get things right feel amazing.

I would have thought that an entire lesson without cantering or jumping would have been boring, but it was interesting; I feel like I'm in the same zone that I'm in when I'm riding Tessa. That in-between state where the magic happens. And Flicker stays engaged and mostly obedient the entire time. He feels more relaxed, and more like a normal horse than he ever has for me.

"All right, that's enough for him today, good job," Elliot says and I look up, coming back to reality with a thud. The entire ride I'd felt like Flicker, Elliot and I were in our own little bubble.

But now I realize that we aren't alone. Lena is gone but

Oliver is still there, and standing beside him are two older people that I don't recognize, a man and a woman. And beside them is Marsha.

I gulp and immediately feel sweat beading on my forehead. I don't want to be yelled at by Marsha for taking Flicker's gear off, even though I know I might deserve it.

"Good job, Kira," Oliver calls, giving me a thumbs-up. The older woman beside him smiles and nods too before turning away. She looks exactly like him so I'm assuming that she's his mother.

Marsha isn't even paying attention to me at all; she's talking to the man in her bellowing voice while showing him pictures on her phone.

Oliver says something and leads them all away and I'm left alone with Elliot again.

"So, how do you think your experiment went?" Elliot asks quietly, pointing at Flicker's bit.

"Um." I gulp, really hoping she's not going to tell Anna about this. "I guess it was mixed. He was way more fun to ride in my lesson with you. He felt like a real horse, not like a robot, and he hardly did that weird tucking his head thing. But, on the other hand, I couldn't stop him at all when he took off. It was like I didn't even exist. I kind of understand why Marsha has all that gear on him. It was scary."

"I'll bet it was. I'm glad you're okay. And I wish you'd waited until I was here before trying it out. That wasn't the safest choice."

"Sorry. I thought it might be my only chance. Do you think he could be trained to go with less gear?"

"Oh, for sure. Any horse can with enough time, patience and a skilled rider. But he'd need to be completely re-schooled and that isn't something that will happen before the clinic. Is it still your goal to ride him in it?"

"Yes."

"Okay, well, I'd suggest a compromise then. How about we ride the first half of your lessons with the gear while we get him warmed up and do canter work. Then we can take it off once he's relaxed and we can do some slower things that challenge his brain. How would that sound to you?"

"Great. Thank you."

"No problem. But you should use it in your lessons with Anna. It would be dangerous to jump him like that, okay? And no more riding on your own with him."

"Okay." I can't argue with that. If I hadn't been able to control Flicker at a canter, then I definitely wouldn't be able to control him while jumping. Anna would never agree to it anyway.

The rest of the week flies by, and every day I can feel Flicker relaxing and becoming slightly more obedient and responsive. I even think he might be starting to like me. He sometimes nickers when he sees me and his bucks and bolts seem more half-hearted now. It's like he's being disobedient out of habit rather than because he hates me.

I don't get the chance to brush or tack him up by myself again. Once the grooms know our new ride times, Flicker is always ready and tacked up whenever I arrive.

I try to spend a little extra time with him afterwards instead, making our way slowly up the hill on a loose rein or letting him graze in hand at the side of the driveway.

At the end of the week, Anna and the rest of the riders, grooms and horses come back from the show in a noisy convoy of trucks and trailers. It is instant chaos, with horses being unloaded everywhere and grooms bustling around unpacking the trailer and trying to keep the horses settled.

Excited kids run around clutching ribbons and rehashing their wins with anyone who'll listen.

I have to wait until the next day for my final lesson with Anna. The clinic will start on Tuesday and run for a week. It is the first time I'll jump Flicker all week and I am dying to see what he'll be like.

I am a little disappointed when he bolts at an easy oxer and cracks his hind hoof into a jump standard, but Anna is more optimistic.

"You're really coming together as a team," she says, as I manage to pull him to a stop nearby her. "He's much better than he was when you first rode him. You're doing a great job, Kira."

I'm not so sure. Some days it felt like we were progressing nicely and other times it felt like we took ten steps backward. My rides with Flicker are certainly never boring, anyway.

<hr>

Chapter 13

<hr>

Kira

On the morning of the clinic, my stomach is churning so hard with nerves that I nearly throw up.

For once my dad doesn't hassle me about not eating breakfast. He seems a little nervous himself.

We'd been invited to a morning brunch for the clinicians, and John Riddle, but I'd already told Anna that I didn't want to go and she'd said that was fine. I just couldn't handle sitting down with all those strangers, and being surrounded by all that food, while my childhood idol sat at the same table. Riding Flicker in front of John Riddle is going to be stressful enough.

I had told my dad six times that he didn't need to come to watch me ride. It wasn't like it was a show with prizes or anything. But, for some reason, he'd decided that this was the moment he needed to show up and support me. Which was odd because he hadn't been to the barn much in years, only once when we'd first bought Tessa.

Maybe he secretly just wanted to meet a real Olympian

too. I mean, I'd talked about John Riddle enough over the years that he probably knew nearly as much about him as I did by that point.

"Do you have everything you need? Did you pack a lunch?"

"Dad, stop fussing. I made a list. I have everything organized. I know what I'm doing."

He looks at me, startled, and then breaks into a laugh. "Okay, I guess you're right. I keep forgetting that you're not a kid anymore. Well, should we get this show on the road?"

"It's not a show, Dad, it's a clinic," I remind him, rolling my eyes.

"Figure of speech, Kira. Okay, let's go."

I sit in the car, half-sick with nerves, and irritated with myself for feeling that way. I am not normally the type of person to get stage fright, but meeting John Riddle…not just *meeting* him but having to ride in front of him…is making my stomach roil.

I don't even see the scenery passing by.

"So, what's with the nerves?" my dad asks casually. "Pretty rare to see you rattled."

Irritation washes over me and I start to say something sarcastic back, but stop myself just in time. He's trying to help, after all.

"I just don't want to mess up," I say honestly. "Not in front of him. I've wanted to meet him for so long."

"You'll do fine."

"Yeah, yeah. I might do fine. But Flicker is a bit…unpredictable. And I've never ridden him in the indoor, or in front of a crowd. He might not be very well-behaved."

"Oh? That's the first I've heard of him being unpredictable. He's not dangerous, is he?"

"No." I slump down in the seat, staring out the window. There is no way to explain to my non-horsey dad about how Flicker behaves well with his awful bit in his mouth but that I hate to use it. And how John Riddle is definitely going to raise his eyebrows when he sees it, or maybe even call me out in front of everyone. He's probably going to think that I'm the one who had Darla design it because I can't handle Flicker without it. And the last thing I want is for John Riddle to lump me in with someone like Marsha.

Things are better when we reach the barn. As soon as I step out of the car, I feel more grounded, more like myself and I'm able to breathe freely again.

My dad gets talking to Anna and I'm able to slip away.

I head up to Barn A to see Flicker first. We won't be riding for at least an hour and I know I won't be allowed to brush and tack him up, but I'd still like to see him and give him a treat, just so we can start on the right foot.

He is still in his stall when I get there, all covered up in a spandex slinky that only leaves his ears, eyeballs and the very tip of his nose uncovered. I duck past the grooms bustling about and head right to him.

"Hey, friend," I whisper, slipping inside his stall before anyone can ask what I'm doing there. I hand him a carrot and smile as he crunches it up and then uses his nose to search my pockets.

"Sorry, I just brought the one. You can have more later."

I don't spend too long there. I know that John Riddle is going to give a short lecture before we have our lessons. Most lessons will only have two riders in them. I'm lucky, or unlucky, enough to be in the first one today, which is good because at least I'll have gotten it over with and can spend the rest of the day watching the other riders. Or hiding in the bathroom trying to avoid all the people.

I'm a little weirded out because the second person booked in my lesson is Oliver's step-brother, Josh, with his stellar horse

Hectic Electric. They are a talented, solid team that will make Flicker and me look like complete amateurs.

The morning lecture is great and I'm too busy taking notes to think about my nerves anymore. The arena is half-packed with people on folding chairs who listen dead-quiet as John Riddle goes over the training scale with them and does a talk on developing young horses.

All you can hear is the sound of pens scratching on paper as people try and soak up as much information as possible.

And then, almost before I'm ready for it, it's time to ride.

As soon as I'm headed to get Flicker, my nerves come back in full force, butterflies jumping so hard in my stomach that I'm on the edge of throwing up.

My hands are shaking as I lead Flicker into the arena, and I find my gaze drawn automatically toward where Josh and John Riddle are standing in the middle of the ring.

Josh is already up on Heck, sitting casually in the saddle like he meets Olympians every day.

Flicker is huffing anxiously under his breath, his eyes wide and his neck stiff, ears swivelling around at the audience. He gulps once and then reaches over to touch my arm with his nose, looking for reassurance.

"It's okay," I whisper. I give him a scratch under his mane and then climb on board, turning Flicker into the middle of the ring.

I glance over at the audience, feeling their eyes staring at me. I don't usually care about riding in front of other people but this is a lot. There are some friendly faces there. My dad and Anna, and the draft-horse-girl, Fina, from next door. There are a lot of nice girls who ride at our barn and, even if we're not best friends or anything, they still are on my side.

Oliver is there too and he gives me a smile and a wink as I catch his eye.

But then I catch sight of Alice, glaring at me like I've personally offended her. And Isla is in the back corner with her arms crossed tightly over her chest and a dark look on her face. And there are strangers as well who are there to learn from all my mistakes and who won't mind too much if I get bucked off and add some entertainment to the clinic.

I now regret skipping the welcome brunch where everyone had probably already introduced themselves because suddenly John Riddle is coming toward me, all smiles.

I half-expect him to stop and look at the bridle contraption in horror and immediately kick me out of the clinic, but nothing like that happens.

"Welcome, Kira. I've heard good things about you," he says, catching me off guard. "Can you tell us a little about your goals for this clinic?"

Luckily, Anna had already warned me that I was probably going to be asked a question like this, so I have practiced my speech about a million times. I open my mouth to talk about how I want to be a more effective rider and to help Flicker be a better horse. But another part of my brain takes over instead.

"Thank you for letting me ride with you," I say, my voice coming out all squeaky. "I...I love you."

I stare at him in horror. Did those words actually come out of my mouth? Had I said them out loud?

There is silence and then everyone starts to laugh. I feel my face burn with mortification and I could easily have just melted off Flicker, into the arena dirt and disappeared into the ground.

Flicker shifts underneath me and I remember again why I'm there in the first place.

"I mean," I say, clearing my throat. "I love the way you ride, and the way you handle your horses. I've spent my whole life watching your showing and training videos. I want to be just like you."

I gulp but John Riddle doesn't look offended or embarrassed. He reaches out and grips the toe of my boot and then pats my knee.

"Well, I'm truly honored," he says kindly. "That's the best compliment I've heard in a while. Now, let's get these horses warmed up."

Flicker does all right on the flat. He still alternates between getting strong and ducking his head in, but I sit calmly and keep a steady, light contact and try to get him to relax. He crunches the bits between his teeth anxiously, making a creaky grinding sound, but, for the most part, he seems content to listen to me.

But, when John sets up a grid exercise for us to work through, Flicker starts to fall apart.

I'd expected that he might try to bolt or buck but I hadn't been prepared for him to jolt to a complete stop and then stand in the middle of the ring, shaking, and refusing to move. It's like he's suddenly glued in place, oblivious to me nudging him or giving him gentle taps with my crop. I have no idea what's going on.

"It's okay, Flicker," I whisper, "it's just a clinic. You don't have anything to be afraid of."

"Crack him with the whip!" I hear Marsha bellow from somewhere in the audience. I glance down at my crop, debating, but Flicker is shaking. He's not doing this because he's bad; he's trying to tell me something.

I look up to see John Riddle striding toward us.

"I'm sorry," I say, "I don't know what's wrong with him. He's never done this before."

Instead of getting mad, John comes over and gives Flicker a reassuring pat on the neck and then carefully looks him over.

"Do you mind if I hop on?" he asks, and I shake my head and slide to the ground.

One of his assistants runs out with a helmet and adjusts his stirrups before giving him a leg up, and John moves Flicker out to the rail.

As disappointed as I am that Flicker is acting up, I love seeing John ride him. Flicker looks like a completely different horse underneath him; his neck is arched and he moves along like a war horse, all puffed up and proud. More like his old self.

But when John points him at the grid again, something that a pony could have easily popped through, Flicker balks again. And this time he doesn't just plant his feet, he rears up in the air and then spins in the opposite direction, throwing out a huge buck for good measure.

John Riddle doesn't even react at all; he just sits calm and relaxed in the saddle like nothing out of the ordinary is happening.

"Good boy," he says quietly when Flicker has all four feet on the ground again. He brings the big horse to a halt, then jumps down and to my surprise, he goes around running up the stirrups, then reaches down to unbuckle the girth and pull the saddle off. That same assistant appears and wordlessly takes the saddle from him, standing back to watch with the rest of us as John Riddle runs his hands over Flicker's back.

He makes a clicking noise when he sees the bump behind the saddle but does most of his poking and prodding up by the withers.

Finally, he turns to me and shakes his head.

"I'm sorry, my dear, but this horse is not sound. Have the vet do some x-rays on his back. I'd bet money on kissing spines or some sort of muscle damage from poorly fitted tack. Do you have someone else you can ride for the rest of the clinic?"

"Hey!" The yell is so loud that half the people in the arena jump in their seats, turning to see Marsha lurching to her feet.

"What do you mean he's not sound? That horse is as fit as a fiddle. He's just bad-tempered and lazy."

I cringe as Marsha wobbles on her crutches. Her face is beet red and she's glaring at all of us. I'm not sure if she's had too many mimosas at the brunch or not, but her eyes are a little vacant and she's sort of swaying from side to side.

All the people in the audience look at her wide-eyed, but there is a feeling of excitement too, like they're about to enjoy watching this drama unfold.

"You must be this nice horse's owner," John says calmly. "He's a lovely mover and I can see why you like him. But his behaviour is not normal, and there are some strong indications when you look at his body that he's been suffering from some sort of physical issues for some time. It wouldn't be fair to ask him to keep going in this clinic when he's so uncomfortable. He won't get anything out of it."

"That's ridiculous," Marsha says, not even taking a second to consider his words. Her voice sounds a little slurred. "That horse has never taken a lame step. If that girl can't handle him properly then put someone else up on him. I knew it was a mistake to let her ride him."

I stare at her, open-mouthed. It had been her idea for me to ride him in the first place.

John Riddle puts a hand out and gives my shoulder a reassuring pat. I feel my eyes sting with unexpected tears. I am normally not a crier, but it just seems like the whole universe has been against me riding in this clinic from the beginning. The one thing I've wanted for so long.

I take a deep breath and give Flicker a scratch on the neck, silently apologizing to him. I should have followed my instinct that something was wrong with him from the beginning. It was true that he was never actually lame. And he'd been checked out by all sorts of professionals. But still, deep down, I'd known that there was something off about him. I'd ignored it because of how much I'd wanted to ride in this clinic.

"Kira, do you have another horse to ride?" John Riddle asks me again gently.

"I…I have Tessa," I say in a small voice.

"Don't think I'm paying for that," Marsha shouts, pointing a finger at me. "I want my money back. I should ask that girl to pay me back for all the lessons too. You probably ruined him. I should have hired a professional in the first place."

I stand rooted to the ground, not knowing where to look or what to say. This is really not how I pictured this clinic going at all. Being yelled at in public is pretty much my worst nightmare.

"Kira, go get Tessa tacked up," I hear my dad say quietly. He doesn't stand up but my gaze moves unerringly toward where he's sitting, looking at me with a mixture of anger at Marsha and concern for me.

I want to ask him if he means it, if we can even afford it, but he gives me a firm nod and then a half smile.

"Go on," John Riddle says, "Josh and I will get on with the lesson. You come back as soon as you are ready."

I move toward the arena door, still feeling numb. It's all happened so fast that I'm not really sure what just went on.

"Here, I'll take him." Oliver appears beside me and pries Flicker's reins out of my ice-cold fingers. He wraps one arm around my shoulder and gives me a brief, sympathetic squeeze that I don't find entirely unpleasant. "Go on, hurry. Take Anna's golf cart. Lena is already getting Tessa ready for you."

I look up to see that Isla is watching us from her place against the wall, her eyes glittering with rage.

"Okay, thanks," I say, looking away quickly. "What's going to happen to Flicker?"

Marsha had looked so livid. What if she sent him for dog food or something?

"Don't worry about that now. It will all work out. Go get your horse."

Suddenly I remember that John Riddle is waiting for me. And that I actually, miraculously, get to ride Tessa in this clinic.

I run the golf cart as fast as I can down the driveway, and when I get to the barn, I am relieved to see Tessa already in the cross-ties with her boots on and her hooves polished.

"Anna sent me a text," Lena says, grinning at me, "no time to braid, but you keep her mane so neat and tidy that I think she'll do. What saddle pad do you want to use?"

"The white one with the blue trim," I say gratefully, "and her gel pad too." I pull a soft goat-hair body brush out of my grooming kit and give Tessa's coppery coat a final polish. She already looks perfect but it settles my nerves.

Lena comes out with my saddle over one arm and my pads in the other. My girth is over her shoulder. She hands me the things one by one as I carefully tack up Tessa.

The mare is sensitive so even though I'm in a hurry I take my time to make sure everything is sitting just right.

"She looks great." Lena appears beside me again with the bridle.

"Thank you so much for helping," I say.

"Never mind that, get going. Enjoy the rest of your lesson."

Tessa is on her toes already, prancing up the driveway and pretending to shy at silly things. Despite being spicy, Tessa is not a spooky horse; I know it's just her way of showing that she's picked up on all the excitement.

We ride up to the side door of the indoor and Anna lets us inside with a smile.

"You two look great. I'm so glad you got to ride her in this. Don't worry about Marsha. Everyone knows you did a great job with that horse. It will sort itself out."

Josh and Heck look like they've had quite the workout. Heck is steaming with sweat and the two of them are standing in the middle of the ring while John Riddle explains something to them, his arms waving as he tries to get his point across.

Before either Tessa or I can lose our nerves, I start right into a warm-up, letting her trot out in some easy circles on a loose rein. It feels so good to be moving again, and to be on Tessa's back, that I forget about the embarrassing parts of the morning. I forget about the audience and that my childhood idol is standing a few feet away.

I block the rest of the world out and keep my focus on Tessa. I can feel her reaching down, seeking the bit now, her back rounding. Without changing the contact, I ask her to canter and she surges forward in that way she does. I move her through the arena in loops and serpentines, letting her power build until she feels like she's about to fly.

"Nice, Kira," John Riddle says quietly and I glance up, startled to remember that I'm not all alone here with Tessa. That I'm still in the middle of a pretty important clinic and have an audience. Josh is still standing there too, watching me with an expression that I can't read. "Take her over the little gate, keep the rhythm exactly like that."

Normally Tessa would get all excited when I point her at a jump, but she feels more warmed up than usual and just incorporates the low gate into her canter stride without any extra fuss.

"Same pace, to the vertical. Don't change anything."

We canter over that one too and then suddenly Tessa seems to realize that she's in the middle of an unfamiliar course and her head shoots up excitedly as she zeroes in on the higher triple bar off to the right.

"Interesting," John says. "If you're comfortable, let her keep going. I'm curious to see what she'll do."

I already know what she'll do and I smile as I shorten my reins slightly and let her keep heading to the triple. She sails over and then focuses on the grid that Flicker had had such trouble with. She flies through it, turning her head at the end so she can hunt down her next obstacle. She barrels to the wall and flies over it.

Laughing, I pat her neck and circle her, bringing her gradually down to a walk and stopping her a few feet away from where John Riddle and Josh are standing.

"She'll jump forever," I tell them. "She loves it."

"I can see that." John steps forward and holds his hand out for Tessa to sniff before moving in to pet her neck.

She hesitates for a second, rocking back a little as if she's not sure she wants to let him touch her. Then suddenly she leans forward and butts him right in the chest with her head, itching her nose on his arm.

"Tessa, no," I start to say, but John just laughs and shakes his head.

"She's all right. I don't mind."

"Sorry, I've never seen her do that before. She usually doesn't like people very much."

"Smart mares are gold when they love and trust you. She can't be an easy horse to manage, Kira. How is it that you ride her so well?"

"Um." I blink at him a few times. This is not a question that I've prepared for. "I just ride her in the way she likes, I guess. I don't get in her way."

"Oh, and how do you know how she likes to be ridden?"

"She tells me...." I break off, feeling my face flaming. I sound like I'm pretending to be an animal psychic or something but really, it's not hard to understand what horses want if you listen to them. I don't want to say that out loud, though.

Someone in the audience laughs and I look down at Tessa's mane, trying to think of the right words.

"Perfect answer," John Riddle says gently. "Riding should be a back-and-forth conversation between two partners. A constant dialog of feel. What you and Tessa have is special, no doubt about it. But you, Kira, should be proud of being such a good listener. Are you planning to ride professionally?"

"I'm supposed to go to university," I say in a low voice. "But yes, I'd rather train horses."

I don't dare look over to where my dad is sitting. Hopefully, we're too far away for him to hear what we're saying.

"Well, you can probably manage to do both, no sense in limiting your options. But, right now let's see if we can give you a few more tools to work with to get the most out of this generous mare."

The next half-hour is the most magical I've ever spent.

John Riddle has Tessa do a series of exercises meant to build her strength over the jumps.

"She likes to fly at them and just barely skim over; she's using that power for speed rather than for height. So, let's convince her to use those hindquarters a little better."

John Riddle has us work through a series of exercises, and gradually I can feel the difference as Tessa approaches each jump. She isn't just flying at them at breakneck speed, she is considering each one as something important, to be approached more strategically.

By the time we are done, I am grinning from ear to ear. And Tessa seems just as happy.

When the lesson is over, she sticks her nose under John Riddle's arm and starts nosing his pocket for treats.

"Tomorrow we'll raise those jumps and see what she can do. I think there is a lot of untapped talent in this horse. Good job."

I kick my feet out of the stirrups and reach down to loosen my girth.

"Thank you," I say to him as he walks away. "Thank you so much for all this."

"You're welcome. Make sure to come back and watch the rest of the lessons. You'll learn a lot."

"I will."

Anna pats my knee excitedly as she lets me out of the indoor.

"Amazing job, Kira. Tessa was on fire. I'm so glad you got to ride her in this. Will your dad let you ride for the rest of the week?"

"Yes, I think so. As long as he didn't hear the part about me not going to university."

She laughs and heads back inside.

Lena is waiting at the barn when we get back.

"Well, how was it?" she asks excitedly.

"Amazing."

"I wish I could have watched it. Maybe I can sneak up tomorrow and see you ride. You do get to ride again, right?"

"I'm pretty sure, yes."

Tessa reaches over and nudges Lena with her sweaty nose, trying to itch herself on the groom's arm.

"She likes you," I say in surprise. "She likes John Riddle too. Two people in one day is kind of a record for her."

"All mares like Tessa want are to be told they're perfect and handled like royalty. It's not rocket science."

That is so accurate that I burst into laughter and a moment later Lena does too.

"Want me to take care of her so you can go back and watch the next lesson?"

"No, I'll do it myself, thanks though."

Lena nods and then starts to turn away.

"Wait, there's something I meant to ask you. How did you know that Flicker wasn't totally sound? You're the only person who thought there might be something wrong with him."

"I don't know." She shrugs. "Just something about the way

he holds his body, I guess. And the way he acts out when he's faced with a jump. And…" She hesitates. "His hooves make a weird sound on the driveway. At my old barn, we had to practice listening to the horses walk down the aisle so we could pick out the smallest irregularities in their gaits. Even being tired or a tiny bit sore changes the way they move. Anyone can hear it if they know what to listen for."

"Wow, okay, thanks. I've never paid attention to that before."

"No problem."

I wash Tessa down carefully and then walk her until she is fully dry. Even though I want to watch the rest of the lessons, she is my first priority and also, I need a few minutes alone in the quiet to get rid of all the excitement and adrenaline from the morning.

My thoughts move to Flicker and what's going to happen to him next. Marsha had been so mad during the clinic. But I hope that once she calms down she will get the vet to do a proper workup on him. Hopefully, whatever is wrong with him is something that can be fixed.

I give Tessa her carrot and turn her out into the grassy pasture with her school-pony friends.

"Have a good day, girl. And thanks."

She flicks an ear at me but doesn't look back, her focus already on the grass in the far corner.

I go back to the barn and change out of my sweaty tall boots into running shoes, grab a juice box and a power bar from the tack room and drive Anna's golf cart back up the hill.

Chapter 14

Lena

The week of the clinic is exhausting but fun too. I have all my regular chores to do, of course, but Anna lets us all take turns going up to watch some of John Riddle's lessons and we're encouraged to take notes.

I've always loved watching good lessons and clinics. I like seeing the horses transform, or suddenly understand new concepts. It's like magic when you see that change come over them; that softer look in their eye when everything stops being confusing and starts to make sense for them. Or when a rocky partnership between horse and rider suddenly falls into place.

John Riddle is an excellent teacher, and it's obvious that he cares for both horses and people. He never yells; his quiet words seem to drive the riders harder than if he was shouting.

Every night I fall onto my saggy air mattress, exhausted, not moving until my alarm goes off before sunrise the next morning.

I have only seen my mom and her boyfriend very briefly

over the last few weeks and I'd assumed that everything was going well between them. But, on the third night of the clinic, I see that the first cracks are forming in Todd and Natalia's relationship.

That night, she shows up at home out of the blue, slamming the front door behind her and stomping into the house, swearing loudly. Todd's truck idles in the driveway for a few minutes before it rumbles away.

"Men are rats," Natalia announces, appearing suddenly in my bedroom doorway. Tears are glittering on her lower lashes and her skin is so pale it's almost translucent. Her long, blond hair is loose and tangled, wisps floating up around her face like they are charged with electricity.

I flinch involuntarily, my heart thundering away in my chest. Every instinct I have is warning me to get away. Fast. She's at her most lethal in these moods.

"Are they?" I say as neutrally as possible, swallowing hard. These conversations with Natalia can be tricky, like navigating a field of landmines. You never know what direction is safe or what will make her blow up.

"Yes." She sighs dramatically and wipes her eyes. "Todd isn't the man he pretends to be. I thought he was smart and strong. It turns out he's just another average rat of a guy. I'm too good for him and he knows it."

There is a long pause while she stares down at me, waiting expectantly, and I gulp, feeling a trap forming around me.

"Well, don't you think I'm too good for him?" she demands.

"Um, yes?" But my words are too slow. I don't even have a chance to see it coming before she's swooped in with alarming speed. The slap rocks my head back before I can react.

Shock washes over me. I should be used to it by now, but the astonishment of being *hit* never seems to lessen, no matter how often it happens. The pain, the anger, my simmering hatred of the situation that I'm stuck in all bubbles to the surface. But I know better than to show that. I know better than to react.

I press my hand gently against my cheek and hold my breath, waiting for the sting to subside.

"That's for being so rude," she says, her eyes flashing at me angrily. "I'm your mother. I deserve to be treated with respect."

"Okay, sorry," I mumble. Lies. But that is literally the only safe response to Natalia when she's in these moods.

She stares at me another moment like she's just dying to pick a fight. But she finally turns away muttering and heads back to her room.

I get up quickly and push the heavy thrift-store dresser, that she'd foisted on me after deciding it was ugly, across the doorway, just in case she comes back. I'm lucky she'd gotten sick of it and made me drag it down to my room. I still don't have a lock on my bedroom door yet so this will have to do.

Twenty minutes later I hear her yelling on the phone to Todd. Then she's crying, and finally, her tears dissolve into murmuring and then soft laughter. So predictable. Her fights at this stage in a relationship are always the same.

A little while later, Todd's truck comes rumbling back up the driveway, just like I'd expected.

I've even expected the gentle knock on my bedroom door that follows.

"I'm headed out, Lena," Natalia calls softly, for all the world sounding like a normal, caring mother. "Todd picked you up some fast food and left it in the kitchen. Just call if you need anything."

She's always a bit nicer after she's hit me or broken my things. I'd like to think that there's a part of her that feels guilty for how she treats me. But I wouldn't count on that.

"All right, thanks," I say, keeping all traces of anger out of my voice. "Have a good time."

That's the best way to survive life with Natalia; spend as little time with her as possible, don't make her mad, and then go along with it when she pretends nothing has happened. I know it's dysfunctional as hell but this is just how staying alive works sometimes.

I don't open the bedroom door until I'm sure Todd's truck is gone. And then I pad into the kitchen, following the delicious smells. There is a bag of fried chicken there and some fries and gravy.

Not bothering with a plate or cutlery, I carry the whole bag back to my room and sit down cross-legged on my slowly deflating air mattress. The feast is almost worth being slapped for. Almost, but not quite.

I look at my reflection in the mirrored closet, noticing the livid red mark on my face in the perfect shape of Natalia's open hand. I hope it's gone by tomorrow. I hate having to make up stupid stories to explain this stuff to other people.

I close my eyes while I eat, practically inhaling the delicious food. I've been living on sandwiches for quite a while so these new spicy flavors hit my mouth in an explosion of taste.

Living with Natalia hadn't always been so precarious. There had been a time, when I was very little, when she'd been a lot of fun. Full of love and laughter. Although my brother didn't have those fond memories of her.

She'd always been harder on him than she'd been on me. I hadn't realized until he was gone how much my brother had protected and buffered me from her rages. He'd taken the brunt of everything on himself so that I could have a some-what normal childhood, and he had paid the price for it in the end.

Natalia had been the best at making up stories, games and songs at the drop of a hat and she'd have me rolling with laughter doing her impressions of other people. She should have been in theater. She had told us both that many times.

"If I hadn't had your brother, I could have been famous," she'd say, loud enough for Garret to overhear. "That pregnancy was the worst thing that could have happened to me. Of course, I love both my children, but my life could have been so much different if you didn't exist."

She took me everywhere with her when I was younger because I was cute and she liked the attention. But the older I got, the less she seemed to like having me around.

"Don't call me your mother," she'd told me on more than one occasion. "I look too young to have a daughter your age, so you just call me Natalia from now on. We'll pretend you're my sister or a needy orphan I've adopted or something."

And finally, she stopped taking me anywhere at all. Many of her boyfriends were shocked when they met Garret and me for the first time because Natalia often forgot to tell them we even existed.

The next morning, my face is puffy and sore and I wince at myself in the bathroom mirror.

There isn't an actual bruise, so I could probably get away with saying that I'm having an allergic reaction or something. And maybe it will be gone by the time I get to work.

I dress quickly and pack my lunch, two peanut butter sandwiches and an apple, and wheel my way out the door. But, when I get to the curb, my front tire is completely flat, and when I kneel to check it, I see that there is a tiny nail stuck near the rim.

I groan out loud and drop my face into my hands, feeling the prick of tears. I'm going to be late now; I hate being late. And my face hurts and I don't want to be living in this stupid house, in this stupid neighbourhood anymore. It all just feels like too much.

"Hey, new girl."

I look up to see Ethen idling some sort of bright orange sports car down near the end of my driveway.

"Oh, hey," I say as unenthusiastically as possible, keeping my head down.

"You have a flat tire?"

"Um, it looks like it." Why won't he go away? I just need a second to *think* so I can figure things out.

The car shuts off abruptly and I hear the door open.

"New girl?" He's right in front of me, standing too close, and I instinctively flinch away. "What happened to your face?"

"Allergies?" I look up to find him staring at me, his expression clouded with concern. He reaches out a tentative hand toward my swollen cheek and I take a step backward.

"That is not allergies," he says in a hard voice.

"I'm fine, really. Sorry, I have to go. I'm going to be late for work."

"Okay." He lets out a slow breath and then steps away, giving me more space. "Get on in then. I'll drive you."

"No," I say quickly, "that's all right. I'll figure it out."

"It's no problem. I don't mind."

I shake my head but then stop. What harm would it do just to let him help me one time? It's kind of an emergency and I don't want to be late for work. He's been pretty nice so far.

"Well, if you're sure," I say doubtfully.

"Of course I'm sure. Push your bike to my house and leave it there. I'll help you fix the tire tonight."

Without waiting for an answer, he gets back in the car and cruises down the road to his house and eases the car to a stop, waiting for me to catch up. I roll the bike right up the walkway and lean it against the faded wooden boards of the house.

"Are you sure it's not going to get stolen?" I ask nervously, looking around to see if anyone has watched me leave it there.

"From *our* yard? Are you kidding? No way. Nobody will touch it."

That doesn't sound shady at all, I think, groaning inwardly.

"Thank you so much for doing this," I say quietly, as soon as I shut the door behind me. "I need this job. I love it. And I don't want to mess it up. I haven't been there that long so I'm still on probation."

"Three Sisters, huh?" he says, glancing over at the logo on my polo shirt. "Is that like some fancy-pants resort or something?"

"No, it's a horse stable. It's a great place, the horses are…"

I break off, embarrassed that I've said too much. As if he wants to listen to me talk about horses the whole way there.

"The horses are what?" he asks curiously.

"Oh, I don't want to bore you."

He frowns and looks out the window.

"New girl, I don't think you could ever bore me."

I freeze, feeling the weight of his words. I really don't want this guy to like me. As nice as it would be to have another person to share all my worries with, it would just be too complicated. Maybe once my life isn't quite so messed up.

"Lena," I say after a short silence. "You can call me Lena. And I was about to say that the horses at Three Sisters are amazing. I never thought I'd find a place that I liked half so much as the old stable I worked at, but this is close."

He listens to me talk about the horses and people I've met with a half smile on his face, nodding at me to keep going whenever I hesitate.

We reach the barn much faster than I'd expected. Anna is going to have to give me that raise if I keep showing up this early. And, I'm strangely disappointed that my short time with Ethen is coming to an end. He isn't so bad after all.

"Wow," he says as the little car crests the hill and the whole farm lies sprawled out before us.

"Isn't it something? You wouldn't believe the work that goes into keeping it looking like this. They have an army of staff."

"Oh, I believe it." He pulls up in front of Barn B and turns to smile at me. "So, what time do I pick you up?"

"You don't have to do that," I say quickly, "I can find a way home. You've done enough already."

"So, like five o'clock, six?"

"Ethen, really." I hear an edge creep into my voice. As nice as he's been, I don't want us to owe each other anything or get too friendly. One car ride in an emergency is fine, but I'm not going to let it go beyond that.

"Look, I know you are perfectly capable of making your way home. I respect that," he says. "I'm heading to work now and tonight we'll get your bike all fixed up. It would be simpler if I just came and grabbed you on my way home. It's even on the way."

I narrow my eyes at him, sure that his innocent grin means that he's lying about that last part.

"All right, fine," I say finally, "but I'm paying you for the bike parts. I don't take charity."

"Deal, no problem. So, I'll see you tonight?"

"Yeah," I grumble, climbing out of the car. Then I duck back in to look at him, realizing how rude I'm being. "Seriously, thank you for helping me. That means a lot."

His grin slips into a genuine smile, and he nods at me.

"Any time. See you tonight."

———

There is a festive feeling in the air as I go into the barn. The driveway up at Barn A is already packed with cars for the clinic, so we've become the overflow parking area and all sorts of strangers are milling around.

I get to work right away, and luckily everyone is kept too

busy to pay attention to my face. I don't even have to use the lie about allergies.

When Kira comes in she looks paler than usual and there are circles under her eyes like she hasn't slept much. I'd managed to catch a few minutes of her lessons over the last few days and she'd looked great; John Riddle was helping her feisty horse to calm down and stop rushing the jumps.

But I'd also noticed that she wasn't up at the ring taking notes all day anymore. The other day she'd left right after her lesson.

Isla and Rebecca come in right behind her and I see Isla's eyes narrow as she zeroes in on Kira.

"Ready to embarrass yourself again, freak?" Isla says loudly. She grins over at Rebecca but the other girl has drawn back, her face troubled.

Kira doesn't look at them but her shoulders sag as she turns toward the tack room. That surprises me; I've never seen Kira react to Isla before.

"Isla," I say sharply, "Samantha is waiting for you, you need to tack up."

This isn't quite true, their lesson isn't for another twenty minutes, but it's enough for Isla to switch her icy gaze to me instead and leave Kira alone.

"I don't need a nanny," she says, rolling her eyes as she sweeps past me.

Rebecca follows more slowly, sending me a tentative smile. She seems like a nice enough girl; I don't know why she hangs out with someone like Isla.

"Lena, could you help Kira get tacked up?" Tonya appears beside me, frowning. She'd definitely overheard what Isla had said. "And then maybe as soon as the chores are done you could go up and watch the lesson. I think she could use some extra support today."

"Okay." I'm not sure what she means by extra support, but I'm not about to turn down the chance to watch the clinic.

Kira stiffens as I approach her outside of Tessa's stall. She looks like she's about to be sick or that she has a headache.

"Tonya asked me to help you get Tessa ready," I say quietly. "Is that okay with you?"

She hesitates and then to my surprise she nods and sends me a half smile.

We get the mare brushed and tacked up together. Tessa seems a little subdued too, which is surprising because she is already very fit and the lessons shouldn't be wearing her out too much.

"Are you doing okay, Kira?" I ask when I'm sure that nobody is within earshot.

"Yeah," she says wearily. "It's just a lot, you know?"

"The clinic? Are his lessons that tough?"

"What? No, the lessons are great. John Riddle is the best. It's all these strangers. I don't like being around so many people."

I look at her in surprise. I don't mind the crowd at all, it makes the barn feel like a party. And everyone is so happy and excited about watching the lessons.

"They all talk so much," Kira adds, closing her eyes for a second. "And it never stops. I can't block them out."

"Are you sure you want to ride today?"

Her eyes flash open in annoyance. "Of course I do. There are only a couple of days left. I can handle it."

"I know you can," I say reassuringly. "You and Tessa are a great team. Tonya said I could come to watch your lesson. If you don't mind."

She blinks at me and then nods.

"I'd like that," she says finally and then leads Tessa away.

I finish the rest of my chores in record time and, as soon as

I'm sure that everyone in Samantha's lesson is tacked up and on their way to the ring, I head up toward Barn A.

I practically run up the hill, only slowing when I reach the towering entryway to Barn A. I can hear John Riddle's voice projecting from the microphone and when I reach the arena, I slip inside to stand against the wall where the rest of the grooms and non-paying auditors are standing.

Kira is walking Tessa around the top of the ring while Josh and Hectic Electric are powering around a difficult course.

The top side of the arena is packed with people, many sitting on folding chairs and the others lined up against the wall like me.

I sidle down further as more people come in. We're all squashed in like sardines.

Kira is up next and I can see now why Tessa is exhausted. John Riddle has set up a complicated course made of poles and grids that were designed so a horse has to back off the jumps and be careful. It's very technical and there is no way for Tessa to just blow through it like a racehorse. She has to pause and think her way through it, and you can tell that her brain is working overtime just trying to figure everything out.

She looks great, though, and it's not like she's hating it. Kira looks good too and you can tell that both of them are working as hard as they can to follow John Riddle's instructions.

"Good job, Kira," I whisper as she navigates the triple bar at a sharp angle.

The girl beside me nudges my elbow and smiles at me. "She's good, isn't she?"

"Yeah." I look over and do a double take. The girl is wearing lime-green leggings and some sort of soft knee-high riding boots trimmed with tassels and beads at the top. I dimly recognize her as someone who takes lessons from Elliot but I can't remember her name.

The rest of the lesson passes seamlessly. Kira looks less pale, more like her old self, by the time it's over and she leaves the ring smiling.

I hesitate, wondering if I should follow her, but there are so many people here that I'd have to push my way through them to get out. And, Tonya had said I could spend a couple of hours here.

The strange girl stays beside me the whole time, watching with just as much fascination as I do. We don't speak again and, when my time is up, I squeeze past her with a nod and a smile and head back down the hill. My head is filled with all the information I've soaked in from watching the clinic and I can't wait to get a chance to write it all down.

But first, the horses need their lunch and I have to see if anyone else needs a hand getting ready.

By the time lunch rolls around, my stomach is grumbling with hunger. We are not invited to the big buffet that is happening at Barn A but, with any luck, there will be leftovers again that we'll be allowed to pick over afterward.

I grab my backpack from the feed room and head outside to eat in the sunshine. But when I walk past the tack room door, I see Kira sitting all alone on her tack trunk, her face pale and miserable.

"What's wrong?" I ask, hesitating in the doorway.

"I can't eat this," she says weakly, pushing the plastic container on her lap aside and breathing deeply through her mouth as if she was trying to keep herself calm, or from throwing up.

"What is that? Leftovers from home? Why aren't you eating at the buffet with everyone else?"

"The smells make me gag," she says, closing her eyes. "I can't go up there right now."

"Oh." I wondered if Isla had been right about her having some sort of eating disorder.

"It's not always this bad." She looks down, scuffing her boot into the concrete floor. "When I'm stressed out it makes it worse. I should have packed a sandwich. I knew better than to bring Grace's gross ravioli. It has actual pockets of meat in it that just burst when you bite into them. It's completely revolting."

She flicks her nails against the container, sending the lid skittering sideways across the trunk. Instantly the delicious smell of pasta hits me.

"I can't believe you think that's gross," I say, raising an eyebrow. I have been starving enough times in my life that I would never, ever, dream of turning down food. "I just have a boring old peanut butter sandwich."

She looks up suddenly, her eyes lighting up.

"We should trade," she says quickly.

"Uh." I look around to make sure we're alone. "I can't take your food, Kira. I'm not sure Anna would like it."

"Why would she care? You'd be doing me a favour."

"Well." I hesitate, eyeing up the container. The smell wafts over me in a delicious cloud.

"Fine," I say, "just this once. Okay, pass it over."

Kira looks like she's won the lottery when I hand her my two sandwiches.

And I retreat to my space in the doorway like a wildebeest to devour the ravioli before she can change her mind. It is full of flavour, and probably homemade, and I lick the spoon and scrape the Tupperware when it's all gone, trying to hold on to the taste of it.

"I can bring you more tomorrow," she says, watching me as she eats her sandwiches in neat little bites. "You bring me two of these and I'll trade you as often as you like."

"Sure," I say shamelessly, because honestly who could turn

down food like this? "But why did you bring something you don't like? Can't you just bring your own sandwiches?"

She frowns and takes another bite. "It's stupid. You don't want to know."

"Sure, I do."

"Well, my dad thinks I eat too many of the same things. I'm supposed to be broadening my tastes a little. It's one of my conditions of getting to spend so much time with the horses. I have to pack nutritious lunches and eat gross things sometimes."

I stare at her in surprise, shuddering a little at the thought of somebody telling me what to do like that. The one benefit of having a neglectful parent like Natalia is that I am nearly completely in charge of my own life.

"Kira, that's awful. You should be able to eat whatever you like. He's like, using horses to bribe you."

"I know. But, it's not like he's trying to be mean. My dad worries about me nonstop and he thinks he's doing the right thing. He's all paranoid that I'll be malnourished or something. Anyway, he paid for Tessa to ride in this clinic when we can't really afford it, so it's the least I can do to compromise. Normally, I can just push through but this week has been kind of overwhelming."

"I suppose so," I say doubtfully. "Well, at least he cares, I guess. My mom doesn't even know what I eat. I do all my own grocery shopping and stuff."

I wisely leave out the part about the food bank.

"Wow, really? I've barely even been to a grocery store. Grace orders all our stuff online and gets it delivered."

"You're missing out then. The bigger stores downtown have sample carts where you can eat free cheese and things. You can practically get a whole meal for free if you visit every cart."

I pause, feeling my face flushing, wondering if I've said way too much. I don't want any of my personal life getting back to Anna. She's not supposed to know how desperate I am. To distract myself, I lean down and unzip my backpack to get my water bottle.

"Hey, is that a model horse?" Kira asks, and I look down to see that Jax's little broken-eared head is poking out.

"Er, yes." I shove him guiltily down to the bottom of my bag, wishing that I didn't have to carry all my worldly possessions around with me all the time.

"Can I see him?"

She's looking at my backpack eagerly and I can't see any polite way to refuse.

"Sure, I guess." I pull Jax reluctantly out and hand him to her, noticing again how battered he's looking. Ears chipped, that broken foreleg and his paint rubbed off in places from living in my backpack.

"This is a limited-edition Breyerfest classic," she says, "there were only a few hundred made. This is a collector's item now. He's probably not worth much in the condition he's in, though."

"Yeah, he's had a rough life. How do you know what type of horse he is?" I ask curiously.

"I'm a collector. And I do some custom sculpting myself. I can fix him if you like." She says this offhand like it's no big deal, flipping him over so she can examine the spot where his leg has been broken off.

"What do you mean you can fix him? How?"

"Easy. Some epoxy for the ears and I probably have a spare leg lying around we can use on him. Or, we can find one online if not."

I stare at her in astonishment. "Spare leg? What, do you have a collection of body parts lying around?"

"Actually, yes. As I said, I do some custom work and I show them at model horse shows. Do you want me to fix it or not?"

I look down to where Jax is resting in her hands, feeling torn. While I would love to see him all fixed up, I also don't want to be without him. He's the last thing I have of my brother's and, as silly as it sounds, he feels like a protective talisman for me. Like I'm safe when I have Jax nearby. Ridiculous, I know, yet there it is.

Kira is staring at me, frowning as she studies my face.

"I can't tell what you're thinking," she says finally. "You can come to see my studio space if you're worried about me doing a good job. You can see some of my other projects."

"Wow, you have your own studio?"

"You could come for dinner after work one day," she says. "Grace would love to cook for someone who actually appreciates her food."

She smiles suddenly and takes a final bite of her sandwich.

I hesitate for a second. Anna has told us that we're not supposed to fraternize with the riders too much. But surely, she meant during work hours, not on our own time. And the urge to have more of that incredible ravioli again is almost overwhelming.

"Okay, that would be great. Whatever night works for you."

"I'll have to ask my dad if you can come but I'm betting he'll be thrilled that I'm having a friend over." She pauses and then frowns, tilting her head to study me as if she's trying to guess what I'm thinking. "We are friends now, right?"

"Of course." I smile at her as convincingly as I can. It's not a complete lie; I am starting to like her and there is no doubt that she's a good rider. But, I don't have the luxury of having best friends who you share secrets with and invite over for movie nights and things. Maybe when I'm eighteen and finally free to live on my own. But not now. It's too risky. That's how I'd been sent into foster care last time. A concerned parent of one of my so-called friends had reported my bruises. I wasn't ever going to let that happen to me again.

Something flickers over Kira's face and I have the feeling that she's not quite buying it. But she doesn't take back her offer for dinner.

"All right, after the clinic then," she says slowly, "next week."

"That sounds great."

She just nods and silently takes back the Tupperware I hand her, not quite meeting my eye.

Chapter 15

Lena

The rest of the day passes quickly. I alternate between working at Barn B and running up to watch some sessions of the clinic. There are fewer spectators as the day goes on and I'm able to sit on one of the folding chairs for a bit rather than standing.

All the lessons have been amazing. With only a few exceptions, all the riders are talented and dedicated and the horses are top-class.

I sit down just as a younger girl who I recognize as Alice Carlisle is piloting a fiery pony around the course. She stands in the stirrups as she passes by me, a determined expression on her face as the pony explodes over each jump in a burst of power.

"Good," John Riddle says, as she canters a circle afterward, "now do it again. Only this time…hey, watch out."

There is a gasp from the remaining members of the audience as she and her pony crash right into a jump standard. Poles scatter and the anxious pony rears and tries to bolt.

Alice steadies him, turning him in a circle and reaching down to pat his neck as he slows.

"Sorry, pony," I hear her whisper, "that was my fault. Please don't be hurt."

"Alice, come into the center for a second."

"Sorry," she calls out, "I didn't see it in front of me. I must not have been paying attention. I'll do it again."

"How about you take a breather while Maggie has a go at it. Let's give that pony a second to settle his nerves."

Alice clenches her jaw as John Riddle turns to the other rider and begins to coach her through the exercise. She rubs her hands across her eyes a few times as though they're hurting her.

Nothing else dramatic happens, though, and I get to sit peacefully for the next hour until it's time for me to get back to my chores.

⸻

When six o clock hits and there is no sign of Ethen, I start to nervously wonder if he's forgotten that he promised to pick me up. I'm about to start walking the long trek to the bus stop when his car comes rumbling up the hill and he parks with a flourish in front of the barn.

"Hey," he says, hopping out with a smile. "How was work?"

"Great, thanks, I wasn't sure if you were coming."

"Of course, I came." He looks offended that I'd even second-guessed him. "I promised I would. I don't break my promises, new girl."

"Lena," I remind him.

"I stopped to get us some burgers and some new tires and

inner tubes for your bike. Those last ones are shot. The rubber is practically crumbling away."

"Yeah, well, it's an old bike," I say. "Wait, you brought burgers?"

"I did. I wasn't sure what you liked so I grabbed fries and onion rings too. And drinks. And dessert."

"Wow, you didn't have to do that. Thank you. I can pay you back when payday comes if that's all right."

"No, don't worry. This one is my treat. Come on, get in and we'll stop at the beach so we can eat."

"The beach?"

"Yeah, it will be too messy to eat in the car. You don't have anything against the beach, do you?"

"No." I get in with a sigh. No matter how well-meaning he might be, I have the feeling that I'm going to have to keep an eye on Ethen. He seems like the pushy type who is going to try and get me to let down my guard so he can work his way into my life somehow.

The beach isn't far and soon Ethen is pulling up next to a grassy area with a picnic table and a view of the ocean. It's not the kind of beach you can walk out on; the site is perched on a high cliff in a cove. You can see right across to the opposite spit of land where the ocean spray crashes upward about twenty feet every time it hits the unforgiving wall of rock.

Despite my misgivings, I can't help but think that it's a beautiful spot. The air smells fresh and salty. Seagulls are spinning and screaming overhead and the waves crash against the cliff face beneath us with a whooshing rumble.

"You were right, this is nice," I say, biting into my burger.

"It's one of my favourite spots. I come here when I need to think about things."

I nod. Watching the endless, rolling ocean does put life in perspective a bit.

"Does your cheek feel better?"

"Yep, it's fine. I hardly notice it anymore." This isn't quite true, but I know that any lingering pain will be gone by tomorrow.

Thankfully he lets it go. And he also pushes his unfinished fries toward me after I've hoovered my own food down and am still looking for more. The feeling of being full puts me in a happy, sleepy mood and I'm able to laugh and joke around with him like a normal person for an hour.

We go back to his front yard after that and I hang out and keep him company while he tinkers on the bike without letting me help. Nobody else seems to be around, but I don't ask him about his family. I'm doing my best not to learn anything more about him. I can already feel myself getting too attached.

Dusk starts to fall and a few early stars flicker in the sky. It's peaceful here, even in a yard full of rusty cars up on blocks in a run-down neighbourhood where I don't want to be. Cars whoosh by every so often but for the most part, it's quiet. For the first time in a very long time, I find myself feeling kind of relaxed and content.

"There you go," Ethen says, flipping the bike upright and rolling it toward me, "good as new."

"Thanks so much. And for dinner too. I will repay you as soon as I can."

"Sure, sure, anytime. Maybe we could go back to the beach again."

This morning, or even an hour ago, I would have said no, but I am feeling strangely mellow right now.

"All right. I'd like that," I find myself saying. And there's no way to take it back.

He grins at me instantly and already I am regretting my hasty words. Ethen is definitely on his way to becoming a complication that I don't need.

Chapter 16

Kira

By the last day of the clinic, I am exhausted. The second my lesson is over I bail without staying to see anyone else ride.

My dad had taken time off work to watch my final lesson, which was a bit of a surprise; he'd even stuck around to have a few private words with John Riddle while I'd gone to untack Tessa, although I wasn't sure what that was about.

John and I had already said our goodbyes since I wouldn't be going to the final dinner that night. I'd thanked him like a million times for all the good advice he'd given me to help Tessa.

"You keep working away with her," John had told me. "And don't give up on your goal of being a trainer. Lots can happen in the next few years. The best thing for you to do is ride as many different types of horses as you can right now. Broaden your scope. Hopefully, we'll see you back here next year for another clinic."

I'd nodded happily and had even let him give me a brief hug. I was fully intending to take another clinic with him in the future. I would just have to find a way to pay for it myself.

"That was a pretty great week, kiddo," my dad says, once we are in the car. "I know events like that can be hard on you, but you did a great job keeping things together. I'm proud of you."

"Thanks," I say, closing my eyes and sagging back against the seat. I guess it's nice that, from the outside, I'd looked like I'd been handling things just fine. Because, on the inside, I'd felt about two seconds away from some sort of minor collapse the entire time.

Whenever I'm under a lot of stress, even when it's good stress like being excited over riding in a clinic, my brain sort of gets hyperaware of every single thing. Every noise, smell and visual thing going on around me, my brain takes in and tries to process.

Most people can block out the sound of a fly buzzing against a window or clocks ticking or the fluorescent lighting humming. Voices, chewing, swallowing, rustling paper, tapping feet. The horses in the barn, the birds in the sky, cars crunching on gravel. Snack wrappers being ripped open and pens scratching across paper.

I hear Every. Single. Thing. All at once, like a symphony of discordant noise threatening to drown me. It's hard to even function sometimes. Not being able to filter things out can lead to a massive migraine that lasts for days if I'm not careful.

The clinic wasn't so bad when I was actually riding, but the rest of the time was a constant struggle to stay afloat.

So, I'm glad my dad is proud of me and everything, but I don't think he has a clue about how hard I'm working to keep myself functional.

"Oh no," my dad says and I open my eyes abruptly to discover that I must have dozed off because we're already home. And, parked in front of the garage is a familiar-looking white Mercedes.

"Not now," I groan. "Can't you tell her to go away?"

It is my Aunt Irene, my mother's sister, the only one from that side of the family who continues to visit us, although I'm not sure why.

"Kira," my dad says warningly and then sighs. "Well, she only shows up once a year. If you see her now then you can probably avoid her at Christmas."

"Please tell me you didn't know she was coming."

"Nope, this is a surprise for me too. But come on, we need to be polite. She's your mother's sister, after all."

I don't see the logic in this. When my mom decided to walk out on us, she'd made a completely clean break. Even though Dad insists that I was too young to remember the day she left, I actually can picture the whole thing perfectly.

It was one of the few times I'd seen her look happy. She'd worn this beautiful white, fitted outfit and I remember thinking how pretty and young she'd looked as she'd packed her suitcase.

"It's best for her if I don't visit," she'd said, standing in the front doorway, not even glancing over at me. "It would be too confusing for me to go back and forth. She wouldn't understand. It's better for everyone this way."

What she'd really meant was that it was better for *her*.

After that, I'd never heard from her again. She never visits or calls at Christmas or remembers my birthday. She is remarried and everything and has two kids, half-sisters that I've never met. She wasted no time in creating a new perfect family.

My dad has told me over and over that she didn't leave because of me, but I think we both know the truth. They'd been arguing about me for months, maybe years, before the divorce. But it's nice of him to try and protect my feelings.

But though Mom and my grandparents could let Dad and me go without a backward glance, my Aunt Irene can't seem to do the same. She usually shows up once a year out of the blue for a weekend, showering presents on me and insisting that I spend quality time with her.

Which would be kind of flattering if she didn't also try to make me do every single one of the things I hate all in one weekend. Shopping, concerts, theatres and strange restaurants. A nightmare.

"Darling!" she calls out in her musical, high-pitched voice that sounds almost exactly like my mom's had. "You've grown."

She swoops down and wraps me in a bruising hug that feels like it's crushing every bone in my body. Then she deposits some air kisses about a foot from my head and turns to my dad.

"I hope you don't mind that I dropped in unannounced. I'm only in town for a few days and I thought it was time for a visit. Life has been just a whirlwind. Your mother sends her love to both of you, of course."

This is one hundred percent a lie. Even when she was around, my mother had rarely shown anything resembling love to me.

"Irene," my dad says evenly, accepting her fake kisses politely. "Good to see you."

"Oh, and you as well. You're looking a bit tired. Have you been sleeping all right? I see this wonderful alternative doctor now and he's gotten me hooked on meditation. And it's like a miracle. I feel years younger. Oh, wow, the two of you really smell like the farm."

"We just came from Three Sisters," my dad says, "Kira was riding in a..."

"Oh, I know, it's always horses, horses, horses with this one. Did you buy those season tickets to the ballet as I suggested? It can't hurt Kira to broaden her horizons a little and it's something cultural that the two of you can do together."

"Um, no," my dad says, sending a warning glance my way. "My caseload keeps my schedule pretty full."

"Oh, you don't have to tell me about that. You wouldn't believe how full my days are. I am on five boards now. Can you believe that? Who knew that volunteering would be such a full-time job?"

"Uh-huh. Will you be staying long?"

"Just a few nights if you can spare the room. I have a plane booked for Amsterdam. Have you been yet, Kira?"

"Er, no."

"Oh dear, you can't be a homebody forever. Almost all the important lessons I've learned in life have been through travel. When you're older we'll do a girl's trip through Europe, just the two of us. How does that sound?"

"That sounds—"

"Right, well, let's get your luggage inside," my dad interrupts. Cutting me off before I can tell her how I'd really feel about spending weeks in her company.

▭

I know that I'm risking a migraine if I don't recharge my batteries with some alone time, so I slip upstairs to shower and change, leaving my dad to entertain Irene on his own.

I don't come back down until dinner time, which I'm pretty sure Aunt Irene would consider rude, but the hours spent just lying quietly in the dark with my noise-cancelling headphones on make me feel so much better.

"There you are, dear, I made your favourite," Grace whispers as I sneak into the kitchen.

I can hear my dad and Irene talking in the den and I'd like to avoid them as long as possible.

"Ooh, macaroni and cheese," I say excitedly because this is something I really love. It's a far cry from the mac and cheese you get in a box. Grace makes it from scratch and there are three different types of cheese in there, plus lobster and a toasted breadcrumb topping. It is ridiculously good but she usually only makes it on special occasions.

"I thought you could use a treat," she says, "considering that you have company."

She waves a hand toward the den and I can tell by the look on her face that she's still not Irene's biggest fan. Grace always grumbles when my aunt is around.

"She's planning to stay for a couple of days," I say, wrinkling my nose. "It's a good thing Tessa is having a vacation after the clinic so I'm not missing any riding."

"You'd think that after all these years that woman would get the hint that your dad just isn't interested."

I nod and then spin around, suddenly realizing what she's said. "Wait, what? She comes here because she's interested in Dad?"

"Shhhh," Grace says, flicking her towel at me in irritation. "Keep your voice down. And you never mind what I said, I was just muttering out loud. How is that other horse you were riding, anyway? Flicker."

I know when somebody is changing the subject on me, but Grace isn't the type to give out any information she doesn't want to part with. I will have to question her again when she's not on her guard.

"He's fine. I mean, he's just hanging out in his stall and the pasture. Nobody has ridden him since the clinic and Marsha hasn't been around at all. I haven't even seen Oliver in the last few days."

"Oliver, hey? That's the cute boy who was watching your lessons?"

"Grace." I groan. "I didn't say he was cute. He's just another rider at the barn, nothing special."

"Uh-huh. So what does this nothing special look like?"

"I don't know. Like a boy. He's all right."

For a second an image of his nice crinkle-eyed smile and the kind way he handles Flicker appears in my mind.

"All right, you don't have to tell me," Grace says good-naturedly. "But if you have questions about anything—dating, kissing and well, *things*—then you know you can always ask me."

"It's really not like that," I say hurriedly, "he's just a friend. Kind of. And he'd never….I mean, we're not… He's like this popular guy that everyone likes and I'm…me."

I look up at Grace, my cheeks burning.

"Kira Anderson," she says firmly, "you are pretty and smart and just as good as any girl out there. There is no reason that a nice boy wouldn't like you."

"Uh-huh," I say doubtfully. I appreciate that Grace is in my corner but I don't think she knows much about how relationships work. It's not like guys are falling all over me in school or anything. Sure, I'm not bullied in my new school, but that's because I am mostly ignored.

And yes, having a boyfriend is nice as an abstract concept. But I'm not sure I could handle that in real life. I still feel like a kid sometimes. A kid who just wants to ride ponies, play in my room working on puzzles and model horses. A kid who likes to watch Disney movies and who definitely doesn't want to talk about fashion, makeup or the latest celebrities. What type of guy would be attracted to a person like that?

Chapter 17

Kira

*D*inner with Aunt Irene goes unexpectedly well. She can be very charming and funny when she likes, especially when the wine is flowing, so she keeps us entertained all through dinner, telling us about all the places she's travelled to and the interesting people she's met.

It almost makes me want to travel to a few places myself, although so far I've never gone further than the Lower Mainland.

But, first thing the next morning, Aunt Irene wrecks the easy, friendly atmosphere of the night before by insisting on taking me shopping.

I am not a shopper. I hate crowds, line-ups, noise and overly bright indoor lighting. The change rooms are always weird, especially the ones where there are flimsy curtains instead of locking doors, and I'm often too afraid to get undressed because I'm paranoid that some stranger is going to barge in and see me in my underwear.

I much prefer to buy my things online. I know my favourite brands and sizes and I'm free to browse dozens of stores from the comfort of my own home. I even buy riding gear that way. I love soft, natural fabrics that aren't too tight.

I try to calmly tell all this to Aunt Irene but she waves me off with a laugh.

"Oh, don't be silly," she says in her high, lilting voice, "every girl likes to go shopping. We can get pedicures afterward and have some girl time. We need to catch up on all the gossip."

I'm not sure what gossip she's looking for from me since I'm only ever at home, the barn or Donna's office, but I finally give in with a sigh.

Aunt Irene doesn't stop talking in the car the whole way to the upscale mall downtown. I would have thought that someone as concerned about fashion and travel as she is would have gone to the boutique stores in the fashion district, but apparently not.

"So, is your father seeing anyone special right now?"

She turns off the ignition and smiles at me innocently but I can see a flash of something else, something predatory, in her eyes as they narrow in on me.

"Um, no." I gulp. "He's pretty busy with work."

"Oh, that's a shame. It would be good for you to have a woman in the house. Someone who can guide you."

I nearly choke at that one. "We have Grace, at least part-time; she's a great cook."

Aunt Irene makes a little, irritated huffing sound.

"Grace," she says sharply, "is not quite who I had in mind. Anyway, we're here to have fun. Let's get shopping."

The next three hours are about as painful and mortifying as I'd anticipated. I *did* try my best to behave like she wanted me to. I trailed her into every store and tried on all the scratchy, awkward clothes she picked out for me without complaint.

I'm sure that Aunt Irene has great taste in clothing and all, but nothing she chooses has anything to do with my own style or is in colours I actually like. I do my best to keep an open mind; she is trying to be nice, after all, but it's like she just ignores every opinion that I have.

"Oh, don't be silly, this colour looks great on you. Not all clothing has to be comfortable. You'll thank me when the boys start noticing you. You'd be such a pretty girl if you had the right clothes and makeup. You don't even look autistic at all, so you have every chance of being a popular girl at school if you'd just make an effort."

"Wait, what?" I'd been trailing after her dutifully, tuning out most of what she said and trying not to hyperventilate in the middle of the crowded mall. "What do you mean I don't look autistic?"

"Oh, well, you know." She flutters her hands nervously and pretends to examine a display of cell phone cases in one of those kiosks next to the food court. "You look *normal*, like everyone else. It's a compliment, Kira."

"Is it?" I'm already irritable and overwhelmed from all this shopping and a headache has begun to pound away behind my right eye. "Aunt Irene, I'm not ashamed of being autistic. It's not a disease; it's just the way my brain is designed. I don't want to be like everyone else."

She stares at me open-mouthed.

"But sweetie, of course you want to be like everyone else. You don't have any friends and you spend all your time with horses. A girl your age should be out partying and having fun with boys. And you had all those troubles in school. I think the other children sense that you're different. If you'd only try a little harder…"

"Wow, thanks," I say, cutting her off. "So, you're saying you want me to be mean and manipulative like the girls at school who bullied me? That's the *normal* you're hoping for me to aspire to?"

"There's no need to get snippy." Her earnest expression falls away and I can see that she's just as irritated with me as I am with her. "I'm only trying to help."

"Thanks, but I don't need help. I like who I am and I like my life."

She raises her eyebrows and crosses her arms across her chest, looking down at me coldly. "Well, I think you're mistaken. You do need my help. Badly. When I think of how wild your father is letting you run, I just shudder. Your poor mother would be horrified."

She breaks off suddenly, her cheeks turning pink, and looks a little guilty.

"I think we should go home now," I say quietly. "I'm not having a good time anymore."

She blinks at me and whatever guilt she might have felt morphs into anger again.

"You are an ungrateful, spoiled girl," she says, loudly enough that some of the shoppers nearby turn to look at her. "I bought you all these clothes. I'm trying to improve your situation."

"You can return them," I say, setting the bags down and backing away from her. "I would have just donated them to charity anyway. Goodbye."

"Kira," she snaps. "Where are you going?"

I speed up, slipping through the crowds until I'm sure I've left her far behind. I push through the heavy front doors and nearly sob with relief when I'm safely outside.

Don't melt down yet, I tell myself firmly. My heart is beating wildly and it's hard to catch my breath, but I still need to make it home. To my right, I catch sight of a bookstore, one that I've been to a few times before, and I make my way to it and slip inside into the cool, blessedly quiet, lobby.

I take a few minutes to calm down, wandering around from shelf to shelf, not even noticing the titles until I have control of myself again.

Finally, I take a deep, shuddering breath and pause by the window to look out at the street. A bus chugs by and I suddenly think of Lena who takes the bus everywhere. She can just jump on any one of these things and go wherever she wants, whenever she wants. I've never even been on one. I wouldn't know how to pay my fare or how to pick one that goes to my neighbourhood.

I sigh and pull out my phone, pressing the button for Blacklock. Right now I just want to get home as fast as possible, but as soon as I have a chance to talk to Lena again I'm going to get her to show me how to use public transit. It's time for me to start taking more control of my life.

The car service doesn't take long to come and I slide onto the polished leather seat gratefully. It isn't Regan driving this time, so we just nod to each other and spend the rest of the ride to my house in silence.

There is no sign of Aunt Irene when I get home, thankfully, and I run up to my room and lock the door firmly behind me. There is a chance that she's going to be really angry with me when she finally makes it back and I don't want to have her barge in and start yelling at me. I slip on my noise-cancelling headphones, send a quick text to my dad to tell him that I'd come home early from shopping, and move over to my workspace.

If I can't go to the barn, then working on the model horses is the next best thing. Something I can get lost in for hours so I can put off thinking about all the uncomfortable thoughts that are suddenly pressing in on me. I'm usually happy with my life, mostly, but the way Aunt Irene had looked down on me, had seen me as something defective, had caught me completely off-guard. Was that really how other people saw me?

I turn the plastic horse between my hands with a sigh. It's my latest entry for an upcoming show and I'd decided to make him an elegant bay warmblood with markings like Flicker's. The plastic body is already prepped and primed; ready for me to apply the thousand layers it will take to make him look like a realistic horse.

The second I sit down, my worries fade away and time just disappears. The familiar work soothes me and I'm so focused that, by the time I sit up and stretch my aching muscles out, I am surprised to see that the sun has faded a little and it's probably near dinner time.

I slip off my headphones cautiously, shaking out my cramping hands to get the blood flowing to them again.

The sound of loud voices downstairs pulls me to my feet and I creep to the door, turn the lock and slowly ease it open.

"She's running completely wild," Aunt Irene is saying angrily. "She has no friends, she dresses like a twelve-year-old, and she's completely obsessed with horses. How is any of that normal? She needs somebody to take her in hand and *guide* her before it's too late."

I grip the door handle, straining to hear my dad's quieter response.

Please don't agree with her. Please don't ask her to stay longer.

"Kira is doing just fine," he says firmly. "She loves being at the barn and she's old enough to choose what she wears, for heaven's sake. And she's a talented rider. I honestly had no idea how talented until this weekend."

"But there's no *future* in horses," Aunt Irene practically wails. "It's fine as a hobby but she needs to grow up. You should have seen her at the mall today; you could tell it was practically killing her to be there. That's not normal. I had to almost force her to…"

"Wait, you saw that being there was causing her pain and yet you didn't leave? You kept shopping?" Dad asks, his voice suddenly icy.

"Well, yes, I suppose. But she has to learn someday. Every girl needs to learn how to suffer a little unpleasantness in order to fit in. You don't want her being a social outcast forever."

There is a scraping sound like a chair being pushed back.

"I think you should leave," my dad says in a quiet voice.

"What? You can't mean that," she says tearfully. "I'm only here to help. I want what's best for Kira. I care about her… about both of you."

"I know," he says quietly. "I appreciate that you've tried to be a part of Kira's life after Cammy left us."

"And yours," she says quickly. "I want to be here for you too."

"Um, yes, of course. But what I was about to say is that if you're going to keep in touch with Kira, then you'll to have to stop trying to change her. She's fine just as she is and she doesn't need you to fix her life. Unless we come to an understanding on that, then I'm afraid you won't be allowed to visit anymore."

I feel a swelling of gratitude in my heart. Irene, on the other hand, makes a sort of choking sound.

"You have got to be kidding," she says incredulously. "After what I've seen today, I have to say that she is a rude, stubborn and ungrateful girl. If somebody doesn't take her in hand soon then she's going to turn out to be completely wild. She'll never be able to hold down a job or have a normal life. Her mother would be appalled with her behaviour."

"Her mother gave up the right to be appalled when she walked out that door," my dad says evenly. "I think it's time for you to leave now, Irene. I'll book a hotel room for you to stay in tonight. My treat. But I think it's best if we don't visit again."

I shut the door carefully to cut off my aunt's outraged

protests. Their voices go on for a few moments longer and then there is silence. Finally, I hear the front door slam and the sound of her car starting.

As soon as I'm sure she's gone, I throw open my door and run downstairs.

"Are you okay, Dad?" I ask when I find him in the den nursing a scotch.

"What? Oh yes. How much of that did you hear?"

"Pretty much all of it." I sit down on the couch beside him. "Thanks so much for taking my side. Today was a nightmare."

"I'll bet. Good thinking on calling the car service. I'm glad you made it home safely."

"So, you think I'm a talented rider, do you?"

He laughs and reaches out to ruffle my hair. He's literally the only person I'd let do something like that.

"Yes, I do. And your John Riddle thinks so too. When you're older he said you should apply for a working student position at his farm."

"Really? I'd love that."

"That's what I figured. Maybe once you've finished university you could apply. Well, you'd better go tell Grace there'll only be two of us for dinner. I bet she'll be thrilled that Irene is gone."

▭

I didn't get off completely free, though. That night, the stress of Irene's visit and the week-long clinic finally caught up with me and I came down with the world's worst migraine. It took me two whole days before I felt somewhat normal again.

Two days before I returned to the barn, and discovered that everything there had completely changed.

Chapter 18

Lena

I stay late on the last day of the clinic, helping to put away all the folding chairs and tables that had been set up for the auditors and participants. And raking the parking lot smooth from where all the extra cars had made unsightly ruts in the gravel.

We had to start packing the trailers too because in three days most of the riders and horses would be off to another horse show again.

"Thanks for all your help, Lena," Anna says just as I'm leaving. "And for working on your days off too. You can have an extra vacation day next week if you like."

"No, that's okay," I say quickly. "I don't mind at all. I love working here."

And the extra pay didn't hurt either. Or being able to avoid my depressing home for a few more hours.

The buses don't run as often at this hour so it's nearly dusk by the time I'm cruising toward my house. I'm so caught up in my thoughts that I don't hear the shouting until it's almost too late.

I skid to a stop when I see Todd's battered old truck in the driveway.

Something smashes inside and I can hear Natalia's sharp voice rising into a screech.

Terror spikes through my veins. Natalia in a rage is something that I will do anything to avoid. The very sound of her raised voice makes me want to ride as fast as I can in another direction and never stop.

Some last vestige of logic makes me pause, though. I do have to work the next day and I can't ride around all night. Better to hide somewhere nearby and keep an eye on the house. There's a chance that she and Todd might leave and I can have the whole place to myself like usual soon.

The park, I think finally, pedaling reluctantly toward the mangy woods at the end of the street.

I pass the rusty, deserted playground and jump off my bike as I reach the edge of the woods. The trees are thinner around the edge of the clearing and I can push easily inside, moving forward until my bike can't go any further and I'm forced to stop.

I look back, sure that nobody can see me from the road, and then I pull my backpack off and crouch down, waiting for my heart to stop thumping so hard.

I hate being overwhelmed with panic like that. I hate not being in control and just wanting to curl up somewhere safe and hide. When I was little it was Garret who took care of me, protected me and hid me away while he took all the brunt of her rage. He did this over and over again until he finally couldn't take it anymore. I didn't blame him for running away. I only blamed him for not taking me with him.

I sit cross-legged on the ground, feeling the cool seeping up from the earth. I lean against the roughened tree at my back and heave out a deep breath.

Safe. At least temporarily. I have a couple of granola bars in my backpack, my phone is charged; there isn't anything to worry about for the moment.

I'm not sure how long I sit there. Long enough for the sun to fade and for shadows to start creeping across the ground. Long enough for my legs to go numb and for me to realize that I'm thirsty.

Back in my old life, when we'd lived on the mainland, I occasionally used to sneak to Gretchen's stable when things like this happened. I could creep in and curl up in the barn and then pretend in the morning that I'd just arrived extra early. Falling asleep with the sound of the horses eating had given me some of the best night's sleep of my life.

But I can hardly do that at Three Sisters. They probably have a security system and cameras and things. They'd think I was breaking in to steal something and for sure I'd be fired, if not arrested.

I don't have money for a motel room, and if I go to a shelter then someone will start asking uncomfortable questions like how old I am and where my parents are.

I stiffen suddenly as soft voices carry through the dusk, getting closer.

Just little kids, I tell myself as their laughter filters through the woods. *Or ghosts.*

I stay frozen, poised and alert, not relaxing again until I'm sure I'm alone.

A branch crackles right near me and I scramble upright, spinning on the balls of my feet with my arms raised defensively. I know how to fight if I need to. Garret had seen to that.

"Are you Lena?"

The little boy stares at me solemnly, dark eyes ringed by even darker lashes. He has beaten-up running shoes, scruffy blond hair and a T-shirt that has more holes in it than fabric. He looks like a feral child that has raised himself in the woods.

"Um, yes?" I say cautiously, reaching for my backpack. Everything inside of me is preparing to run.

"My brother said to tell you that the police are at your house. You're supposed to stay here for a while until he comes and gets you. Okay?"

"The police," I say, feeling numb. Police ask questions sometimes and might alert a social worker if they discover that I'm living there.

"Domestic disturbance," the kid stumbles a little on the second word, "the old guy across the street called it in because the fighting sounded bad."

"Is Todd hurt?" I ask woodenly, wondering if Natalia will have to go back to jail.

"No, just a black eye. Your mother is really mad, though. She's kind of scary. You can stay with us tonight. You'll be safe there."

Adrenaline floods through me and, with it, the urge to run. I need to get away from this nightmare.

"Wait," the kid says as I start to push my bike back through the woods. "You're supposed to stay here. Ethen says...."

But I can't stick around. Suddenly I feel like the whole world is pushing in on me, like I'm trapped and I just have to get away. To go anywhere but here. I jump on my bike as soon as I'm clear of the woods and start to ride as fast as I can, the pedals pumping in rhythm to the pounding of my heart.

What if I keep going? What if I ride and ride until I find a new place? A new town to live in where nobody knows my name and I could just start over fresh. No Natalia, no grinding worry about money, no going to bed hungry. Just a place where everything is taken care of and I don't have to always live so close to disaster.

That place doesn't exist, I remind myself firmly. There is no magical place where things will suddenly be easy for me. I have at least another year of this drama with Natalia before I'm legally allowed to be on my own.

Eventually, my breakneck pace eases. I have no idea where I am but I also don't care much. The streets are wide and nicely paved, lined with big trees. The houses are large too, with lush lawns that come down to touch the sidewalks. There is nobody outside to see me pass by.

I will spend the whole night riding around and eventually I will go home and things will be back to normal. Or as normal as they'd ever be.

I can feel how tired I am now, my legs burning with the effort of pedalling and the cold seeping into my bones.

A car rumbles up behind me and then slows.

"Lena, wait," a familiar voice calls when I start to pedal harder.

Ethen. I sigh, feeling a strange mix of irritation and almost tearful gratitude that he found me.

I roll to a stop and let him catch up, watching him cautiously as he shuts the car off and comes toward me with his hands raised like I'm a wild horse that he's afraid of spooking.

"Hey," he says quietly, stopping a few feet away, "you shouldn't have run off. We would have come to get you."

He watches me patiently, his expression full of compassion and understanding.

"I don't need your help." The words are an automatic reflex and even as I say them, I know that I'm lying. I do need help.

"I know," he says, surprising me.

I study his face under the glow of a nearby street lamp. He looks a lot like his feral little brother right now; big eyes and an unkempt, wild look about him.

I'm not sure what to do and the silence stretches out until

he closes the distance between us and then reaches out to place a warm hand on my arm.

"It's okay," he says softly, "everyone crashes at our house when they need to. My mom has an open-door policy. She's making up a big spaghetti dinner tonight too. You don't want to miss that."

I open my mouth to remind him that I don't need his charity but my stomach makes a loud, protesting growl.

We both stare at each other for a second and then he bursts into laughter. And after a minute I smile reluctantly.

"All right," I say, sighing in resignation. "Thanks."

He somehow wrestles my bike into the tiny trunk of his car and we ride silently back to his house. I lean back against the seat, overwhelmed with relief that I don't have to spend the night on the street by myself. I impatiently brush away a couple of stray tears before Ethen can catch me crying.

When we reach his house, I can't help but peer longingly down the street toward my own home. As dilapidated as it is, it has started to grow on me. And, since Natalia has almost always been away until now, it feels pretty comfortable. Like a bit of a sanctuary. But I guess that had been a complete illusion; there will be no safe place in the world for me until I am old enough to have a house of my own.

The lights there are blazing and I can hear loud, thumping music blaring. There is a pile of something at the front door but it's too far away for me to tell what it is.

"She threw some of his stuff out on the street," Ethen says quietly.

"Our stuff," I say dully, because Todd doesn't really keep anything at our house.

"Don't worry about it tonight. Come on in. I can smell dinner."

Suddenly I can smell it too and my mouth waters. I hadn't realized how tired and hungry I am until just that moment.

I step inside after Ethen, pausing in the entryway.

The house is identical to ours except that it has furniture, smells like good cooking and is full of people.

"Oh, you must be Lena." A heavy-set woman with a smiling face bustles over to me, wiping her hands on a messy apron that's tied around her waist.

Before I can move, she reaches out and squashes me into a hug. There is a second where I feel smothered, trapped, but it quickly passes and I feel tears prick my eyes as I lean into her comforting bulk.

She steps back and holds me at arm's length, staring at me with such kindness that I nearly start bawling like a little kid.

"Well, aren't you a pretty thing. Ethen says you need a break from your home for a bit. Well, you've come to the right place for that. We're always overflowing with friends and cousins so you'll fit right in. Ethen, show her where to wash up and then introduce her to everyone."

She gives both me and Ethen a little shove down the hall and heads back to the kitchen.

"Your mom is so nice," I whisper.

"Told you you'd like her. Here's the bathroom. Don't use the Superman soap. It's Milo's and he can tell if anyone's touched it. It's like he's psychic."

"No Superman soap. Got it."

I use the bathroom and then take my time scrubbing my hands and washing my face. I pluck the leaves out of my hair and re-braid it as neatly as I can. My reflection in the mirror looks pale and scared. There are dark circles under my eyes.

That's as good as it's going to get, I think with a sigh. I'm still wearing my dirty work polo shirt and I realize suddenly that I don't have any more clean ones at home. I'd planned to do laundry tonight but it doesn't look like there is any chance of that now.

Pushing my shoulders back, I step out of the bathroom and

make my way down the short hall to a living room that is full of noise and people.

A pile of kids are heaped on the nearest couch having a loud fight over the television remote, but they all stop and look at me silently when I step forward.

"Uh, hello," I say, gulping.

"Introduce us to your friend, Ethen."

I glance up shyly at the older man who is sitting in an upright chair across from the television with a brightly coloured blanket on his lap. No, I realize, he's in a wheelchair.

His eyes are a lot like Ethen's, bright and kind, but one half of his face droops ever so slightly. His words are just a little slurred too.

"Everyone, this is Lena," Ethen says, getting up from the couch not piled with kids and coming to stand beside me. "Lena, this is everyone. That pile there is mostly cousins but Milo and my sister Rosie are under there somewhere. And you remember my older brother, Owen. Those are his friends."

At the table by the window is Ethen's alarming older brother with the silver teeth and his silent, brooding friend. There are two more older guys with them, sitting around the table wordlessly playing a game of cards. Ethen doesn't tell me their names and I don't ask.

"Hi, hi, hi," the kids say in chorus, their eyes all fixed on the television again.

"All right everyone," Ethen's mother bustles in. "Listen up. I want you to remember that Lena is our guest for tonight. You all give her a warm welcome and if I hear of any of you not being polite then you don't get any dinner. Understood?"

Everyone laughs at the fierce expression on her face but it all sounds good-natured. Even the dubious-looking guys at the table nod politely before ignoring me.

"Here, take this chair," Ethen says, ushering me into a

battered chair that looks like it has seen better days. "You look exhausted."

"I am," I admit. "Thanks. I don't want to get in the way, though."

"You're not. We have a sort of open-door policy here. Even Owen's friends are welcome any time."

"Haha," Owen says, drawing out the words sarcastically but not looking up from his handful of cards.

"Ethen, be nice," their dad says. "Lena, we try and make this a safe place for our kids and cousins, and their friends. There is no judgement here and everyone is welcome. And we don't ask too many questions. You stay here as long as you need to."

"Thanks," I say quickly, flushing with embarrassment. "I'll go home tomorrow though. Natalia should be okay by the morning. She's just…"

I break off, wondering why I'm still trying to think up ways to defend her or make it sound like she's not so bad. It's an old habit from childhood.

"Well, you know best," their dad says, smiling kindly. "Ethen says that you work at a horse stable."

"You do?" All the little kids turn to look at me at once, their television show forgotten.

"Yes, at Three Sisters. I haven't been there that long but I really like it."

"Do you get to ride them?" a little girl with huge dark eyes asks excitedly. "Do you gallop like in the show Spirit? Do you jump?"

"Um, I have. At the last barn I worked at. I mostly just take care of them here, though. That's the best part, anyway."

"Do you have any pictures on your phone?" an older girl asks, trying not to look too eager. She looks a lot like Ethen and I wonder if she's his sister.

"Just a couple. See, this is Flicker, he's sassy but has a good heart."

"Just like Spirit," a tiny girl says dreamily.

"This is the horse you ride? He's so big."

"No, a girl named Kira rides him."

"Oh, is she your friend?"

"Well," I hesitate. "Yes, I guess she is."

They spend the next twenty minutes peppering me with questions until finally Ethen's mom comes in and shoos everyone away to wash their hands before dinner.

"Everyone just eats where they sit," she explains to me. "We have lots of food but a very small table. We usually put a movie on while we eat too."

"Great," I say, sniffing the air eagerly. I am equal parts hungry and tired and I doubt that I will make it through even half a movie without falling asleep.

Ethen's mom dishes up the littlest kids and then everyone else lines up, grabbing plates from the stack on the counter, and taking turns ladling up pasta, sauce and garlic bread. I'm practically fainting with hunger by the time I sit down again to devour my food.

I try not to hoover it all down or embarrass myself, but the food tastes as good as it looks and I practically inhale my whole plate.

"Go get seconds, Lena," Ethen's dad says. "We never hold back on food in this house. Those are the rules."

I don't feel so guilty when I see that there is still lots of food left. I can't imagine what it would cost to feed a family this big.

After dinner, Ethen's mom doesn't let me help wash the dishes so I return to my chair and curl up, my eyes half-closed as I nap my way through their movie. Despite all the dramatic things that have happened tonight, a feeling of sleepy contentment washes over me. I feel safe and well-fed for the first time in a while.

Some of the little kids are sent off to bed once the movie is over and I half-listen to the older ones talking with Ethen and his dad about some car. The card-playing guys at the table are talking in low murmurs too.

Suddenly, a series of rings and chimes go off and I jerk back to wakefulness, half-sitting up and looking around.

All the guys at the table have stood up and are tossing down their cards and heading for the door.

"Gotta go, Dad," Owen says. "Cars are coming in. See you tomorrow."

"Be safe. Make good choices," their father says, a shadow of concern washing over his face.

"Always. I'll see you in the morning. Bye."

Owen nods at me briefly before heading outside after his friends.

"A car coming in?" I ask, still muzzy with sleep.

"Uh yeah, emergency repairs at the garage." Ethen looks away quickly, a faint blush staining his cheeks.

"All right, you kids." Ethen's mom bustles back into the living room. "It's getting late, off to bed. Ethen and Lena need to get up early for work. Ethen, you make up the couch for Lena and make sure she has a pillow. With a *fresh* pillowcase, mind you."

"Good night, Lena," Ethen's dad says. "Hope you like pancakes because that's what's for breakfast."

He gives me a kind smile and a wink and propels his wheelchair past me into the hall. Only one of his arms seems to be working properly so it takes him a while to get there. Ethen's mom doesn't help him but you can see that she wants to. Her hands keep twitching at her sides and she has to look away when he bumps roughly into the wall.

"We're saving up to get him a power chair," Ethen says softly beside me. "His arm barely works anymore and every day it gets harder for him to manoeuvre around. He's too proud to let my mom help."

"What happened?" I keep my voice low too.

"Work accident." Ethen turns away to look out the window. "He broke his back and had a lot of nerve damage. And then he had the stroke."

"Oh, I'm so sorry, that's awful. Insurance won't pay for the new chair?"

"No." Ethen looks down at his hands and clears his throat. "And the one he needs costs nearly ten thousand dollars."

"Wow, that's crazy."

"Yeah, well, we'd better get to bed."

He's standing close to me when he turns to study my face and I automatically stiffen, wondering if he's going to expect me to kiss him or something in repayment for letting me stay here. But he just reaches out and tugs playfully on my braid before stepping away.

"I'll get your stuff. Mom laid out a towel for you in the bathroom and there's an extra toothbrush too."

"Um, thanks," I say, flushing with embarrassment. Why do I always have to expect the worst from people? Ethen has been nothing but nice so far. "It's okay if I use the shower?"

"Of course," Ethen grins at me. "I was going to mention that you kind of smell like a horse but I thought it would be rude."

"Haha, you're very funny."

Ignoring his laughter, I shut myself in the bathroom, locking the door carefully behind me before undressing quickly and jumping into the shower. It feels so weird to be doing this in someone else's house and a part of me feels like I'm back in foster care again. At the mercy of strangers.

But, as the soothing hot water rains down on me, I push that thought away. Ethen's family aren't strangers anymore; they are neighbours and friends. They aren't helping me because somebody's paying them to look out for me, they're doing it because they care. They care about *me*. It's a strange feeling.

I get out of the shower reluctantly and then stare down at my dirty clothes with a sigh. I don't have anything else to change into so they will have to do. I'm certainly not about to sleep on Ethen's couch wearing only a towel.

As if he's guessed my thoughts, there is a light knock on the door.

"Hey, Lena?"

"Yes?" I say cautiously.

"I left you a sweatshirt and shorts just here in front of the door, okay? You don't have to wear them if you like but they're clean."

"Um, okay, thanks," I say, staying rooted in place.

"I'll just go back to the living room. They're right here."

As soon as I think he's gone, I inch open the door, stick my hand out and snatch the clothes from off the hallway floor.

They are too big for me, of course, but they are soft, cozy and, best of all, clean.

Ethen is sitting back in the living room and he smiles as he looks up and catches sight of me.

"That's a good look on you," he says, laughing at the sweatshirt that is hanging nearly to my knees over the baggy jogging shorts.

He looks so nice and normal sitting there, and so kind, that a warm feeling of gratitude wells up in my chest.

"Thank you so much for this," I say quietly, "you really saved me tonight. It means…a lot."

He's silent for a moment.

"Any time, new girl," he says finally. He stands up but doesn't come near me. "Well, get some sleep, I'll see you in the morning."

He's gone before I can answer and I sigh and climb onto

my temporary couch-bed. The sheets smell freshly washed and tinged with something like lavender and vanilla. It smells nice and homey.

I don't think there's any way I'll be able to fall asleep after my crazy day, but I do. The second my head hits the pillow, I'm out like a light.

Chapter 19

Lena

Despite my protests, Ethen insists on coming with me to my house first thing in the morning to get my stuff. Just as he's already insisted that he's driving me to work after breakfast.

"You had a rough night," he says firmly. "Let me help you just this once."

"You've already helped me like ten times this month," I mutter. But I decide not to argue too much. I'm still tired and sore after all the biking I did last night and the idea of climbing that hill to Three Sisters is making me a little ill. So, accepting a lift from Ethen is way too easy.

It is early dawn, and the sun is barely up, but my heart is still beating hard as we approach the house. I ball my hands into fists, not wanting to show Ethen that I'm afraid.

He must sense it anyway because he walks close to me, hovering protectively, his shoulder brushing mine at every step.

The screen door is hanging at an odd angle and there is a

big dent at the bottom like somebody kicked it. Thankfully it's not *my* clothes that have been dumped on the walkway out front. They're Natalia's, all things that Todd has bought her in the last month. And on top is a pile of her books, all torn up, their spines broken and pages fluttering in the breeze.

Two of the dining room chairs have been tossed outside and smashed, their legs lying at sharp angles.

"Leave it," Ethen says quietly as I bend down to start scooping up Natalia's things.

"What?" I look at him in confusion, then blink at the tight, angry look on his face. "I can't leave this stuff outside for the whole neighbourhood to see. It's embarrassing."

"Don't take on other people's stuff, Lena." He reaches down and holds his hand out for me to take. "This is not your problem. Let them clean it up themselves. Their mistakes are not yours."

I stare at him for a second in surprise and then I drop Natalia's things and slowly reach out to rest my hand on Ethen's. It closes tightly around mine, warm and gentle, as he pulls me carefully to my feet.

"I guess you're right," I say slowly.

I've been cleaning up, or hiding, Natalia's embarrassing messes my whole life. Afraid of being judged, of being painted with the same brush that she is. Maybe it is time to stop.

Inside, the house isn't as bad as I'd expected. The fridge door is open and there are empty beer bottles all over the kitchen table, which explains why Natalia exploded last night. She doesn't drink often but when she does, she's a mean drunk and capable of anything.

Otherwise, things look pretty undamaged, and my own room is surprisingly untouched. Todd must have taken the brunt of her anger this time.

From down the hall, I hear Natalia's drunken snores and breathe a sigh of relief. She's alive, so that's good. And she's also out cold so I can get changed and make my lunch in safety.

Ethen trails after me closely, like he's a bodyguard on high alert. Which I don't blame him for. I'm used to tip-toeing around in the aftermath of Natalia's rages. He's not.

I grab the cleanest clothes that I have, wishing again that I'd done laundry earlier in the week when I'd first thought of it, and then head to the kitchen to make my lunch.

Ethen makes grumbling noises when he sees our near-empty fridge.

"Is that seriously all you're going to eat for lunch?" he whispers.

"What, it's a peanut butter sandwich. What's wrong with that?"

"You work hard all day outdoors; you can't keep your strength up with that."

"I'm fine, Ethen, stop fussing. You'll wake up Natalia."

He mutters something under his breath but doesn't bring it up again.

When we get back to his house, everyone is awake and Ethen's mom is already cooking pancakes. Some kids are eating sticky platefuls of food on the couches and the littlest ones are seated at the table.

"Order up, Lena," she calls as if she's the line cook at a restaurant, "syrup is on the table. Find a seat somewhere."

I sit down at a vacant seat at the crowded table, staring at the stack of pancakes in front of me with disbelief. It's about six inches tall.

"Don't pretend you can't eat that," Ethen says, sitting beside me and giving me a nudge. "I've seen how you inhale your food."

"I don't *inhale,*" I protest, poking him in the ribs.

"Like an anteater vacuuming up an ant hill."

"Hey! I do not…"

"Children," his mom says firmly, "there is no fighting in this house. Eat your food or I'll take it away."

"He started it," I whisper under my breath, soft enough so only Ethen and the giggling kids next to us can hear.

He raises an eyebrow and sends me a wicked grin.

The pancakes are light and fluffy and loaded with syrup. I scrape my plate clean and, once I'm sure everyone else has been fed too, I go back for seconds. I feel like one of those anacondas at the zoo who only gorge on a giant meal every few months.

Ethen disappears to get ready for work and I help his mom to load the dishwasher and scrub the pans while I wait for him.

"Everything okay over at your house this morning?" she asks casually, not looking at me.

"Um, yeah, Natalia, I mean my mom, was asleep. There's not much damage; just the front door and some furniture."

"The police didn't stay too long. I think they just gave a warning."

"I hope Todd is okay." I chew my lower lip, thinking of how he'd brought us donuts, fast food and furniture. "He's not a bad guy."

"I saw him drive away." She takes a clean pan from me and vigorously rubs it with the drying cloth. "He looked all right. He might have a few bruises, though. Is your mother always like that?"

I look up at her quickly, suddenly on guard. I had been so overwhelmed last night that I hadn't even considered that these people might report Natalia to family services. That they might think foster care was a safer choice for me than staying at home.

"No, not at all," I say, my voice coming out a terrified squeak. "She's usually very responsible. She…"

"Lena," Ethen's mom interrupts firmly, laying a hand on

my shoulder. "You don't have to do that here. You don't have to pretend things are all right."

"Okay." I fidget under her gaze, suddenly needing to get outside. The house feels too small, like it's closing in on me.

"Thanks so much for breakfast. Tell Ethen I'm waiting outside," I say in a rush and bolt for the front door. I almost grab my bike and pedal right out of there but I know if I do then I'm going to be late for work.

After a few minutes, the front door opens behind me and Ethen steps outside.

"Ready to go?"

I nod, still not fully trusting myself to speak without my voice wobbling, and get in the car.

It is strangely comfortable driving in the car with Ethen. I could get used to this. And that realization makes my belly churn with fear. Because it's way too easy to be around him, to just let him be nice and help me. And what if whatever is wrong with Natalia is something genetic? What if I become a monster too and start hurting him on purpose? What if I'm using him right now and I don't even know it?

I clasp my hands in my lap and look miserably out the window.

"Are you okay?" Ethen asks quietly.

"I...don't know," I say honestly. There are too many feelings bubbling up in me that need to be sorted out. I wouldn't even know where to start.

"Lena, when your face was swollen the other day. Did Natalia hit you?"

Shock and anger buzzes up inside me at the question and I sit bolt upright, ready to tell him to mind his own business. But just as suddenly it fizzles out and I sag back against the seat. I really don't have the energy to keep pretending.

"Yes," I say in a small voice. "But you can't tell anyone. I don't want to get taken away and put into foster care again."

"I won't say anything if you don't want me to." He hesitates, tapping his fingers on the steering wheel. "How bad is it at home?"

Part of me can't believe that I'm openly, casually, having this conversation. But the other half of me is so relieved to stop lying.

"Right now it's not awful," I say carefully. "She stays with Todd most of the time and she only slipped up that one time and hit me."

"It wasn't a slip-up, Lena. People don't accidentally hit people. Even when they lose control, they're making a choice."

"Yeah, well, Natalia always chooses violence. She's been like that almost my whole life. My brother, Garret, sort of stood between us while I was little but when he left, all her anger fell on me."

"I'm sorry, Lena. You deserve better."

The words are said so quietly that I have to strain to hear them. Ethen looks sad when I glance over.

"Um, well thanks. We don't always get what we deserve in life though, do we?"

"No, my dad didn't deserve to get hurt and put in a wheelchair either."

"It was an accident at work?"

He shoots me a sideways look and a muscle in his jaw flexes. "You can keep a secret?"

"All my life," I say dryly. "I'm kind of an expert."

"My dad didn't have an accident, he was shot on the job."

"Oh, no, that's awful. What sort of job was he doing?"

"Um, well, he was working on a stolen car at the time."

I stare at Ethen, certain he's kidding, but he looks dead serious.

"Okay," I say slowly.

"My dad isn't proud of his past. He always tries to tell us right from wrong. But he needed the money and my uncle had a quick job for him. He was working on the car when the cops burst in and there was a lot of shooting. One of my cousins was killed. And my dad was shot in the back and ended up doing time in prison."

I think of how nice Ethen's dad had been to me the night before. And how kind and patient he'd been with the little kids. "Your uncle steals cars for a living?"

"Kind of. Sometimes. But you need to forget you heard that. And don't talk about it to anyone, and definitely not in front of my family. It's a touchy subject."

I'm silent for a moment, thinking over everything I'd seen and heard the night before.

"Your brother and his friends work for your uncle, don't they?"

There is a flash of alarm in his eyes but I hold up my hand to stop him from saying anything.

"It's okay, it's not like I have anyone to tell. I don't care what they do as long as they don't do it around me. I don't want to get near anything illegal. I don't want to lose any chances at having a good future."

"Don't worry, they'll keep it clean around you, just like they do around the younger kids."

I nod, not sure if I like being lumped in with the small children, then glance over at Ethen. "You're not involved with any of that, are you?"

I'm relieved when he shakes his head.

"I do work with cars but not for my uncle. My dad pretty much forbids me from having anything to do with my uncle's garage. He doesn't want me getting mixed up in everything like Owen is."

His hands tighten on the steering wheel and I reach out without thinking and touch his shoulder. After a second, he loosens his grip and sighs, leaning into me slightly.

"My brother, Garret, is an addict," I say quietly. "He lives on the street in Vancouver, or at least he used to. I haven't heard from him in over two years. He's been sent to jail for stealing too."

I hesitate and then plunge on.

"When I was eight years old, my mom went to jail for a few months for fraud. Garret and I were split up and put in different foster homes. It was terrifying not to know what was happening with either of them. Nobody would tell me anything."

"That's why you're so worried about anyone finding out what Natalia's like?"

I shake my head. "No, a few years ago I was over at a friend's house and her mother saw the bruises on my arms. She was concerned enough to call child protective services and a social worker came to our house and found Natalia passed out drunk. It was enough for me to get taken away again and put back in foster care. Garret was already long gone by then."

"And they were mean, your foster parents?"

"No, they were nice enough. But by that time I was already working at a stable and being around the horses was the only thing that was keeping me from having a complete breakdown. But my foster parents didn't understand that. They didn't want me to work, they said I should just concentrate on school and not worry about having a job, and they wouldn't listen when I said that I needed the barn more than anything. That it was the only thing keeping me sane. Keeping me from hurting myself. So I ran away. Twice. And by that time Natalia had convinced the social workers that she was reformed and ready to be the world's best mom. So, they put me back with her."

"But she hadn't changed?"

"No, not for a second. But she likes the money I bring in. And she needs someone to handle the rent, bills and groceries. That's about it."

We've reached Three Sisters by now and I stare at the

beautiful stables and rolling green pastures still empty of horses.

"Now we both know each other's secrets," I say quietly. "So you know that I won't tell anyone yours. And you know why I will do anything to work in a place like this. It's as essential to me as breathing."

Ethen nods and then reaches out to take my hand, giving it a soft squeeze, little currents of electricity flowing between us.

"Here," he says, reaching into the back seat and handing me a large paper bag. "My mom made you lunch. I'll see you tonight."

Before I can stop him, he leans across the seat and softly kisses my cheek.

I stare at him in shock, not sure how to react, and then slowly climb out of the car, not looking back as he drives away. I reach up to touch the spot where he'd kissed me and I realize that I'm smiling for some reason.

A horse nickers softly when I roll back the big door, then another and another. I inhale deeply, letting the tensions of the last day flow out of me. Here, at least for a few hours, I can forget about everything but the horses.

Chapter 20

Kira

"Bye Regan, see you tonight," I call, practically launching myself out of the car before he has a chance to stop in front of Three Sisters. I am dying to see Tessa. It has been four long days since the clinic ended, and since I'd last been at the barn. It seems like a lifetime ago.

But, when I get inside, the first thing I see is Flicker's big head looking over a stall door halfway down the aisle. His ears are pricked and he nickers happily when he catches sight of me.

"Hey, big guy," I say in astonishment, coming slowly forward to scratch his neck and give him a small piece of one of the carrots I've brought for Tessa. "What are you doing here?"

I step back, realizing for the first time that he is in Hilty's stall, or at least it used to be. Her nameplate is gone and has been replaced with a shiny new plaque with Flicker's name on it.

I peer into his stall, noticing the churned-up bedding and the strands of loose hay scattered everywhere. It looks like he'd spent the night there anyway. He must have moved this weekend.

"Hey, you're finally back." Lena appears beside me, grinning. "And you discovered our new guests."

"Guests?" I look over and see that Bluebell's elegant head is poking out over the next stall door beside Flicker's. "Oh, wow, what are they doing here?"

"You didn't hear the news yet?"

"Obviously not. What?"

"Oliver bought Flicker. And he moved both his horses here."

I just stare at her, trying to process her words.

"It's true," she says. "Flicker's old owner, that loud lady with the cast, had this big workup done on Flicker at the vet hospital over the weekend. She made a big deal about it too, saying that she was going to prove John Riddle wrong and sue him for slandering her horse or something. Anyway, they x-rayed his back and found out that he actually has kissing spines near his withers."

"Oh no." I put my hand over my mouth. I don't know exactly what kissing spines is except that is painful and that some horses had to be put down because of it. "Poor Flicker, he was trying to tell us that he was hurting all along."

Lena nods. "Anyway, the lady—"

"Marsha," I interrupt.

"Yeah, her. She starts freaking out and telling everyone how the girl who sold her Flicker in the first place must have known he was unsound and just wanted to dump him before he completely broke down."

"Oh, boy. I doubt that. I'd heard Flicker was going well for Clara when she sold him."

"Well, that's not what Marsha thinks. She was threatening

to just put Flicker down without even trying the cortisone injections and the rehab that the vet suggested. So, Oliver made her an offer and she took it."

"Wow." I just stand there for a second, petting Flicker and trying to absorb all that information. "But why would Oliver buy a lame horse with kissing spines who he can't even ride? Even if Flicker was sound, he's a lot of horse; too much for Oliver."

"That I don't know. You'll have to ask him yourself when he gets here."

I frown, trying to puzzle everything out. I knew that Oliver liked Flicker for some reason, but his family could afford to buy him all sorts of expensive horses, why pick one who was lame and difficult to ride? It didn't make sense.

"But, wait, where is Hilty?" I ask finally. "Why is Flicker in her stall?"

"Um," Lena breaks off abruptly and looks at something over my shoulder, her eyes widening.

"What's it to you?" Isla stalks past me with an armful of saddle pads. Hilty's bridle is hanging over one arm. "I hope she's dog food by now. Good riddance."

My fingers clutch the stall door, and all the blood rushes out of my head so fast that I'm left dizzy.

"What did you do to her?" My voice comes out a croak.

"None of your business," Isla says over her shoulder. "See you, freak. Have fun riding with all the other losers."

"Don't call her that," Lena says sharply, and I look at her in surprise. Her face is suddenly blotchy with anger and her fists are balled at her sides.

Isla turns slowly on her heel and gives Lena a look of pure loathing. "Watch it, groom," she says in her deadly voice. "One word from me and you'll be fired so fast you won't even know what hit you."

Lena says nothing and Isla finally flounces out without a backward glance.

"It's best just to ignore her," I say quietly. "She's been awful for a long time. Poor Hilty."

"Oh." Lena shakes her head as if to clear it. "Don't worry about Hilty. She just went to a sales barn on the mainland. She's a nice horse; I'm sure she'll find a good home."

"Right." I feel sad that the big mare is gone. She'd been at Three Sisters a long time and I'd liked her. I'd always felt sorry for Hilty for having to put up with such a crappy owner. She was a sweet mare. Hopefully, now she'd have a chance at a better life.

"So, wait, does that mean Isla is gone for good?" That sounds like a dream come true for me.

"Kind of. She's going up to Barn A to lease Marsha's new horse, Sonata. The mare arrived yesterday and, since Marsha's still on crutches, the horse needed someone to keep her exercised."

"Oh, poor horse. She gets both Marsha and Isla in her life. Oh, I almost forgot, do you still want to come to dinner tonight? My dad and Grace said it was okay. Sorry about the short notice but I don't have your phone number."

Lena looks so pleased that her whole face lights up.

"Sure, if you still want to. I'm off at five tonight."

"Sounds good, I was planning a long trail ride anyway, to make up for missing so many days."

Lena smiles again before getting back to work so I go to find Tessa out in the pasture.

Tessa, always the drama queen, throws up her head when she sees me and lets out a piercing neigh. She gallops toward me, skidding to a stop a few feet away, bobbing her head and snorting like a circus horse.

"Hi, pretty girl." I feed her the carrot she's waiting for and then throw my arms around her neck and press my face against her soft coat, inhaling deeply. She stands rock-still and I feel all the anxiety left over from Aunt Irene's visit just melt out of my body.

I love my sessions with Donna, but Tessa is nearly as good a therapist, maybe better.

I take my time brushing and tacking up, running the soft body brush over the mare's silky coat until she's glistening. It just feels so good to be reunited with her.

"Let's try the upper trails today, Tessa," I say out loud. I hardly ever ride in the woods behind Barn A but I am feeling adventurous for some reason. Tessa pricks her ears, always up for trying something new and I have to work to keep her at a calm walk while we head up the driveway.

As soon as we reach the trails, I let her go, and she flies along at a brisk trot, ears forward and snorting happily ever so often.

This is what she loves best and it is a long while before she slows down on her own, puffing and blowing like she's just finished a race.

"Does that feel better, girl?" I scratch her slightly damp neck and kick my feet out of the stirrups to stretch my legs.

Suddenly Tessa stiffens and throws her head up a little, ears pinning. Hooves thud behind us and the neighbour girl, Fina, comes trotting up behind from around a bend in the trail.

"Oh, sorry," she calls out, "I'm always startling you, aren't I? I didn't expect anyone to be out this far in the woods."

I look around, realizing for the first time that I had no idea how much ground we'd covered. I'm not very familiar with these trails, and I'd been daydreaming a little as Tessa had trotted along. Which is probably an excellent way to get lost in the woods.

"Oh, that's one of your draft horses," I say, gazing at the powerful creature. She has a thick, long mane that falls to her shoulders and each trunk-like leg has a fluffy tuft of feathers that fall right over her hooves.

"Yep, this is Naomi." She reaches down and tousles the horse's mane affectionately, and I realize for the first time that she's riding bareback and has shorts on instead of breeches.

I do my best not to stare. But I have never seen anyone be this casual around horses. At Three Sisters we have to be in proper riding clothes at all times. We're not even allowed to ride in tank tops when it's really hot. This girl has an aura of freedom around her that I instantly envy.

"Did your other mare have her foal?" I ask.

"Not yet. You should see how big she's getting, though. It won't be long. I can't wait to meet the baby. Hey, do you want to come and see the farm? We're really close."

I hesitate only a second before nodding. Something has changed for me this past week and I'm not sure if it's from riding in the clinic or because of that incident with Aunt Irene. But, for whatever reason, I feel a bit reckless and adventurous all of a sudden.

The sun filters down softly through the trees. They buffer the worst of the heat and a cool breeze stirs through the leaves. It's like being in an enchanted forest; the light makes everything glow a soft green and gold, and I can hear the leaves rustling gently around us.

We come to a little open clearing with a few rusted old farm implements scattered around. Tessa eyes them up suspiciously but the big mare that Fina is riding just marches past without blinking.

There is a fence up ahead, and when we reach a shiny metal gate Fina leans down to pull a rope that swings it wide open.

"My grandpa put in a new gate so that I don't have to get off the horses every time I open it. Go ahead, I'll shut it behind us."

Tessa goes hesitantly through the gate, pinning her ears briefly at the solid mare before she thinks better of it, and we stop a few feet ahead on the trail to wait for Fina.

"We're almost there. And since you're here, I'd love for you to watch me ride Rune if that's okay. My grandpa and Dale are on the mainland looking at a couple of new mares and I don't feel comfortable riding him on my own without anyone else around. He's a great boy, but he's still so green, anything could happen."

"Okay, sure."

The short trail opens up to a gravelled driveway and it's not long before we're turning into a small, tidy farm yard with a long, low barn that probably only would fit a dozen horses. It looks cozy, exactly like something I'd pick for my future barn.

"This is all yours?" I ask incredulously, "no boarders?"

"Yep, well, it's my Grandpa Max's place. But my brother and I live here and help our caretaker, Dale, with the horses. Do you like it?"

"I love it. It's so quiet."

She laughs. "Not when my younger brothers and sister are visiting. It's chaos then, but right now it's pretty peaceful. Come on, you need to see Beatrice first."

We ride around behind the barn to where there are some small pastures filled with draft horses. Most are black but there are two bays and one of them is heavily pregnant.

Fina jumps down off the mare she's riding and leads her into the nearest pasture, taking off her bridle and letting the mare amble away with a final pat.

"Don't you need to brush her first?"

Fina laughs and shakes her head. "She didn't exactly get sweaty on her ride. She'll just have a roll and be good as new."

"Oh." The rules about grooming are very strict at Three Sisters. I've never even heard of *not* grooming after a ride, unless you're like Isla and don't care about your horse at all. But the horses here look clean, shiny and content.

"Come on, Beatrice," Fina calls and the pregnant mare throws up her head and saunters over, taking her time. Her round sides sway as she walks.

"She's beautiful," I say as the mare puts her big head over the fence and whuffles at me softly. Tessa does not agree, though, and she pins her ears and gives an angry stomp followed by a squeal of irritation. "Sorry, she's not the best with other horses."

"No worries, she sort of gives off that lead-mare vibe, doesn't she? I have an extra paddock for her if she wants to graze for a while. If you think she'd be settled."

"She does like grass. I could try it."

Feeling like one of the heroines in the pony books I used to read as a kid, I follow Fina to a small, grassy paddock, pull off Tessa's tack and leave it hanging on the fence. I can almost hear Anna groaning in horror. Our gear always stays in its temperature-controlled tack room when it's not actually on a horse. I'm just breaking all the rules today.

Tessa does a quick canter around the paddock and then immediately puts her head down to graze, shooting sidelong looks at the horses in the pasture next to hers as if telling them to stay away from her food.

"Great, she looks okay. Why don't you ride Kona while I ride Rune? She's already bred so he won't act silly around her."

"Rune's a stallion?" I ask in disbelief. I've never met a stallion before, although I know that some top riders compete with them. I always had the impression that they were slightly dangerous.

"Yep, he's the biggest softy. He's my favourite after Beatrice. I don't bring him to Three Sisters yet because he's young and can still be a bit silly when he sees new girls. He's coming along, though."

She leads me around the barn to another paddock where two jet-black horses are grazing quietly together.

"That's Rune and Kona," she says proudly. "I can't wait to see their baby next year. It's going to be stunning."

"He's not dangerous?" I ask hesitantly. "He won't hurt the mare?"

"What, Rune? No way. He loves his girls. And besides, he doesn't have a mean bone in his body. You'll see."

She whistles low under her breath and the big horse throws his head up, long mane and forelock swirling through the air like he's some sort of fashion model. He nickers, a low deep rumble that seems to come from his chest, and trots over, his heavy hooves shaking the ground.

He stops in front of Fina and dips his head, breathing gently against her cheek before reaching down and quietly accepting the small treat she offers him.

"See, a gentle giant."

I slowly reach out and touch his mane and then the soft hair on his neck. His huge eye rolls toward me, studying me calmly and I am instantly in love.

"He's one of the most beautiful horses I've ever seen," I say truthfully. Three Sisters is full of stunning, well-bred, expensive horses. But this guy is something else. "What breed are they again?"

"Shires. Grandpa Max has some really nice bloodlines. Next year we're going to have a whole crop of amazing foals."

"How long do horses stay pregnant?"

"About eleven months. It's a long time to wait. We can ride them almost the whole time, though. Isabelle's been helping me school them but she's doing an internship this summer at a research lab so she doesn't have as much time. Now, come on, let's get these two tacked up."

I didn't remember agreeing to ride a strange horse but, twenty minutes later, I find myself at the mounting block hopping up on the widest back I'd ever sat on. Kona is shaped like a barrel.

It's only awkward for the first couple of minutes, but I get used to the feel of her pretty quickly. She is the complete opposite of Flicker and Tessa. She is obedient and moves forward nicely without plodding, but she doesn't have the best work ethic. You have to keep on top of her or she'll just slow down and stop, and you can tell she'd rather be out grazing than trotting around the ring.

But it is still a lot of fun. I realize within the first few minutes that she is a safe and uncomplicated lady, unlikely to pull anything tricky on me. I haven't ridden a horse like that in a long time. Even with Tessa I still have to pay attention the whole time I'm riding, I can't just relax and forget about her; I have to ride every step. But Kona is the type of horse that you could daydream a little on.

Rune is a bit spicier, although he is very well-behaved. They have a nice, newly built sand ring with cedar fencing. A few sets of jumps are stacked off to one side but, for the moment the ring is wide open.

"Do you jump?" I ask curiously. "I only usually see you school on the flat."

"I do, I love jumping. But Rune's still young so we're just doing flat work for now. Beatrice really enjoys jumping but she's on a break to have the baby. I've just been doing so much dressage work with everyone lately that I moved the jumps aside. Sometimes there's a horse for me to ride at Three Sisters, though, and I get to jump then."

"Do you like riding other people's horses?"

"I do. I love how they're all so different. I learn something new every time."

"Do you want to be a professional trainer?"

"Maybe. I haven't decided yet. I take some university courses from home just so I don't rule out any options. So far I haven't found anything I like better than working with horses. But it's a big world, you never know."

"I've wanted to be a trainer my whole life."

"Well, you should do that then. You certainly ride well enough."

"I hate showing, though; Anna says that showing and networking is a big part of being a trainer."

"Yeah, but that's only one type of training. There are all sorts of people out there who never see the inside of a show ring. Some trainers start young, wild horses, or train race-horses, ranch horses or even circus horses. There are a million different options that don't involve showing. There's more to the world than Three Sisters."

I nod, taking in her words and savouring them. They are exactly what I needed to hear, although I'm not sure how it changes things. I'm still expected to go to university and find a job that will pay good money.

"I'd better get back," I say finally. "I still have to find my way through the woods."

"Don't worry about that. I can ride with you most of the way."

We untack and groom the horses outside at the hitching post before turning them out and then I go get Tessa who is still happily grazing away. She looks relaxed and totally at home here.

The ride back is peaceful too. Fina rides another dark mare with us down the trails and then leaves me at the hill over-looking Three Sisters.

"Thanks again for helping me out. Come anytime. I always could use a hand with them. Especially as my grandpa and Dale will probably bring some new horses home with them."

"Thanks, I'd love that. See you later."

I ride down the hill, humming away quietly to myself. It

had been the best day I'd spent in a while and was exactly what I'd needed after a stressful week.

And now I have dinner with Lena to look forward to. I wasn't sure how I'd gone from zero friends to two in such a short time, but I was glad that things were looking up.

____

Chapter 21

____

Lena

*K*ira comes back to the barn looking triumphant and a little sunburnt.

"Oh, there you are," Samantha says, "I was about to send out a search party. You really shouldn't trail ride alone."

"I wasn't alone, I was with Tessa." Kira drops to the ground and scratches the mare on the neck. "And I met up with a friend."

"A friend?" Samantha looks a bit incredulous.

"Yes, Fina from next door."

"Oh, that's fine then. Just tell someone next time when you're going on a long trail ride. Otherwise, we worry."

Kira shoots her a surprised glance. "Okay, sorry. Are you off work now, Lena?"

"Almost. I'm just doing dinner feeds and then we can go."

"All right, I'll get Tessa settled and then call the car service."

"Car service?" I say doubtfully. "I have my bike with me."

"That's fine. I'll get them to bring an SUV. They don't mind."

I stare after her but she's already leading Tessa away, leaving me with so many unanswered questions.

Forty-five minutes later I find myself sliding onto the expensive-looking leather seats of a black luxury SUV. My battered old bike had looked pretty outclassed when the smiling driver hoisted it onto the bike rack on the back. I'm kicking myself for not letting Ethen drive me this morning like he'd been doing for the last few days.

"Lena, this is Regan. He's an old friend. Regan, this is my friend Lena."

"Well, hello there," he says, smiling at me so warmly that I can't help but smile back. He looks like he'd be a nice grandpa to have. "It's nice to meet you."

"You too. Thanks for driving us."

"It's a pleasure. I've been driving Kira around here since she was a little kid."

"Regan is basically family," Kira says. "He's a great listener if you ever need someone to talk to."

"I feel like I know a very great deal about horses after all these years," Regan says dryly. "Kira keeps me fully informed." He sends a wink at her to show that he's just teasing.

"Come on, you love it," Kira jokes back at him and I look at her in surprise. It's the first time I've seen her relaxed and joking around, like she's let her guard down all of a sudden.

We drive to a fancy area of town near the golf course. Regan drives us through a huge black gate and down a wide street lined with trees and borders of flowers. The houses are big, the lawns are tidy. Nothing is out of place; no drug dealers are standing on corners or broken cars up on blocks. In fact, there aren't any people on the street at all. There aren't any cars in the driveways even. It is like a movie-set subdivision, not a real one at all. Still, it is miles better than where I live and I can't help but feel a pang of jealousy.

"I know, this is the most boring neighbourhood you've ever seen, isn't it?" Kira says, studying my face. "I don't like it either."

"But it's beautiful."

She shrugs. "I guess so. I'd much rather live in the country on a small farm where I could keep Tessa. And maybe get a dog or even a cat. This place is all right if you like golf and nosy neighbours."

"I've never played golf," I say slowly. "I've actually never even seen a golf course."

"Well, you're not missing anything. Horses are a million times better."

We pull up to a house that looks nearly identical to all the others and I slide out hesitantly, cringing a little in mortification as Regan pulls my bike down off the rack. It does not look like it belongs in this neighbourhood at all.

"We can leave it on the porch," Kira says once we've said goodbye to Regan and watched him pull away. "Come on, did you bring your model horse with you?"

"Yes, he's here."

No point in explaining that I *always* have him with me. I already feel completely out of place here.

"Great, well, come see my workshop. Or do you want a snack first?"

I'm about to lie politely and say that I'm not hungry but the rumbling of my stomach gives me away. "Um, well if you're having a snack, then I guess I could too."

"Sure, chips and dip? A cracker and cheese platter?"

"Yeah, whatever. It all sounds good."

Their kitchen is huge and looks like it belongs on one of those television shows about high-end interior design. There are sprawling granite countertops and miles of tiled floor.

Kira opens up a massive, double-doored refrigerator that is packed, I mean just stuffed full, of food of every shape and size. The whole bottom is full of more vegetables than I would see in months. And there is an entire middle drawer devoted just to cheese. And much of it has been pre-cubed and put into tiny Tupperware containers.

She pulls out a few packages to set on the counter and then goes to an upper cupboard where there are multiple boxes of different artisan crackers stacked. There must be over a hundred dollars worth of just crackers there.

She deftly assembles it all on a plate and then grabs some sort of dip container to place in the middle.

"I'll add some nuts too. I can cut up some fruit too if you like."

She wrinkles her nose distastefully at this last part so I shake my head. "No, this is more than enough. I haven't eaten this well in weeks."

She gives me a considering look and then shrugs.

"Okay, follow me."

We go through the kitchen, past a massive den and then head up an elegantly curled staircase with a polished wooden banister.

"Is this seriously your room?" I say when we get to the top.

"Do you like it?" Kira looks around proudly. "I designed it myself. I mean, I picked out the paint and decorated and everything. That part is my studio."

"Wow." The huge room takes up the entire second floor and is partially divided here and there by Japanese screens. Horse posters and pictures cover the walls. And one whole end is covered by shelves and shelves of model horses. There is a work desk right by the window and one end holds neatly stacked paints and brushes and a weird-looking contraption that looks a bit like a tattoo gun.

"Oh, I used to have a little collection of horses," I say in delight, staring at Kira's rows of lifelike plastic horses. "I mean, not nearly as impressive as this, of course, but my brother used to get them for me on special occasions."

There is no need to mention that he'd most likely stolen them rather than bought them for me. It was the thought that counted, after all, right?

"You don't have them anymore?"

"Uh, no, just Jax here. He's the last one left. The rest of them…broke."

I don't tell her about how Natalia had systematically gone through my collection after Garret had left, snapping off their legs and smashing their heads, screaming like a lunatic the whole time. Only a few pieces had survived and she'd taken the rest of her anger out on them over the years until only Jax was left. Or most of him was left, anyway.

"I used to break things," Kira says, turning to look out the window, and I realize that she must think that *I* had broken them. That I'd been so careless with my things. "Not on purpose, but I'd get so mad when I was little that I'd just fly into a rage and not know what was happening. I'd feel so bad afterward, though."

"That must have been awful," I say, clearing my throat. "Is that because of the autism thing?"

I stop abruptly, worried that I've sounded insensitive or something, but she just breaks into startled laughter.

"Possibly. Or maybe that's something all kids do when they're little. It's hard to say. I was just so mad all the time back then. It was riding that helped me."

"Me too," I say in surprise. "Being around horses is probably the thing that keeps me calm and from freaking out all the time. They just make the world make sense, you know?"

"I do. They're so much simpler than humans."

"Oh, yes, definitely." I think about my complicated mother and her tragic boyfriends, and nasty Isla, and even about not knowing whether having Ethen in my life is a good thing or a bad thing. I never feel that way about the horses.

"So, you have this massive collection of horses," I say, trying to lighten the conversation a little. "What do you do with them all?"

"Do with them? I don't know. I collect them and customize some and show them. There are exhibitions all over the country."

"Kira, this is seriously amazing." I move over to the shelf to examine them more closely. There is one section where the horses all have ribbons hung up behind them. "Are these the ones you made?"

"Yep, those are mine."

I lean forward to study them in disbelief. They look incredibly real. As if they'd come alive at any second and prance right off the shelves. "You are so talented. You could make a fortune off of these."

She stares at me for a long second, blinking slowly. "I don't make money off them," she says finally. "It's just a hobby."

"But they're so professional."

She looks away quickly, her face flushing. "It's just a hobby," she says again firmly.

Hmm, that's interesting. Why would she not want to make money off of all her talent?

If I could do something like this, you could bet I'd be selling them for as much cash as I could.

"So, you'll leave your horse here for me to fix?" she says, changing the subject.

"What? Right, Jax. Sure." I'd almost forgotten why I was here in the first place. "I can't pay you, though. At least not right away. I have a lot of other bills."

She blinks at me in surprise and I wish that I could take back that last part about the bills.

The confused look on Kira's face is a little infuriating too.

I'm guessing that her dad just pays for everything she wants and she's never had to stress over money or struggle a day in her life.

I have to take a deep breath to keep from feeling angry. It's not Kira's fault at all that she's rich and I'm poor. And I need to stop veering off from my cover story; I'm supposed to have a dad in the military and a hard-working but well-meaning mother. Not be a poor, neglected kid loaded with emotional baggage.

"You don't need to pay me at all. It's easy for me to do. I can even paint him if you like. I can look up his original coat colour online."

I hesitate, wondering if he'd even be the same Jax if he was all painted up with his leg fixed. Or would everything that made him special be gone.

"Let me think about that," I say slowly, and she just nods like she understands exactly.

We hang out a bit longer, looking at horse videos and gossiping about life at the barn, but suddenly Kira looks at the wall clock and stands up abruptly.

"Sorry, I'm supposed to help Grace with dinner. It's nearly time."

"Is Grace your step-mom?" I ask, following her down the stairs.

"No, our part-time cook and light housekeeper. But she's been with us forever so she's pretty much family too. Like Regan."

Uh-huh. I wonder just how many staff these people have working for them? Is there a pool boy and a private pilot hidden around here too?

My sour thoughts lift though when we reach the kitchen and an older woman turns to me with a delighted smile that lights up her whole face. Before I can move she swoops over and wraps me in a tight hug.

"Lena, this is Grace. Sorry, she's kind of a hugger. She'll stop if you tell her to, though."

Laughter rumbles through Grace's body as she gives me a tight squeeze and then holds me out so that she can stare into my face.

"Lena, it is so nice to meet you. I'm so happy that Kira finally has a friend. It's like a miracle after all the trouble she went through last year."

Kira makes a protesting, choking noise but Grace doesn't bat an eye.

"Girl," she says to me, "you are thin as a rail. You look like someone who needs some fattening."

"Grace, that's body shaming," Kira says, rolling her eyes.

But, I honestly don't mind Grace's assessment. If somebody out there wants to fatten me up then I'm not about to stop them. There is hardly a day of the week that goes by that I don't feel starving at some point.

Grace sets us up making salad and garlic bread while she bustles around mashing potatoes and occasionally checking on a large, fragrant roast that is cooking away in the oven. My mouth is watering just smelling it.

The front door clicks and Kira looks up eagerly.

"Oh, my dad's home. Come meet him, Lena."

I followed her across to the den, feeling awkward and out of place again. I would much rather stay in the cozy kitchen, near Grace and the food, than talk to somebody else's dad. He is probably going to ask me questions about my life or something.

But he doesn't do any of that. He just looks up tiredly from a spreadsheet that he's laid out across a low table in the den and smiles kindly when Kira introduces me.

"Nice to meet you, Lena. I've heard good things about you. Apparently, if Tessa likes you then you're a good person."

"Oh, Dad," Kira says, rolling her eyes, but they're both

smiling fondly at one another and you can see how much they like each other. Like they're actually glad to be related and live in the same house together. I'd bet Kira's dad would sacrifice a lot of things to make her happy. Must be nice.

Dinner is just as delicious as I'd expected it would be. And despite my vow to be polite and not take too much, I can't help piling second and then third helpings on my plate. Something that Grace encourages.

I'd been surprised when Grace had sat down with us to eat. I'd assumed that she'd be expected to serve us or something, but that wasn't the case at all. And after dinner, Kira and I helped her with the dishes and to tidy the already immaculate kitchen.

I had such a good time that it wasn't until Kira's dad offered to drive me home that I had a mild panic attack. I could not let them see where I lived. What if Natalia was home and in a rage again?

"Where are we dropping you off, Lena?" Kira's dad asks after we've loaded my bike into his trunk. I'd winced as it had gone in, worried that its sharp edges would chip the perfect paint job on his car.

"Um," my mind whirrs for a second and then settles. "Actually, you can drop me off at the church on Hammington Street if you don't mind. They have a youth group that runs late and I'm supposed to meet a friend."

It's the best lie I can come up with on short notice; it even has the side benefit of making me sound a bit religious which is something parents often like. I have never been to a church in my life but there are posters up for this free drop-in youth group all over town, so it sounds like as good a cover story as any.

But I don't miss the hurt look that flits across Kira's face.

"It's the pastor I'm meeting," I add, trying to soften the lie a little. Just in case she's upset that I didn't invite her to an imaginary youth group. I can't quite look her in the eye. "I have to ask him something or I'd invite you to come along."

Her eyes widen for a second as she studies me and then she looks out the window without saying a word.

The rest of the ride is mostly silent, some of the happiness of the evening spoiled for both of us. I hate lying; I only do it in an emergency. But, I genuinely like Kira and I hate to repay her hospitality by being fake.

The church has a huge parking lot and there are lots of young people outside playing basketball on a court.

"So, see you tomorrow?" I say, trying to pretend that a rift hasn't opened up between us.

"Sure." She nods and doesn't look back as the car pulls away.

I wait until they're around the corner before I start the long ride home.

It isn't quite dark out, just that nice dusky time of evening when the whole world is tinted blue and purple. It's one of my favourite times of day, when everything seems peaceful and the air is cooling off.

Despite the awkwardness at the end of my visit, I still had a great time. And I hope that I can repair any misunderstandings with Kira tomorrow.

Chapter 22

Kira

I stare up at the ceiling, my brain working overtime as I churn through all the events of the day. The fact that Lena had lied to me when we'd dropped her off didn't bother me as much as it once would have. I'd known her long enough now to tell that she was a good person. The horses loved her, *Tessa* loved her, and that was all the proof I needed.

No, whatever had made her lie to my dad and me hadn't had anything to do with us. She'd been scared of something. I just hoped she wasn't in some sort of trouble.

But, despite Lena's oddness at the end, this has pretty much been one of the best days of my life. My trail ride with Tessa, helping Fina with her horses, and hanging out with Lena has been more excitement than I've had in a while.

Actually, it feels like this whole last month, from the moment Anna had offered me the ride on Flicker, has been sort of life-changing. Like something big has shifted inside of me and I've gone from a person living a boring existence to somebody who has adventures, friends and opportunities thrown at them from all directions.

Aunt Irene's visit had changed something else in my life too. I'd had the sudden realization that if I didn't take charge of my future, then other people were always going to try and manage it for me. Pushing me in whatever direction they saw fit.

Even well-meaning people like my dad. He might think he knew what was best for me but he really didn't. He couldn't see that I'd rather die than do something boring like accounting or finance. And since I like horses more than anything else in the world, didn't it make sense that I make a career out of working with them?

I sit up suddenly, my heart beating with excitement. My dad is set on me going to college or university but maybe there is a way to compromise.

I scramble up and grab my laptop off the desk, hauling it back into bed with me.

A long time ago I'd discovered that some colleges actually had equestrian programs. My dad had dismissed them right away, though. Because they were all far away and he wanted me to go to a school nearby so he could watch over me just in case I couldn't handle the pressure. And also, because he was sure that I wouldn't be able to make any money with horses. At the time I'd given in and agreed with him. But what if he'd been wrong?

I pull up my bookmarks, relieved to see that the lists of schools are still there. I'd never even looked at them again once I'd known that my dad wouldn't pay for me to study at a place like that.

But, what if...I look up at my wall of horse sculptures, remembering what Lena had said about me selling them. What if I could pay for school myself? This collection is worth tens of thousands of dollars if I find the right buyers. I don't know why I didn't think of making money off them before.

I bounce a little on the bed with excitement, plans falling into place like missing puzzle pieces.

I will need to do lots of research, to figure out the perfect school, and I'll have to find out how much money I'd need to take Tessa there too. There's no way that I would leave without her.

Luckily, research is something I'm a bit of an expert at. I pull up a blank word document and get to work.

Chapter 23

Kira

The next day I am tired but exhilarated too. I stayed up half the night going over the different school programs and weighing their pros and cons. I sent off emails to a dozen schools asking about costs and about the possibility of bringing Tessa.

There is still another year of high school ahead of me before I have to make any big decisions, but it can't hurt to be prepared.

There is still no sign of Oliver when I get to the barn, but Flicker has been turned out in one of the big grass pastures with a group of other horses and is grazing happily.

I duck through the fence and walk the short distance to where he's grazing, pleased when he lifts his head and makes a familiar little rumbling sound under his breath. It's a little like the sound Fina's stallion, Rune, made when he was happy.

"Hey, big guy." I run my hands over his silky coat and then step back to take a look at him. He looks good; a week without riding has softened some of the sharp lines down his neck and back. And he's lost that tense, vacant expression on his face. His gaze is softer, more relaxed. "I'm sorry you were in pain all that time. You were trying to tell us, weren't you?"

He snorts, lipping the carrot I offer him gently off my palm, and then ambles away back toward his friends.

I crawl back through the fence and go to get Tessa, wondering again about Oliver's mysterious purchase of Flicker. What had motivated him to buy an unsound horse that he couldn't ride?

Tessa demands my whole attention after that and I brush her carefully and tack her up for our lesson with Anna.

There is no sign of Lena, although I know she is scheduled to work today and I'm a little worried about her. She'd looked so sad last night and I wonder if we'll ever be good enough friends for her to confide in me.

This is my first time jumping Tessa since the John Riddle clinic and, right from the start, I can feel a difference in her. She is more relaxed, and less likely to rush. Anna has set up ground poles in front of some of the fences and has made a slow and technical course for us to work through.

"Let's keep up the good work you've started with her," Anna says, rubbing her hands together in anticipation. "I think she had a breakthrough in that clinic."

She's right, Tessa's first choice was always to go fast, but now she is approaching the jumps with new respect, and a new interest. She is tackling them as if they are individual problems to be solved, not just objects to get over as fast as possible.

It's like Tessa has levelled up into a calmer, new version of herself.

"Wow, Kira, that was fantastic," Anna says at the end, grinning as she comes toward me. "I know you don't want to show but, if you did, you two would clean up."

"Thanks." I reach down to scratch Tessa's neck. "That was a great lesson."

A car door slams and I look up to see a familiar black Volkswagen cruising slowly out of the parking lot.

Oliver, I think with a pang of disappointment. He hadn't even come over to say hello and now he's leaving. *Maybe he's only been hanging around to watch Flicker all this time. He never had any interest in me at all, as a friend or otherwise.*

The thought is depressing and I do my best to forget him as I give Tessa her bath and put her out on pasture.

"Hey, have you seen Lena around?" I ask Samantha as I get back to the barn.

"She went up to Barn A to help out. One of the girls quit suddenly so they needed a hand."

"Oh, thanks." I clean my tack as slowly as possible, trying to draw out my time at the barn as long as I can. But finally, there is nothing more to keep me here.

I sigh, wishing I had Flicker back to ride, that I had my own barn with a dozen horses to school. I haven't asked my dad yet about Fina's offer to help her ride her horses. I know that he wouldn't approve. Not of me going off-property and not of me spending more time with horses.

But it's my life, not his, I think as I pull out my phone and dial the number for Blacklock. *Why does he get to decide what I do with my time? Why shouldn't I pour all my energy into horses if it makes me happy?*

It's not Regan who comes to pick me up. It's a strange driver who just nods to me politely but is pretty much silent the rest of the way home.

I sigh as I look at my perfect house in my perfect neighbourhood, wondering if my dad even likes living here. Maybe I should start printing off real-estate ads for farms and leaving them strategically around the house.

I shuffle into the kitchen and start randomly opening

cupboards, listlessly looking for a snack that I'm not even hungry for, when suddenly the doorbell rings.

I jolt at the unfamiliar sound. We rarely have unexpected visitors and salespeople are not allowed in this neighbourhood.

Instead of going to the door, I tap the security panel on the wall to bring up the camera for the front door.

Oliver? As I watch, he takes a step back and looks around, then rings the bell again.

"Um, yes?" I say into the intercom.

"Oh hey, is this Kira?"

"Yes."

Through the camera I see him start to laugh, although I'm not sure what is so funny.

"Hey, it's Oliver, I probably should have called but I thought it would be easier to talk in person. Lena told me where you live. I hope you don't mind. I want to talk to you about Flicker."

"Okay," I say finally, "hold on, I'm coming."

His face lights up when I open the door. "Hi, I was worried that you wouldn't want to see me. I'm sorry that you had to stop riding Flicker."

"That wasn't your fault. That was all Marsha."

"Well, kind of. Can I come in? That lady next door is giving me a weird look."

I lean outside to see Mrs. Harris staring at us over her watering can while she pretends to take care of her flowers.

"Come in, quickly before she tries to come over to talk to us."

I usher Oliver inside and lock the door tightly behind him.

"Nice place," Oliver says, edging past me into the front hall and turning in a little circle so he can take it all in. A lot like Lena had done when she'd first seen it.

"It's all right. I suppose. Would you like something to drink?"

"Sure. It's hot out there."

"Right." I hope this is not going to be one of those social visits where we sit and talk about the weather or politics or something equally boring.

I pour us both iced teas from the pitcher of iced tea Grace had made the night before and usher Oliver to sit down at the table.

"Thanks," he says, his eyes widening as he tastes his drink. Grace makes it with crushed mint and real lemons and it's pretty amazing. "So, you've probably heard all the gossip by now."

"I've heard some stuff," I say slowly, wondering which gossip he means. Stories fly around at Three Sisters like wildfire sometimes. "I know you bought Flicker, and you moved him and Bluebell to Barn B. And that you've been away all week. But I'm not sure why."

"Oh, did you miss me?" he says, grinning. But luckily, he doesn't wait for me to answer. "It's kind of a long story. But I've been thinking about moving Bluebell for a while now. She's getting older and it's time to step down and let her have an easier life. I'd already stopped showing her when I was at boarding school; I was too busy anyway, what with the battle robots and everything. And I…"

"Wait, hold up," I say, raising a hand to stop him. "What robots?"

"Battle robots, you know, for fighting in tournaments." He looks at me as though I should know exactly what he's talking about. "I'm on a professional team. That's where I've been the last few days. At a tournament in New York. I just flew home."

"Oh." I stare at him blankly, my mind working overtime to try and process this new information with everything I knew about Oliver. I thought he was a lacrosse-playing jock with popular friends. Robot building just doesn't compute.

"How do you not know this about me?" he asks, looking a

little offended. "There was a public assembly for me in the school auditorium when I won Nationals. It was televised. And I earned that full ride to Starling Academy to study robotics and engineering with an international team. It was all over the internet."

He looks so baffled that I'm not leaping up to ask for his autograph or something that I can't help but laugh and roll my eyes.

"I don't know, Oliver, I was probably busy living my own life and not paying attention to yours. We moved in totally different circles and your friends made my life a living hell. So, I'm sorry if I haven't kept track of all your hobbies."

He frowns and rubs a hand across his face in frustration. "First of all, those weren't my friends; they were just people I hung out with. I haven't talked to any of them in over a year. And I'm sorry that you were bullied. I didn't know how bad it was until you'd already left."

I shrug and take a sip of my iced tea. "It doesn't matter. I don't blame you or anything. As I said, we moved in totally different circles."

More like I'd been in a circle of one, and he'd had dozens of people orbiting around him like adoring satellites.

"Yeah," he says glumly, "I guess so."

"Anyway, you were telling me about Bluebell and Flicker."

"Oh, right. Well, the second I moved back to Three Sisters with Bluebell, Darla kept putting all this pressure on me to either sell her and get a younger horse or push her harder so she'd be worth more. It was relentless."

"But you didn't want to do that?"

"No, of course not. I'm not driven to succeed like Josh is. I don't have any inner fire burning to be this top show jumper or make money off my riding. I just want to have fun, go to a few shows, collect a few ribbons and enjoy my horse. I've had Bluebell since she was three; I'm not about to sell her just so I can have a new toy."

"Lots of people would. Isla was thrilled to dump Hilty."

"Well, do I seem anything like Isla?"

"No," I admit. "Not at all. Your horses really like you."

"Thanks. Did you know Flicker's old owner, Clara, when she lived here?"

"No." I shake my head. "I've seen her ride, of course, but I've never had anything to do with her. I know that she's Isabelle and Alice's sister. And I heard all sorts of wild rumours about her. But that's it."

"Well, some of those rumours were probably true. But Clara is kind of a genius. She and my step-brother were friends for a while so I got to know her a little bit. And then, she just showed up one day as a guest lecturer at Starling Academy."

"Oh, wow, that's weird."

"Yeah, it was a strange coincidence. She lectured there a few times and she even coached our team at some competitions. She is a ruthless competitor and showed us how to get every last drop of talent out of a robot."

"Wait, what exactly are we talking about here? Is there some secret, underground robot fighting network? Is it run by gangsters or something? Do they cut off your thumbs if you lose?"

Oliver snorts back a laugh and shakes his head.

"Oh, probably somewhere. But the stuff I do is on the up and up. They're legal competitions with sponsors and everything. Anyway, Clara remembered me from Three Sisters, and she asked if I'd keep an eye on Flicker when I got back. She said she'd been forced to sell him and that Marsha was the worst possible choice for him. She was really angry about it; it was a bit scary how mad she got when she talked about having to sell him."

"Being forced to sell your horse to a horrible person would

be the worse punishment ever. What could she have ever done to deserve it?"

"Um, I'm not supposed to talk about it," Oliver says, flushing a little. "My step-brother told me that nobody is supposed to know."

I look at him with my eyebrows raised. He'd brought it up in the first place, not me.

"Fine. All I know is that she planted some small explosives as a joke. But one of the riders got hurt and a horse too. She had to sell her horses and go quietly overseas so nobody would press charges."

"Oh," I say quietly. I had already heard that story but had thought it was just made-up gossip.

"Anyway, Clara asked me to keep an eye on Flicker. And I've been keeping tabs on him since I've been back. She was so relieved when you started riding him, you know. Apparently, you made a good impression on her at some point."

"Really? How would she even know I existed?"

Oliver shrugs. "You're more memorable than you think, Kira. Anyway, she was glad you were riding him in the clinic because she was hoping John Riddle might be able to help find Flicker a new home. But, when it turned out that he had kissing spines, she knew that Marsha was going to bail on him. She'd either just put him down or dump him on an unsuspecting new buyer. So, Clara asked me to buy him. She paid me to buy him, actually."

"Oh." Suddenly the pieces fall into place and it all makes sense. That's the reason Oliver had been hanging around so much. It wasn't because he liked me, or even because he liked Flicker, it was because he was doing a favour for Clara. My breath catches a bit in my throat, and I feel my face start to heat with embarrassment.

"Why are you here then?" I ask, my voice coming out more sharply than I'd intended.

"Well," he looks at me uncertainly, "I was hoping to get your help with him."

"Oh. With what?"

"With his rehab plan. The vet did all these diagnostics on Flicker. She thinks that the kissing spine thing can be improved if he's brought very slowly back into work. He's only to do flat work for now and he has to build his muscles up properly so they can support his spine. He might be sound forever if we are careful about it."

"Really? I'd thought kissing spines was sort of career-ending."

"It can be. It depends on where it is and how severe. The vet said that Flicker might even be able to start jumping again. But he'll need regular cortisone injections and bodywork, and at least a year of rehab on the flat. And that's where you come in."

"Me?" My heart takes a little jump. "You want me to ride him?"

"Yes, I want you to ride him and work with Elliot on his rehab program. And, I want you to teach *me* how to ride him too."

I look at him blankly, trying to find the kindest way to tell him that it's a bad idea for him to ever get on Flicker.

"Okay, you don't have to give me that look. I'm well aware that some people think I'm a crap rider with a good horse. Do you know how many times my step-brother has told me that Bluebell is a saint for putting up with me?"

I shake my head.

"Lots. But, I've come to like Flicker. And I think he and I get along pretty well on the ground. I'm certain he likes me. So, I've made it my mission this year to level up my riding. It's win-win for everyone. So, what do you think?"

"I...well, I definitely want to ride Flicker. I like figuring him out and he's very fun when he's not being naughty. And

I'd like to find a way to ride him in less gear without him trying to kill me."

"Yeah, Clara was really mad about that bridle."

"I'm just not sure why you don't ask your brother for help. He's a much better rider than me. Or Anna or Elliot."

"Have you met my step-brother? He can't stand to be anywhere near me. He'd never stoop to help me with anything."

"Are you sure?" I ask with a frown. "He was really nice to me at the clinic."

"That's because you're talented and you push yourself hard to succeed. Just like him. You're not a lazy weirdo whose mother married his father. He's not thrilled that I'm part of his family."

"You're not lazy…or weird."

"Well, Josh thinks I'm both. His dad made him start riding lessons before the wedding, you know. So that we could have something to bond over. Josh hadn't even been near a horse before that. But it turned out that he is some sort of genius or something because he was a better rider than me from almost the first time he sat in a saddle. He's never let me forget it, either."

"Oh," I say thoughtfully. There is apparently more to Oliver's story than I'd expected. "Look, I'd like to help you but I'm not a teacher. You have Anna or Elliot to help you ride better."

"I don't want *lessons*, Kira. I've been riding in lessons since I was six years old. I want to know your secret."

"Secret?"

"Yeah, we've both ridden at Three Sisters a long time. And, don't take this the wrong way, but you were a really bad rider when you started. Like really bad. Hopeless. Much worse than me. I remember that."

"Gee, thanks."

"Wait, I'm getting to the compliment part. I just mean, that you're not a natural intuitive rider like some of the people are here, like Josh is."

"Oh, right." I nod in agreement. "No, I had to really struggle to figure things out."

"Exactly, and I want to know how you did it. How did you go from not being able to steer a school pony over cross rails to riding like you do now?"

He stares at me fixedly, waiting for me to spout some words of wisdom, and I half expect him to whip out a notebook and pen to start taking notes.

"I…" I hesitate, trying to formulate my thoughts. "I'm not sure I have the answer you're looking for, Oliver. I just worked hard, that's all."

His hopeful expression falls and I feel a stab of remorse.

"All right then." He pushes himself slowly to his feet. "I'll figure something else out. I just thought it was worth a shot. I thought you might have had, like, a system you followed or something."

A system? I frown, thinking it over. I hadn't just worked hard; after all, it hadn't been brute effort that had made me improve. Anna had tried her best to teach me for years. And I'd suffered through so many frustrating lessons where I never seemed to understand, or be able to make my body do, what she was talking about.

It hadn't been until later that I'd accidentally found my learning style. I was a visual thinker, so when I'd watched that first video of my lesson, a whole bunch of concepts had suddenly fallen into place. And then I'd begun watching clips of successful riders over and over again and copying them. Studying their positions, their timing, and their breathing until I was able to incorporate that into my own riding.

All the tiny things that some riders did by feel, I'd had to focus on and fix one thing at a time. The left foot that wanted to turn outward no matter what I did, my clumsy fingers that couldn't keep the reins, me ducking forward at every jump. It hadn't mattered that Anna had tried to correct me a million times. I hadn't understood what she'd meant until I'd studied the videos.

And maybe Oliver is a little bit the same way. Maybe he doesn't learn by feel either but needs something more visual.

"Wait, Oliver," I say as he puts his cup in the sink and turns to leave. "I can't make any promises, but maybe I can help you."

"Really?" His whole face lights up and I can't help but be struck by the way the sunlight from the window washes over his cheekbones. He has the nicest eyes. Kind and full of humour. I've never really noticed that before.

"Well, I can try anyway. Come on upstairs."

Oliver is whistling happily under his breath as he follows me upstairs. I have a brief moment of wondering if it is the wisest move to be taking a near-stranger up to my room when nobody else is home but I push it away.

Oliver doesn't strike me as much of a fighter and he's pretty out of shape compared to me. I am fit and toned from riding Tessa. I can probably out-muscle him if it came down to it. And it's not like it's a secret that he's here. Mrs. Harris from next door has probably already told the neighbourhood watch that I have a guest.

"Wow, you have this whole floor for yourself? This looks great. You're lucky."

"Thanks, my dad was pretty amazing to let me design the whole thing how I wanted."

"Nice." Oliver zeroes in on my puzzle table and then turns to the media station.

"Kira." Oliver stands there gaping at the shelves that hold my old-school DVD's and ancient VHS tapes. "What is all this?"

"Movies, mostly. But there are horse training and riding

videos too. Lots of the older trainers never put their stuff online at all so this is the only way to watch it. You can learn a ton from watching them. I'll make you a list of things to look up online too."

I watch him warily, not loving the fact that he is running his unwashed hands across my collection. I've only brought a handful of people to my room before and it feels weird, like I'm exposing my secrets or something.

Oliver turns, surveying the rest of my room, and zeroes in on my puzzle table again.

"Wow, this looks complicated. What is the picture supposed to be?"

"I don't know." I shrug. "It's a mystery puzzle. You don't get to see the picture until the end. It's usually some sort of landscape, though. Or abstract art. Never horses."

He laughs and shakes his head. "You kind of have a one-track mind when it comes to horses, don't you? I remember that from school."

I raise my eyebrows and cross my arms over my chest. Liking horses too much was one of many things I'd been teased about in school.

"So? That's why you're asking me for my help, aren't you?"

"Yes," he says quickly, his smile dropping away. "Sorry, I was just teasing. You should be able to like whatever you want. Nobody in my family appreciates my interests either."

"The battle robot thing?"

"Yes. You don't have to sound so skeptical. There's nothing wrong with robotics."

"Sorry. You're right. I just didn't picture you into nerdy stuff, that's all. You seemed more…sporty when we were at school. You were with that popular crowd."

"Robots aren't nerdy." He looks at me, raising an eyebrow. "And what rule says I can't like sports *and* building things? You like horses *and* puzzles, right? It's the same thing."

"Sorry," I say again, because I'm realizing that I'm kind of being mean here. And judgemental. "Look, your friends were awful to me in school and I can't help but lump you in with them. It's hard to forget something like that."

His face falls and he looks down at the puzzle table, reaching out a finger to nudge one of the pieces.

"Yeah, I wondered about that. Sorry, I was sort of focused on my own stuff back then. I knew they were being mean to you, but I thought it would just go away on its own. You never seemed to mind anyway; it drove Katie crazy that you'd never react to any of the nasty stuff she said."

"Never seemed to mind?" I say incredulously. "Oliver, every day at that school was a living hell. I cried in the bathroom between every class. I forced myself not to react because it only made things worse. I became an expert at squashing down every feeling and masking every thought. That isn't a good thing, Oliver. I was this close to breaking down that whole year. I finally did break down."

I am gasping for breath and I look down to see that my hands are tightly balled into fists. Oliver is staring at me like I've grown two heads.

"Sorry," I say, pushing back the sudden urge to cry. "I shouldn't have said all that. I try not to talk about this stuff too much. You can leave if you want."

There is a long silence and I finally look up to see Oliver staring at my John Riddle poster on the wall.

"Are you still willing to help me?" he asks quietly. "Even after all that."

"I am." I take a deep breath. "What you did for Flicker was amazing. You probably saved his life."

He turns, sending me a half-smile. But his eyes look a bit sad.

"Okay," I say, clapping my hands together suddenly. "If you want to ride that horse then we need to get to work. That shelf to your left is mostly all horse videos. Old ones. Mostly by famous riders who are now dead."

"Um, okay."

"When I first started riding there were a lot of concepts that I couldn't understand, no matter how Anna tried to teach me. One day my dad videoed my lesson. And when I watched it, what Anna was saying suddenly made sense. Hearing the instructions didn't work. But when I watched them, things started to click. I do better if I can watch things done properly first and then I can figure out how to coordinate my body to do it."

"Oh," Oliver says, frowning. "I have no idea how I learn best."

"Well, probably not being shouted at by Darla, for starters. But, it's not like you're a dead-awful rider, Oliver. Bluebell obviously likes you. You stay out of her way and you talk to her and pat her all the time. I've seen you."

"Oh, been watching me, have you?" he says, leering at me and wiggling his eyebrows in the most bizarre way.

"Yes, I just said that I've seen you ride. Why are you moving your face like that?"

"Sorry, never mind. I was making a joke."

"Anyway," I say, letting that one go. I don't understand half the weird stuff people say or do, so I'm going to ask him to explain his joke. He's here for a reason and, if he really wants help, then we have our work cut out for us. "I have thousands of hours of instructional videos from riders around the world."

"Thousands of hours?" he says, wincing. "That sounds like a lot."

"Are you serious about riding or not, Oliver? You don't sound very committed."

"Yeah, yeah. Okay, but can I put the video thing in the machine? I've never even seen one of these before."

"Sure." I sigh. "Just don't break anything."

We completely lose track of time because it is hours later when my dad comes upstairs to find us sitting on the floor in front of the oversized television screen streaming John Riddle videos.

"Oh hey," I say, glancing up from the screen long enough to see that the sunlight has faded outside and my dad is staring incredulously at us from the doorway.

"Hello. Aren't you going to introduce your friend, Kira?"

Oliver scrambles to his feet, nearly knocking his drink off the table in the process.

"Oliver, sir," he says, sounding all polite. "Nice to meet you. Kira is just helping me with some riding issues I'm having."

"Ah, a horse friend." My dad smiles, sounding relieved for some reason. "Well, it's getting late. Time to start getting dinner ready, Kira."

"I'm not hungry," I say, sitting up reluctantly. "We are having fun."

"I see that. Well, you still need to eat and Grace just arrived. Oliver, you can stay for dinner if it's okay with your parents."

"Can I? That would be great. My mom has her book club tonight so it would just be fast food for dinner anyway. I'm starving."

My dad laughs and grins over at me.

"Well, I guess you two had better start cooking then. Grace is ready and waiting.

"Okay, fine," I sigh, "come on, Oliver. I hope you're good at chopping salad."

Dinner is actually both delicious and entertaining. Oliver and my dad seem to hit it off. They talk nonstop about both robotics and the environmental protection act that my dad is helping to draft up in his spare time.

Normally, both those subjects would bore me to tears, but it's nice to see my dad so happy and animated. For once he doesn't look tired and worried.

And, since Oliver has somehow charmed him into such a great mood, I decide that the dessert course is a good opportunity to set part of my plan in motion.

"Dad? Do you remember that girl, Fina, that I told you about? The one with the draft horses?"

"Yes, of course. The one who you said wears the unconventional clothes."

"Uh, yes. Sometimes. Well, she's offered to let me ride some of her horses for free. She lives right next door to Three Sisters. I rode Tessa there on a trail ride the other day."

I hadn't mentioned to him yet that I'd ridden one of Fina's horses already. And now doesn't seem like the time.

"Oh," he says, looking a little startled. "I don't know about that. Do they have insurance? Would it be safe?"

"It's definitely safe. Her horses are well-behaved. And she treats them like gold."

"Fina's grandfather breeds Shire horses," Oliver adds. "Their farm is kind of famous around here. And Fina is very responsible."

I grin at Oliver and then we both smile hopefully at my dad.

"You two are laying it on a little thick," he says dryly. "Well, if you want to, Kira, then I'm not going to stand in your way. I'm glad to see you playing outside rather than being on the internet all day."

"Thanks, Dad," I cut him off before he can launch into another lecture on how the internet is ruining my generation. As if he doesn't spend nearly every day glued to his phone or laptop himself.

The rest of the summer suddenly seems a lot more inviting. I'm already figuring out how I might be able to keep riding at Fina's even once school starts.

▭

Later that night, long after Oliver and Grace have gone home, my dad knocks on my bedroom door.

"Hey, just wanted to check on you. Oliver seems like a nice boy."

He gives me a meaningful look and smiles hopefully.

"Dad," I groan, "don't make a big deal out of this. Oliver is just a friend and he was only over to get help with Flicker."

"Is that so? Well, he looked like he was having a good time."

"He always looks like that. Seriously, Dad, there is nothing to see here."

"Okay, okay. I'm just pleased that you're happy, all right? You've made quite a few friends lately. I'm just glad, that's all."

He smiles down at me fondly.

"Thanks. It has been a good week. You're really all right if I ride more at Fina's?"

"Yes." He nods and sighs. "I don't seem to be having much luck limiting your horse time, do I? It's something that really makes you happy? Even after all these years?"

"More than anything."

"Well, do as much as you like this summer then, there's plenty of time to get serious about your future once school starts. You might as well enjoy your holidays."

I open my mouth to tell him about my new plans, about how I'm not going to university for accounting or whatever horrible thing he wants me to study. That I want to work with horses. But I shut it again without saying a word.

"Thanks, Dad. Goodnight."

After he's gone, I lie back in bed and stare up at my John Riddle poster.

At some point, I'm going to have to have a hard conversation with my dad about my future. Horses are the only path forward that I can see. I just hope he's not going to be too disappointed in me.

Chapter 24

Lena

I do my best to focus on the horses for the next week but my anxiety over Natalia's behaviour hums in the background like an ever-present noise.

She and Todd have made up, sort of, but you can tell that it's only a matter of time before things will start deteriorating again.

She's been spending more time at home, unfortunately, and I've had to do my best to stay out of her way.

"Why is there no food in this house?" she'd shout, slamming cupboards and kicking the fridge door as if she expected it to magically dispense a meal for her if she kicked it hard enough.

Luckily, I'd had another payday so I have been able to stock a supply of snacks around the house for the times when Todd isn't around to feed her. The one night she really started to rage, I'd managed to slip over to Ethen's house and crash on his couch again.

It hadn't been nearly as embarrassing the second time. His family was so nice and non-judgemental, and they made sure to let me know that I wasn't the first person they'd taken in and I wouldn't be the last.

Natalia hadn't even noticed that I'd spent the night elsewhere and, in the morning, Todd had shown back up at our place with a peace offering of muffins and coffee. He'd had tears in his eyes as he'd apologized to my mother, like somehow, *he'd* been the one to blame for Natalia raging at him the night before.

"How do I even avoid being that dysfunctional?" I ask Ethen on our drive to work. "I mean, it's all I know. Am I going to wake up and discover that I'm that messed up too? Or that I'm an abuser in a broken, toxic relationship?"

"No," Ethen says firmly. "You won't. You're a good person, Lena, and you're allowed to make mistakes. If you mess up and do something dysfunctional, then you'll just apologize and fix it. It's going to be okay."

He reaches out to squeeze my hand and I grip onto it like a lifeline for just a second too long, loving the way that our hands fit together perfectly. I don't let him drive me every day, because I don't want to get too used to depending on him. But, once in a while, it's nice to give in.

"You say that now. Maybe I'll be a complete witch in a few years. I'll probably even look like Natalia."

"No way, you're way prettier."

"I'm not." I look at him incredulously.

"You are. Because you're good inside and your heart shines out through your eyes and your skin and your fingertips. You're the most beautiful, kind person I've ever met."

I stare at him. Stunned. Nobody has ever said anything like that to me. Even if it's far from the truth. I've spent way too much of my life lying to be called a good person.

"Ethen…I'm not…"

"I'll see you tonight," he says, and I realize we've pulled right up to the barn. "Here's your lunch. My mom packed you extras. Don't get into any trouble. And don't overthink things too much."

Before I can answer any of this he leans over and cups my cheek in one hand and then plants a searing kiss on my lips that leaves me weak all over. Then he unclicks my seat belt and shoos me out the door.

I walk into the barn, feeling like I'm floating, and it's not until hours later that I stop feeling the impression of that kiss on my lips.

Once I've fed and helped with cleaning, I spend most of the time helping Samantha organize the little kids and the ponies.

I have found myself looking forward to this part of my job more and more. The kids now greet me by name and laugh and joke with me like they do with Samantha. With Anna and most of the older riders away showing, the kids are much more relaxed. We keep the radio in the barn on almost all day. And watching them sing and dance along to their favourite songs while they get the ponies ready is pretty darn cute.

I wish that Ethen's sister, Rosie, could have a chance to ride here. And his little cousin Ally likes horses too. I can totally see them here with the other kids. Maybe I can talk to Anna one day to see if they have any staff discounts for family.

They're not actually your family, I remind myself. But honestly, Ethen's house feels homier to me than any of my own many houses ever have.

"You're so good with them," Samantha says to me, as we're helping her lesson kids get untacked. "Have you ever thought about teaching?"

I look at her in surprise. "I haven't actually. I only thought about being a groom."

"Well, there's no saying you can't do both. There's a camp

coming up next month and I'm going to ask Anna if you can be my assistant if that's okay."

"Wow, sure," I say, totally taken off guard. "I mean I'd like that. Thanks."

"No problem. Don't thank me until it's over, though, you don't know how much work these kids are yet."

"Hey!" Paxton, a little blond girl with her hair braided in pigtails, is lugging her saddle toward the tack room. She glares up at both of us.

"Not you, of course," Samantha said quickly, "just all the others. You're a treat."

Paxton considers this and then nods in agreement. "Yes, I'm very advanced for my age."

I have to bite my cheek to keep from laughing, and Samantha sends me a meaningful look as she heads to the tack room to make sure the kids are staying on task.

Still, I'm excited by her offer. I've never tried teaching before but suddenly I want to try. That is a whole other career path I hadn't even thought about.

Hooves clop in the aisle and I look up to see Isla leading a thin, nervous-looking bay mare toward where her friend Rebecca is tacking up Rio.

"There you are," Rebecca calls. "I thought you'd bailed on our lesson."

"Whatever. I'm barely late. It's this stupid horse's fault anyway. She's so nervous about everything. I had to lead her down instead of riding her because she didn't want to leave the barn."

I look over the mare appreciatively. Despite her rolling eyes and nervous expression, she is very pretty in a fine-boned sort of way. She has a long neck and a sloping shoulder. Her coat is silky smooth and her eyes are huge and expressive. She looks intelligent but very, very sensitive. I'm not sure how either Marsha or Isla will get along with her. She looks like she needs a tactful sort of person to handle her and neither of them exactly gives off that vibe.

"What are you looking at?" Isla snaps, making the mare jump.

"Sorry, your horse is really beautiful, it's hard not to look at her."

"Oh," Isla says, looking slightly less irritated. "Yes, Sonata is pretty. But she doesn't always act that way. She spooks at everything. It almost makes me miss that slug, Hilty."

"Hmmm," I say noncommittally because what can you say? There is no tactful way to tell Isla that she probably would have been better sticking with kind, long-suffering Hilty.

"So, is Oliver around?" Isla says casually.

"No, he and Kira went on a trail ride, I think."

"Ugh, how can he stand hanging out with that weirdo? She's such a freak."

"Don't call her that," I say sharply, before I can stop myself.

"Why?" Isla narrows her eyes at me, ignoring the mare who has started shifting around beside her. "Don't tell me you're friends with her or something."

I consider not answering. Or punching her in her scheming little face, but I love this job and I have no idea if Anna would take her side or not if Isla complained about me.

"Yes, I'm friends with her," I say through gritted teeth. "She's a fun person and she's one of the best riders here. That's why John Riddle invited her to be one of his working students after she graduates."

Maybe I shouldn't have added that last part. I also don't bother to squash down the smile that tugs at my lips when her face goes white with rage.

The mare beside her senses the change and skitters backward nervously, nearly hauling Isla off her feet.

"Stop that," Isla shouts, which is enough to send Sonata crashing sideways into the wall.

The tack room door opens and Samantha flies out, along with the little kids from her lesson. All of them are just staring at Isla, open-mouthed, as she jerks the mare's reins sharply over and over. But Sonata has had enough and she half-rears, knocking Isla sideways. The reins rip out of Isla's hands and the mare trots right toward me.

She is probably heading toward Rio for comfort, but it is me who reaches out to grab her reins and soothe her softly, petting her neck and murmuring to her gently.

"Isla, control your temper," Samantha snaps. "That is not even your horse. If you can't handle a sensitive mare like her properly then you'll have to find another horse to lease."

"I'm sorry," Isla says quickly in a meek voice. "She just got away from me. It won't happen again."

Samantha crosses her arms over her chest, not looking convinced.

"All right, well, let's get to the ring for your lesson. We're already running behind."

"Of course," Isla whispers, but when she snatches the mare's reins out of my hand her expression is murderous. I have the feeling that I've just made a very bad enemy.

———————————————

Chapter 25

———————————————

Kira

"I'm warning you now that it's going to be a long, boring process at the beginning," Elliot says, looking between me and Oliver. "Now that his cortisone injections have had a chance to kick in, the vet said that Flicker needs to do a lot of slow lunging work to build up his core strength. He's allowed to be ridden, but only on the flat, and, again, it needs to be slow, correct work. We have to encourage him to stretch down and use his back and his core in order to rebuild his muscles from the bottom up. And he should be turned out all day in between his sessions. Standing around in his stall doesn't do him any good."

Oliver and I both nod.

"Oliver, I know you plan to ride this horse eventually but he's a lot…"

"Don't worry, we've already got that part covered," Oliver breaks in. "I'm going to let Kira ride him most of the time and then I'll hop on to cool him out once he's tired. And, in the meantime, I was going to ask you about taking some lessons on Bluebell."

Elliot furrows her eyebrows, tapping her fingers on her hip as she studies us.

"That could work. But, just remember that Flicker is a lot of horse; even cooling him out could be a challenge if you're not prepared."

Oliver makes a low, grumbling noise in his throat. "I'm not *that* terrible of a rider. I have been showing for years. I want to do this."

"Okay, okay." Elliot holds up her hands in surrender. "Let's give it a try then. But, today we're going to see how Flicker is on the lunge. It would be ideal if you two could do the lunging work on days when he's not being ridden. You have lunged before, right?"

"Er, a few times last year," I say slowly, and Oliver shakes his head.

"Oh well, you're about to learn. I'll do it this week and you guys can watch me and practice with Bluebell and Tessa in the meantime. Next week I'll have you take over if he's well-behaved."

Flicker, predictably, is not good on the lunge at all. He is so excited after all his time off that he pretty much bolts away at a gallop the second Elliot sends him out on the circle.

"Whoa," she says sharply, digging her heels in and stepping sideways so that he has to slow down to avoid hitting the arena fence.

After a few wild circuits, the crazy look in his eye mellows and he is able to find a canter rhythm.

"Good boy," Elliot calls, "easy, tarr-ottt."

Somewhere in Flicker's past, he must have been taught voice commands because he slows instantly to a trot when she says the word.

"Good boy, and walk. Whoa, now."

Flicker jerks to a stop and looks at her expectantly, his ears suddenly pricked as she reaches into her pocket for a treat.

"Somebody treated him well at one point," Elliot says, scratching the big horse's neck while he crunches his piece of carrot. "I think he knows all this stuff deep down. We just have to remind him that we're not his enemies."

She sends Flicker out in the other direction and this time he is much more relaxed and happier. It's like he's suddenly figured out what we expect from him. He only does one small bolt in this direction, but after that, he listens nicely.

"All right, that's enough for him. Put him away and let him have all the turnout he likes. I'll see you both tomorrow."

Lena is grooming one of the older ponies in the aisle when we get back and she looks up, sending me a small smile.

She has been kind of quiet lately, and she seems a little sad, but she still acts friendly with me. We eat lunch together on most days and she's still been true to her word about bringing me peanut butter sandwiches in exchange for my home-cooked lunches.

Every day I give her updates on the progress of her model horse, although at this stage there's not much to tell. The bodywork is done; his leg has been replaced, as have his chipped ears. And his battered body has been sanded down smooth and primed. Now I'm working on the many layers of paint he needs since Lena had given me permission to freshen him up.

"He should be back to you by the end of the month," I tell her after I've shown her the pictures I'd taken of his progress with my phone.

"Oh, there's no rush," she says, biting her lip and frowning. "He's probably safer with you right now, anyway."

"Safer?" I exchange a look with Oliver over Flicker's broad back.

"Oh, I just mean that he's in good hands," she says quickly. "Are you going to Fina's this afternoon?"

"Yes, we're both going to ride over right now. I just texted her to ask if we could practice lunging her horses since they're so quiet and steady. Tessa's not that keen on lunging."

"Oh, okay."

I don't miss that wistful tone in her voice and I wish that she could ride with us. Maybe that would cheer her up.

"Hey, I bet that Fina would let you ride her horses," I say. "I could ask her today when we're there."

"Oh, thanks," Lena says, shrugging. "I'm okay, though. I get my horse time in just taking care of these guys." She gives the senior pony that she's grooming an affectionate hug around the neck. But that aura of sadness around her doesn't lift.

Oliver and I ride side by side up the hill toward Barn A, heading to the upper trails that lead to Fina's house.

"Here, look at this one. This is the fight we nearly lost," Oliver says, leaning sideways on Bluebell to show me the video he's popped up on his phone. I glance over with a sigh to see yet another robot fight.

"That's great, Oliver. But we really shouldn't be riding and watching videos at the same time. It's kind of basic horse-manship."

"Yeah, yeah, safety-police. But did you see this move here? We completely destroyed his blades."

I shake my head, not being able to keep from laughing. I have been subjected to hours of robot destruction videos in the last couple of days. And yes, it's pretty impressive that he'd helped build these machines. He is probably some sort of genius. But I could not muster up a lot of enthusiasm after the first few videos. There were only so many ways a battle robot could explode, be torn apart or catch on fire. But, I was doing my best to sound mildly interested and be a supportive friend. Which, honestly, was a lot more work than I'd expected.

"Where are you two going?" a voice to our right calls sharply.

We are passing Barn A and I look up to see Isla standing in the open doorway, her eyes blazing with anger as she catches sight of Oliver.

"Oh, hey Isla," he says, his laughter fading. "Just going on a trail ride."

"So you're riding with *her* now, are you?"

She shoots a vengeful look at me, flexing her fingers like she is itching to wrap them around my neck.

"Uh, yeah. Kira and I are hanging out today. See you around." He gives Bluebell a little nudge to hurry her along.

I don't look back but I can feel Isla's fiery glare burning into my back long after we've passed.

"What was that about?" I whisper.

"Nothing," he says, his cheeks turning a tomato red. "She, just um, sort of asked me out the other day and I said no. I don't think she took it well."

"She asked you out? That was brave of her. I don't think I'd risk it."

"Why not?"

"Because they might say no just like you did to Isla. That would be mortifying."

"Being turned down is not *that* bad. Besides, they could say yes."

"But, most likely they'd say no if it was *me* asking."

"I doubt that. You should give it a try."

"No, too risky."

"Kira, you have to take a chance if…"

"If I let you show me another robot video will you let this go?" I interrupt.

"Yes," he says laughing. "I happen to have a good one right here."

<hr>

We spend the rest of the morning at Fina's, playing with her horses. It turns out that she is a bit of an expert at lunging and ground driving so she gives us a crash course.

The mares are all fairly easy, although the bay, Briar, keeps liking to stop suddenly and switch directions. Nobody bolts like Flicker had but, by the time a couple of hours have passed, I feel much more confident about my skills. Fina even has us practice ground-driving with two reins. Which is a bit of a challenge for me to coordinate, even at a walk.

"Next time we can try some actual driving," Fina says enthusiastically. "Wait until you use a cart. It's addictive."

We promise to come back and I leave with my head practically overflowing with information. Luckily, I'd videoed our training session so I could watch it all later.

"That was fun," Oliver says. He has dropped the reins on Bluebell's neck and is letting the mare pick her own way through the woods.

"You know you can't do that with Flicker, right?" I say, raising my eyebrows.

"Yeah, yeah. But this is Bluebell, the world's best mare, she knows what she's doing."

He is probably right. I have the feeling that Bluebell has spent her entire career taking care of him.

Chapter 26

Lena

"Are you ready to head out?" Samantha asks, smiling at me as I sweep the last speck of dust out of the aisle.

"Yes, Ethen should be here any second. We're going out to dinner tonight."

"Oooh, like a date?"

"Well, kind of. He wants to take me mini-golfing, of all things. I made the mistake of telling him that I've never been."

"Aw, that's adorable. He sounds like a good guy."

"He is. I'm actually enjoying spending time with him."

"You sound surprised," she says, laughing.

"Well, I kind of am. I'm not exactly sure how he ended up in my life. I didn't plan for that."

"Well, just relax and enjoy it. You deserve to be happy. Have fun and I'll see you tomorrow. Don't forget that you're on kid-duty with me."

"Yes, I'm looking forward to it."

I smile as I watch her leave. Samantha has turned out to be

a great person and she is insistent that I'm going to get my instructor qualifications and start teaching. I am slowly warming up to the idea, but I have to admit that I love helping her with the little kids.

Ethen's car rumbles up the driveway and my heart gives a little leap when he parks and steps outside into the sunshine.

Despite all my initial resistance, I am enjoying the time I spend with Ethen. He has worked his way around most of my defenses somehow and I am finding myself looking forward to seeing him more and more every day. He has become a refuge for me, a port in the storm. I have taken to retreating to his house more and more often whenever Natalia is home.

"Hey you," he says, coming over and kissing me softly. First on the lips, then the forehead and then the tip of my nose, making me laugh. "Ready to go?"

"Yep, I just have to lock up. Do you want to come in and meet the horses? There's nobody around."

"Sure," he says, his eyes lighting up.

I grab his hand and tug him into the barn, going from stall to stall to introduce him to my favourites.

"So this is the famous Tessa," he says, slowly holding up his hand so she can sniff it suspiciously.

Her ears pin back threateningly for a second and then she abruptly changes her mind, making a little nickering noise and softly nuzzling his arm.

"Wow, she never does that. She likes you."

"Yeah, well, I happen to have a way with beautiful women."

"Haha. You do know how to lay the charm on pretty thick. Come meet Flicker and Bluebell."

"Hang on, I have to take a picture of Tessa first. Rosie and Ally insisted."

"You know, I don't want to get their hopes up. But Samantha told me that Three Sisters has a small fund to sponsor a few kids at camp. I was wondering if your parents would want to apply for them."

"Oh, really? Yeah, that would be great if you could find out more. All Ally talks about is horses."

We finish our barn tour and then Ethen follows me outside while I carefully lock up the barn.

"Can we go see the other barn too?" he asks. "I want to take a couple of pictures of that fancy indoor arena you told me about."

I hesitate. I'm not as comfortable up at Barn A as I am here, even though I've filled in there a handful of times. And I'm not sure they'd want us poking around.

"I'm not sure if anyone's up there, but we could probably take a quick look."

"Great, let's go."

Luckily the barn door is still open and Ben's pickup truck is in the driveway when we get there. I relax, not feeling so awkward bringing Ethen in for a tour if there are other people around.

"Hello?" I call as we go inside, but there is no answer.

"Wow, this place is intense," Ethen says, staring down the wide aisle at the polished rows of stalls.

"Yeah, it's a little over the top compared to Barn B, that's for sure. You should see it when it's full of horses. Right now most of them are away showing. Come on, I'll show you the indoor."

Ethen takes a few photos as we walk down the aisle, but as we near the tack room the door flies open and Isla marches out into the aisle, her face twisted in anger.

"What are you doing here?" she snaps. But when she catches sight of Ethen her contorted face smooths out and she seems to shrink. Her eyes widen and she blinks at him tearfully, sniffling a little.

"Are you okay?" I ask tentatively.

"No. I just got a lecture from that stupid Ben. He was so mean to me."

"Ben was mean? Why?"

"He's all weird about how I handle Sonata." She makes a little hiccupping sound and wipes her eyes, shifting a step closer to Ethen. "He says she's getting stress ulcers or something. He threatened to talk to Marsha about how I'm too rough on the horse. Can you believe that?"

"Oh, well, maybe it's not the best match," I say diplomatically. "There are plenty of other…"

Isla spins and fixes me with a murderous expression and I break off with a gulp.

"Sonata and I are fine," she says, her voice low and deadly. "If anyone is giving her ulcers, it's Ben. I should talk to my friend Alice about getting him fired."

"Uh-huh. Well, I hope you feel better soon. I'm just giving Ethen a quick tour before we head out for dinner."

That look of anger flashes briefly over her face again before it's gone.

"I have a date too," she says quickly. "So I have to go. Oh, Lena. Would you do me a favour and make sure Sonata's bridle is hung up properly in Marsha's locker? It has her name on it. Thanks so much."

She turns on her heel and marches out before I can say another word.

"She's different," Ethen says, raising his eyebrows.

"She's something all right," I grumble. "Come on, I'll just check on the bridle thing and then we'll check the indoor out and go."

Isla's bridle is hanging in Marsha's locker in perfect order, so I let Ethen take his picture of the tack room for the girls and then I shut the door carefully behind me and we head to the indoor.

"All this just for horses," Ethen says, whistling under his breath as he takes in the massive arena.

"I know it seems extravagant, but you really need an indoor on this coast if you plan to show all winter. It's just too rainy otherwise. Trust me, it gets well used."

We take a couple of photos and then head back outside.

There is still no sign of Ben and I have a brief worry that maybe Isla had been mad enough to knock him over the head and stuff his body somewhere. I push the thought away with a laugh, shaking my head at how silly I am being. I mean, Isla is crazy but she's not *that* bad.

"Ready to watch me crush a mini-golf course?" Ethen says as we get into the car.

"Um, yeah. Let's go get it, killer," I say, rolling my eyes and laughing.

Ethen starts the car and looks over at me, grinning. And for a second everything in the world seems just perfect. I blink at him, waiting for the feeling to go away, but it doesn't.

"What?" Ethen asks, staring at me quizzically.

"I...I'm just happy, I guess. I think you make me happy."

Ethen's expression melts and in the next second, he's pulled me into a tight hug.

"You make me happy too, Lena. I can't remember what life was like before you."

He reaches out to squeeze my hand and I link my fingers tightly with his. We stay that way for the entire drive.

Chapter 27

Kira

The next day the weather takes a sudden turn, and instead of blazing heat, we have the mother of all thunderstorms crashing down on our heads.

Water runs in rivulets everywhere, pouring down the driveway and making deep ruts in the carefully manicured gravel.

The power flickers constantly, threatening to go out, and all the lessons in the outdoor ring are cancelled, including Flicker's.

All the horses stay inside instead of going out on pasture, which makes Tessa extremely grumpy. So Oliver and I decide to make a run for it up to Barn A to use their indoor to let both mares stretch their legs.

Most of the riders from both barns are away showing on the mainland again so the indoor is miraculously free.

We trot up the hill as fast as we can but we are still soaked to the bone by the time we got there. Even my saddle is squelching with water and I make a mental note to give it an extra good clean and oil as soon as our ride is over.

Tessa and I have been making steady progress on our lateral work under Elliot's careful eye. I can now do a somewhat decent shoulder-in and haunches in. My leg yields aren't as crooked and Tessa has stopped springing into a canter the second my leg goes back behind her girth.

Bluebell looks like she is half asleep but Tessa is on fire, excited by being in the indoor for the first time since the clinic and by the sound of the rain drumming relentlessly on the metal roof.

I've grown to enjoy riding with Oliver. He has a good eye for things, and if I get stuck on something it is nice to have a second pair of eyes to tell me what Tessa is doing. We've been going over our videos at night too.

After every ride, I send him a copy and we stay up late on the phone, pulling our rides apart and figuring out how we could do better next time.

The rain grows heavier in the middle of our ride and it is so loud that it takes both of us a minute to realize that someone in the barn is shouting.

I draw Tessa to a halt, staring over the half-door that looks into the aisle. Oliver pulls Bluebell up beside me.

"They're gone!" Isla shrills at the top of her lungs. "Sonata's things are gone. They've been stolen. And Alice's stuff too. We've been robbed."

I roll my eyes and turn away, certain she is freaking out over nothing as per usual. But then I see Alice stomping out of the tack room behind her with a dark look on her face. She already has her phone pressed to her ear, and she is barking orders to someone on the other end.

Then she shoves it in her pocket and glares around at everyone in the aisle, her gaze moving to the ring and resting briefly on me and Oliver.

"My things are gone and I want them back," she says coldly. "I've already let my father know, and he's on his way here. We will be reviewing the security footage. And then we will be calling the police."

"I know who did it!" Isla shrieks so loudly that Alice grimaces and puts a hand over her ear. "It was that groom, Lena. Her boyfriend is practically a criminal, and I saw them sneaking around here last night when there was hardly anyone else around. I bet they broke in and sold all your stuff."

Alice looks at her skeptically.

"It's true," Isla sobs hysterically. "They were creeping around. I didn't want to leave while they were still here but my dad came to pick me up and I had to go."

"Lena would never do that," I say loudly, my voice rising over the thudding rain on the roof. I hop down off Tessa and lead her into the aisle. "You have no right to accuse her without proof."

"You're just saying that because she's the only one who puts up with you, freak. She's as weird as you are so that makes sense. Why would they be in here last night if they weren't up to something shady?"

"Lena works here," Oliver says coldly, coming up to stand beside me. "She's allowed to be in the barns."

"Could everyone just shut up?" Alice says, half-shutting her eyes like she's in pain. "Why do you all have to be so loud? We'll know exactly who did it after looking at the security footage. Now, if nobody has any answers as to who took my stuff, then please go back to what you were doing. Quietly."

She turns into the tack room, holding up her hand abruptly to keep Isla from following, and slams the door behind her.

Isla balls her fists and makes a face at the door as if she is silently showering down curses on Alice.

"Is your tack really missing?" Oliver asks quietly.

"Yes." Isla spins around. "You heard what I said. Are you calling me a liar?"

"Whoa." Oliver steps back, holding up his hands in surrender. "I was just asking."

Isla mutters something angrily under her breath and then, not looking at us again, she charges up the stairs to the lounge.

"Wow, she's lost it," Oliver says. "I've never seen her like that before."

"I have," I say grimly, "lots of times. But she usually hides it better. I wonder what's going on with her. Do you think the stuff was really stolen?"

"I guess so. Unless it's some sort of bad prank."

Oliver and I lead the horses down the aisle and then huddle in the barn doorway, staring out into the stormy afternoon, waiting to see if there will be a break in the weather so we could make a run for it.

"Do you think we should tell Lena that Isla is telling everyone she's a thief?" I ask quietly.

After a minute, Oliver shakes his head.

"It will probably come to nothing. And we'd just upset her. I'm sure it will all blow over. I bet they just took the wrong tack to the show or something. Maybe it was just an accident."

I nod uncertainly, not able to shake off the memory of Isla's triumphant, glittering eyes. It felt like she was definitely up to something.

The rain is clearly not going to let up so we run with the horses out to the mounting block, jump aboard and trot at a good clip down the hill. Despite it only being late afternoon, the sky is so dark that it feels like dusk. The rain slants sideways so hard that I have to close my eyes and hope that Tessa stays on the driveway.

She stiffens suddenly as lights flash across us and a golf cart sloshes carefully by us on its way up the hill. I squint but can't make out who is in it.

When we get back to the barn, there is hardly anyone around. And there is no sign of Lena or Samantha.

"I hope everything is all right," I mutter as I untack Tessa and carefully towel off her dripping coat.

I pull out my phone, cursing to see how fast the time has passed. I have hardly any time before the Blacklock car will arrive to take me to my appointment with Donna. And I still need to get Tessa settled and take care of my tack.

"So, my robotics club is meeting tonight to do a trial run before our tournament," Oliver says, leading Bluebell to her stall. "You could come if you like."

"Sorry, I have an appointment with the therapist, and honestly, I think the robots are kind of boring."

I glance up to find him staring at me, frowning.

"What?"

"You really just say whatever you're thinking, don't you?" he says, his mouth twisting into a wry smile. "Do you have like Asperger's or something?"

I blink at him in surprise.

"Asperger's isn't actually a thing anymore, scientifically speaking; so it's just plain old autism for me. I thought you knew I was autistic."

"Oh." He shrugs. "I guess I forgot."

"No big deal. I just prefer to be upfront and honest, I guess. But I don't mean to be rude. Did what I said sound rude?"

"Yes, kind of."

"The therapist part or the robots?"

"Pretty much everyone I know is in some sort of therapy, I don't care about that. But, these competitions are important to me and I want you to be there. As a friend."

"Can't friends have their own separate interests sometimes? Like, I don't force you to watch online model horse competitions."

"Well, I'd go to them if you asked me to."

"Why?"

"To be a supportive friend. That's what people do."

He rolls the door shut harder than necessary, making Blue-bell jump.

I groan inwardly and then finally give in to the inevitable. It won't kill me to be bored for just a couple of hours.

"Oliver, I like you and I'm sorry if I hurt your feelings. If you really want me to go to one of these robot things then I will. Just not tonight. Okay?"

"Really?" His whole face lights up and I bite back a sigh.

"Yes, fine, if it's important to you. But you owe me one."

"Deal," he says, grinning at me. "I'm going to hold you to that."

Chapter 28

Lena

"Lena?"

I look up from where I'm crouched over the feed buckets, mixing dinner, and stare at Samantha in surprise.

She looks pale and her eyes are huge like she's had a shock of some sort.

"Hey, are you okay?" I ask, slowly standing up and moving toward her. "Has someone been hurt? Are the horses okay?"

"Yes," she says, still staring at me, "everyone's fine. Did Ethen go up to Barn A last night?"

"Yes, he picked me up and I gave him a tour of the barns. He wanted to see the indoor. Was that not okay?"

"I'm sure it's fine," she says, sending me a tight smile. "I just need you to come with me to Barn A. Some tack has gone missing and they're questioning everyone who was here last night."

"Oh," I say, an icy spear lodging itself in my chest. "Okay, I'll just finish mixing…"

"No, leave it," Samantha cuts in. "They want us there right now."

"Um, all right." I follow after her wordlessly, my heart lubbing away in my chest. I know that neither Ethen nor I had anything to do with missing tack; it's probably just a misunderstanding. But I still feel scared for some reason. I love this job and I'd never do anything to mess it up.

I feel even more scared when we get up to Barn A and the first person I see is Isla standing in the open doorway. Her face sort of twists in evil delight when she sees me and for a second, she looks unhinged. Then she catches sight of Samantha and the look is gone.

"I'm so glad you're here, Samantha," Isla sniffles. "Alice is so upset. Her dad is here. In the tack room."

Samantha grits her teeth and narrows her eyes suspiciously at Isla.

"You'd better not have had anything to do with this," she says in a low voice and Isla startles backward, her eyes wide.

"What? No. I'm the victim here. I've been robbed."

"Uh-huh," Samantha says and tugs at my elbow to keep me moving.

The nervous feeling in my stomach ratchets up a few notches when I see the expressions of the people waiting in the tack room.

"Lena, this is Mr. Carlisle," Samantha says quietly, "he owns Three Sisters. And his daughters Alice and Isabelle, who I think you've met."

I haven't met them, not really, but I've seen them around so I gulp and nod, my throat too constricted to speak.

Isabelle sends me a small smile before looking away but Alice, the younger one who always looks ill and irritable, stares at me coldly.

"Lena, were you here last night?" Mr. Carlisle asks. His voice isn't mean but it's not exactly warm either.

"Yes…" I squeak. "I worked yesterday and then Ethen picked me up. He wanted to see the barn so I gave him a tour. Isla was here, she saw us."

"She mentioned that. She said that your boyfriend made her feel 'uncomfortable' and that she left quickly while you were still here."

"What? No, that's not true. Ethen is nice. She acted like she liked him."

"Well, we'll set that aside for now. What reason did you have to come into the tack room?"

"I…ah…Ethen asked for a tour. I showed him the horses, and the indoor and the tack room. We were only here for a second."

"And your friend took pictures while he was here?"

My heart sinks and I nod.

"For his sister and cousin. They love horses."

Mr. Carlisle frowns and sighs. "Lena, last night the tack room window was pried open and some expensive tack was taken. I have to ask you, how long have you known Ethen?"

"What? We were only here for a few minutes. We didn't take anything. And besides, Ethen would never do something like that. He wouldn't steal anything."

"Maybe not while he was here with you," Mr. Carlisle says heavily. "But he could have come back later and used the photos he took to case the place. I know it's hard to always have good judgement when you're young and when there's a good-looking boy involved. Isla was saying that he looked a little rough around the edges."

"He'd just come from work," I say incredulously. "He works with cars so he had a bit of oil on him. He's a good guy. He would never…"

"I saw the video. He looks like a classic criminal." My gaze snaps toward Alice who is staring at me with a contemptuous look on her face. "One of the saddles that was stolen was my mother's. She left it for me when she died. It is completely irreplaceable. Bottom line is that you took your sketchy boyfriend onto private property where he didn't belong and then our saddles were stolen a few hours later. How do you explain that?"

"I...I can't. But, look, if you have security cameras then you must be able to see who stole your things. Because it definitely was not us."

"Normally, yes," Mr. Carlisle says with a sigh. "But the camera in the tack room has been down for a few weeks. The cameras in the aisle are working but that's it."

"Which is pretty convenient," Alice snaps. "Maybe you took care of that too."

"Alice, that's enough." Her father sends her a sharp look.

"Lena would never be involved in this," Samantha says, clearing her throat. "She is a hard worker and all the horses love her. She's great with the kids."

"Anna said the same things when I spoke with her," Mr. Carlisle says. "But we still need to get to the bottom of this. Perhaps this Ethen..."

"He's saying your ghetto boyfriend there probably used you to steal our stuff," Alice snaps. "So either you were in on it or you were too stupid to know better."

"Okay, that's enough," Mr. Carlisle says warningly, laying a hand on her shoulder.

She turns on him sharply but suddenly her flushed cheeks go pale and she puts her hand to her face, closing her eyes.

"Dad?" she says, sounding faint and nauseous. "I don't feel very well."

And then suddenly she slumps backward in her seat, her eyes rolling back and her body going limp.

"Alice!" Her dad and her sister are at her side in an instant and Samantha is calling an ambulance while I just sit there, staring in horror at Alice's limp body. A tiny trail of blood runs down from one of her nostrils and I have to look away.

I don't move until Samantha is pulling me gently upward by the shoulder, moving me out of the way so the ambulance attendants can get to Alice. I let myself be led back to the golf cart, hardly hearing anything Samantha is saying.

"Lena, can you hear me?"

I shake my head to clear it, drawing my gaze to Samantha with effort.

"What?"

"It's just for a week, until Anna gets back and we get things sorted out. You'll be back to work in no time."

"Wait, did Mr. Carlisle fire me? But I didn't do anything."

"Didn't you hear him? It's just until things settle down. We'll figure it out, don't worry. If there's a way to bring you back then I will. You have my word."

I stare at her, my mind numb with shock, hardly able to process a single thing that's happening. An hour ago I'd been happily mixing feed and now…everything I'd built is crashing down around me.

"It will be okay," Samantha says gently. "Just get your stuff and I'll drive you home in the truck. You can't ride your bike in this rain."

I don't have any energy to argue. Woodenly, I walk into the aisle, staring straight ahead, not daring to look at the horses who I will probably never see again. If I do anything else but put one foot in front of the other then I am going to lose it. I will collapse in a puddle on this concrete floor and never get up again.

Keep moving, keep moving, I tell myself. I pick up my backpack and then head outside and around the side of the barn to where my bike is parked back out of sight by the manure bins. The handlebars are slick with the rain that is sheeting down all around us but I grip them tight, using the bike to keep me upright.

"Here, let me take that," Samantha says sympathetically. She pries the handles out of my stiff hands and lifts the bike into the back of the truck. When I don't move, she gives me a little push toward the passenger side.

I get in, still not saying anything, staring out the rain-spattered windshield.

Samantha tries to talk to me a few times but I can't even really hear her. I just give her the directions to my house and then lean my head against the window and stare out into the dark afternoon. Inside my head is just one vast void of nothingness. I know that the pain will come eventually but right now it's like I'm filled with novocaine. There is nothing left of me but a shell with all the good parts scraped away inside.

"Is this one yours?" Samantha says, peering out at my house doubtfully.

The house looks even more depressing in the pouring rain and concern flits across her face.

I nod and push the truck door open, grabbing my backpack. Samantha gets out too, arriving just in time to help me get my bike out.

"I'll...I'll call you, okay?"

"I have to go," I say miserably. "Goodbye."

"Lena, this isn't...."

A sharp sobbing sound comes out of me and I turn away quickly before I start bawling. I push my bike toward the house, not looking back as her truck rumbles to life and drives away.

For a second I can't breathe and I lean against the wall, struggling to make my lungs work, to make my heart stop shuddering in my chest. It's like my whole body is shutting down.

I close my eyes and gradually the feeling fades.

"What the hell are you doing here?"

My heart sinks as I shut the door quietly behind me, pausing so I can assess how bad the situation is. I hadn't even registered the music blaring from the living room or the fact that all the lights are off and the place reeks of alcohol, even though it's only early afternoon.

I should have had Samantha drop me off at Ethen's house in the first place. But I hadn't felt up to facing him yet. To explain to him that I'd been fired because some people thought he was a thief.

"Get in here."

Natalia's voice is slurring and that is never a good sign. Todd's truck isn't in the driveway so that means that she is drinking alone and listening to sad music. All very bad signs.

I tiptoe across the cracked linoleum, heading for my room so I can at least change my clothes before I can make my escape. Hopefully, she'll forget she heard me.

"Lena!"

Pushing down my fear, I step into the living room and force a smile. Sometimes if I pretend that everything is normal then it will calm her down. She seems to feed on fear sometimes. Showing her how scared I am will only make things worse.

"Hi," I say cheerfully, keeping my gaze fixed on her wild, bloodshot eyes. I do my best not to let on how shocked and terrified I am.

Sometime after I left for work this morning, the living room has been destroyed. The two lamps have been smashed to the floor, books lie everywhere, and a couch cushion has been ripped apart, balls of stuffing scattered across the floor. Various bottles of alcohol lie smashed or tipped on their sides all around the room.

I can't tell if Natalia did all this herself or if there'd been some sort of fight between her and Todd.

"He left me," she says blearily and then hunches over, clutching her stomach.

"Todd?" I take a cautious step closer, licking my lips nervously, feeling sorry for her despite the danger. She looks devastated.

"That rat. That bottom-feeding scum. He didn't even have the decency to dump me to my face."

"Oh." I can feel my heart speeding up again in my chest. Natalia has rarely been broken up with in her life. Usually, she is the one doing the dumping. But, on the rare times it has happened, it usually pushes her completely over the edge. Big time. I don't blame Todd at all for dumping her over the phone. He probably saved himself a trip to the hospital.

She sits up abruptly, her gaze narrowing in on me.

"You knew he was going to do this, didn't you?"

"What?" I take a few hasty steps backward. "No, of course not."

She rises slowly to her feet, like a puma locking in on its prey. Even at her worst Natalia has all the grace of a dancer or an apex predator. When I was younger, I secretly wondered if she might be some sort of vampire. She's always had that type of deadly, ethereal beauty.

The strike comes before I can move. She's across the room and my cheek is stinging, my eyes are watering before I even registered that she's hit me.

"That's for laughing at me," she says, her face inches from mine. "And this is for being on his side. You're always on his side."

Pain explodes in my right eye and I fly backwards, my head hitting the edge of the doorway with an audible crack.

She's going to kill me this time. I curl up in a tight ball to avoid her blows while she screams and rants. It seems to go on forever but finally, there is just the sound of crying, and I don't know whether it's mine or Natalia's, and then silence.

After a while, I uncurl painfully and pull myself unsteadily to my feet, whimpering as pain assaults me in dozen places. My ears are ringing. And there is something wrong with my vision that makes the whole world seem lopsided and distorted. My breath makes a rasping noise when I inhale and I wonder if my nose is broken.

My phone vibrates in my pocket but I ignore it. I don't know where Natalia is. She's probably passed out on the couch, but there is a chance that she'll appear at any second and drag me back for round two. I need to get to my room so I can figure out how badly I'm hurt.

My backpack is lying beside me where it fell. I loop a strap over my arm and make my move. I stay crouched down low until I'm in the hallway and then stumble the rest of the way to my room. At least nothing else feels broken. I remember that one summer she broke my wrist and I couldn't work at the barn for weeks. This is probably just bruises. These I can handle.

Something in my elbow twinges sharply when I push open the door to my room but I force the pain away.

There is a grumbling sound from the living room and something, probably a bottle, shatters abruptly against the wall.

I have to hurry.

I slam the door shut and push the lock on the knob. I know from experience that a flimsy lock will not be enough to stop Natalia when she's in a rage. But it might slow her down.

It takes everything in me to reach up and fumble the bolt high above my head into place. I'd installed the extra lock above the door just a few weeks ago when I'd sensed that things between Todd and Natalia were shifting. My entire body spasms in agony, especially my ribs where she'd kicked me. But I push through it, knowing I only have minutes to get to safety.

My face is wet and I'm not sure if it's from tears or blood but I make myself forget about it and keep moving.

The dresser feels like it weighs a thousand pounds. It barely moves when I press all my weight against it. But finally, it shifts, the legs inching across the unyielding carpet until it is fully blocking the doorway.

I sag with relief, my whole body shaking hard. I know that this will be enough to stop Natalia even at her worst. There is always the slight possibility that she will try and come through the window. But my room looks out over the neighbour's back yard and I'm pretty sure that even she won't be crazy enough to climb their fence just to reach me.

Right on cue, my bedroom door shudders and, despite my precautions, I feel a jolt of fear. She's shouting something but between the blaring music and the constant ringing in my ears, I can't hear the words.

Grabbing my blankets off the air mattress, along with my backpack, I drag my way to the closet and curl up inside in the furthest, darkest corner.

"You'll be okay, just lay low and it will all be over soon," I whisper. That is what my brother Garret used to say to me, back when we were little and we'd hide in the dark together. Back when he'd try to protect me.

Gradually the shouting and the banging at the door eases and I let myself relax, just a little.

It might be hours until Natalia has truly passed out and I can consider escaping through the front door. Although the idea of having to move that heavy dresser again makes me feel ill. I might be able to try and pry the window open after I rest for a bit, but it's painted shut and I don't know if I'll ever be able to lift it.

But right now I can't make myself get up. My body begins to shudder with pain as the adrenaline leaves me and my teeth chatter. Everything hurts. I run through a mental checklist of my injuries, wondering how bad it is. And how bad I'll look in the morning. Will I even be able to ride my bike to work?

Work. The memory hits me like a hammer. The saddles being stolen, Alice passing out and sliding to the floor, the ambulance. The fact that I'll probably never be welcome back there again.

Tears sting my eyes and I wipe them away, sucking in my breath as I touch the puffy skin around my eye.

Weariness settles over me but I can't sleep. I have to stay up and keep watch, just in case Natalia comes back for round two. But, despite the fear and the pain, or maybe because of it, I drift off into a dark and dreamless sleep.

Chapter 29

Kira

I have spent all night tossing and turning and worrying about Lena. She hasn't answered any of my texts or phone calls and she hasn't answered Oliver's either.

I think about the message Samantha had sent me earlier and flip over angrily.

There is no way that Lena was involved in anything to do with stealing tack. Especially not anything belonging to stupid Isla.

I look over at my work table to where her model horse Jax is waiting for another layer of paint and then push myself to my feet. I'm not going to be able to sleep so I might as well work on him some more. He's almost finished anyway; he'll be a surprise for Lena when she comes back. There is no way that Anna will just let Lena be fired based on accusations from awful Alice and Isla.

I work on Jax for hours, until my eyes are sore and I have a headache from the paint fumes, but finally I set him aside to dry. He looks much improved from the broken sculpture she'd brought me. But you can still see that it's him; I've managed to keep his personality intact.

I flop back down onto my bed, stretching out my cramped muscles and staring at the ceiling. Even though I'm exhausted, I feel nowhere close to falling asleep.

Climbing under the covers, I lift my phone from the nightstand and scroll through my library of videos. I stop on one from last week, one from my lesson with Elliot, and idly watch the screen, still half-thinking about Lena.

Suddenly something at the very edge of the video catches my eye. It's a person, moving furtively toward the back of Barn B. They stick tightly to the side of the barn, moving carefully as if they don't want to be seen.

I pause the video and take a screenshot and then zoom in as far as I can.

Isla. I'm almost positive it's her. But why would she be lurking around the back of Barn B? There's nothing back there besides the big manure bins where we dump all the bedding.

The manure bins, I think suddenly, already forwarding the video and the screenshot to Oliver. I have no idea if he's still awake, but if not he's about to be.

"Hello," he answers blearily on the fifth ring.

"Oliver, I think I know who stole the saddles. Check your messages."

"Kira?"

"Come on, wake up. This is important."

"All right, all right."

He's awake after that and we stay on the line for another hour before we finally hang up.

I get dressed, waiting for the sun to come up so we can execute our plan. We need to be the first ones to get to the barn before it officially opens. And I need to be there before Isla does. It might already be too late.

As soon as it is light out, I creep downstairs, leave my dad a note and trot down to the road and past the main gate which is luckily never closed.

Oliver's car is already there, pulled over to the side of the road.

"That's hot chocolate since I know you hate coffee," he says, pointing to the to-go cup in the holder."

"Thanks, you remembered."

"Whipped cream and raspberry drizzle," he says with a grin.

"I hope we're right about Isla," I blurt nervously.

"Me too. It's worth a shot anyway, right?"

"Right." Despite being not a bit superstitious, I cross my fingers and toes for luck just in case.

━━

Please be there, I think, swishing after Oliver through the wet grass until we reach the metal manure bins out behind the barn. One is standing open, half-filled with manure at the back corner, but the other one, the unused one, is still shut. And that's where we head.

It takes us a minute to struggle with the rusty, dirty latch. But finally, the door opens with a loud screech of metal.

"Is that what we're looking for?" Oliver whispers as we both creep forward toward a heap of bright blue tarps.

"I hope so."

Everything is wet and dripping as we peel back the layers of tarps and, by the time we unwrap the bundle like a present, our legs and shoes are soaked with rainwater.

But, as we pull back the final layer I heave a sigh of relief.

"They're here," I squeal excitedly, impulsively reaching out and hugging Oliver. "We were right."

"*You* were right," he says, hugging me back tightly. "Quick, send some pictures to Anna and Samantha. We need someone else to see this before we move it."

I send the pictures out, plus the video and photo of Isla from the night before. We wait five minutes and then I call Samantha.

It doesn't take long for things to start happening after that. The tack gets moved back to Barn A. And shortly afterward, Anna calls to say that she's on her way home and that I should call Lena and tell her not to worry, that she should come back to work and they'll sort it out later.

"Mr. Carlisle is still with Alice at the hospital," Anna says, "so he won't want to be bothered with this now. I'll talk to Isla myself when I get back."

"Wait, Alice is in the hospital?"

"Didn't Samantha tell you? Alice is quite sick. They're running a bunch of tests right now but it looks like she might need surgery. I might talk to you about riding one of her ponies while she's out of commission. But we'll deal with that after I talk to Darla."

"Oh, okay," I say slowly, guessing that she probably means the excitable Jiggs. "I don't understand why Isla did it, though. What does she have against Lena?"

Anna sighs heavily on the line. "She's a very unhappy girl, Kira. And she's always been jealous of you. Maybe she thought that hurting your friend would hurt you too? Who knows? She definitely needs some help, though."

Jealous of me? I think in shock. Isla had always acted like I was dirt under her boots. I'd never dreamed she was jealous.

"I guess I'd better call Lena and tell her the good news."

"Yes, we'll have to do something nice for her to make up for the misunderstanding. She must have been so upset."

I keep waiting for Lena to answer my texts or call me back. Or just show up at the barn, all smiles and excitement that everything has been solved.

I can't help but be distracted as I ride Tessa so I am lucky that she is in a mellow mood and takes it easy on me for once. Afterward, I lean on the fence while Oliver lunges Flicker, only half paying attention, my anxiety notching steadily upward the longer that I don't hear from Lena.

"Do you know where she lives?" Oliver asks as he leads Flicker back toward the barn. "We could go find her."

"No. Samantha does, but she took the kids on a trail ride already."

"We could look in Anna's office."

I stare at Oliver in surprise. Anna's office is pretty much off-limits to everyone unless she invites you there.

"What, like hack into her computer?"

"If we have to." He shrugs. "But it won't come to that. Anna is old-school. I've seen her use an actual address book. And it's not like we're going to rob her. We're doing it to help Lena."

"Right. Okay, but if we get in trouble then you're telling Anna that it was your idea."

It doesn't take long to find Anna's address book. It's black with a fake leather cover with the words *Address Book* stamped on the front. And it's lying right on her desk.

"See, easy," Oliver says, whipping out his phone to take a picture of Lena's neatly written address. "Come on, let's go."

Chapter 30

Lena

I wake to the sound of loud banging and jerk upright, my heart already pounding. I stagger to my feet in alarm even though every inch of my body hurts. I lean against the doorway to my closet, waiting for my heart to stop jolting in my chest and my legs to feel less wobbly.

Gradually my terror eases. The noise is not coming from my bedroom door, it's from the front door, from outside. So, not Natalia then. Is it the police? Or Todd?

The sun outside streams in from my curtainless window.

Something is wrong with my vision; everything looks blurry. I crouch down in the closet to find my phone but stop in horror when I see the state of my hands. They are red with blood and I can see bruises trailing from my wrists up my arms. What does the rest of me look like?

My face throbs, everything hurts, but at least I'm alive. And nothing feels broken. Despite the pain I can move, slowly. So that's something.

That banging is coming again and I can hear people, their voices getting closer.

Why won't they be quiet? They'll wake up Natalia. I still need to get out of my room and use the bathroom and find my bike.

The room sways around me as I gingerly pick up my backpack and stuff my phone inside.

This is all going to be okay, I tell myself firmly. *Just one step at a time. You can do this.*

But it is so hard to make myself move. All I want to do was curl up and sleep forever. But not here. This place isn't safe. I need to figure out a plan of where to go next.

I should go to Ethen's but I hate to just show up like this. Even if his mom had promised to not call social services on me, she might not want to keep her mouth shut anymore if she sees me in this state. She'll probably want to call the police.

I wish more than anything that I could be at the barn right now, listening to the horses eat their breakfast, watching the swallows swooping through the air outside the barn and hearing the laughter of the kids as they get their ponies ready.

Shadows block the sunshine for a second and I look up in alarm, not able to hold back my scream as a face looms up against the glass. Not one face but four of them. Ethen I recognize, and then Kira and Oliver, but I have no idea who the elderly man in the hat is.

It's the shocked and horrified expressions on their faces that sort of undo me. I can take almost anything in the world, but not pity. Closing my eyes, I back up until I bump into the dresser and then sink to the floor, wishing that they'd all just go away.

"Stand back." Ethen's voice sounds distant through the closed window. And it's followed by the sound of shattering glass and lots of crunching.

And then he's in the room, kneeling beside me, touching

my face and my hair so softly, so gently that I start to bawl. He's saying all sorts of nice things to me, reassuring me. The love and worry in his voice are like little daggers against the protective shield I've built up around myself. I can't afford to be weak right now.

"I'm fine," I sob, "I can handle this. I don't need your help."

But he doesn't listen to me. Instead, he reaches down and swoops me into his arms.

I know he's not trying to hurt me but my body screams in protest and I start to cry harder.

"I know, I know," he says into my hair. "I've got you. Nothing bad is ever going to happen to you again."

"You can't promise that," I whisper and then everything goes black for a moment as he hands me through the window to the people waiting outside.

Chapter 31

Kira

I am pretty sure that I am in shock. There is no other explanation for the feeling that I've left my body and am floating about three feet from it right now. I am numb all over and time seems to have slowed down.

I have never seen anyone hurt as badly as Lena is. Not even when one of the girls in my lesson was thrown face first into a jump and had to have one of her cheekbones reconstructed.

And what if Ethen hadn't seen us drive up to Lena's house and come over to help? Oliver and I would have never thought to go around back and break into get her like that. She would have still been lying there, hurt and bleeding.

I feel a sob rise up in my throat.

The neighbour, the old guy in the hat, is saying something to me but I can barely register it.

"I've called the police," he says again. "I should have called them last night when I heard all the shouting. But I thought it was just that awful woman and her boyfriend again. I forgot she had a daughter, poor thing."

"Lena's mother is passed out on the kitchen floor," I say dully. My voice sounds muffled in my ears. "She threw up."

I don't think I'll ever be able to get that image of the woman sprawled out on the linoleum in a sea of vomit and empty bottles out of my head.

"Well, I know the landlord and I'll do my best to get her kicked out. We don't need that sort of trouble around here."

But then what happens to Lena? I think, although it's obvious that she can't stay here. I still can't believe that that woman was actually her *mother*. As cold and aloof as my own mom had been, she'd never done anything like this. I couldn't even imagine having to live with someone like that.

The sound of sirens wails toward us and both Lena and her boyfriend Ethen lift their heads at the same time, wearing identical looks of panic.

"We need to get out of here before they come," Ethen says.

"What?" Oliver looks nearly as disturbed about the whole thing as I feel. His face is pale and he looks like he's about to be sick. "Lena is hurt. The police will help. They'll call an ambulance."

"They'll put her in foster care, you idiots. They'll take her away. That's how it works. We should hide out at my house instead. My brother has a friend who can patch her up."

For a second there is complete silence.

"No way, she needs a proper hospital," I say firmly. "We can drive her there right now if you want to avoid the police. My dad's a lawyer. I'll call him while we drive over. Don't worry, Lena. We'll take care of everything. You're not going anywhere."

I don't even know where the words I'm saying are coming from. Or how I sound so composed when inside I'm falling apart. But, for once, everyone listens to me and we pile into

Oliver's car, leaving the poor neighbour to deal with the police on his own.

I dial my dad as soon as we're moving.

"Hey, it's me. I need your help," I say, miraculously keeping my voice from wobbling. "Can you meet us at the hospital?"

Chapter 32

Lena

I want to argue about going to the hospital but I'm too exhausted. And I'm worried that there is something seriously wrong with me. Like maybe some organs or something were damaged. I'm not sure if I trust some random friend of Ethen's brother to patch me up either.

The ride to the hospital is mostly silent except for Kira whispering urgently into her phone. Ethen keeps his arm gently around me the whole time and I lean against his chest, wondering how my life has reached this new, embarrassing low. I'd tried so hard to keep everything on track. It had all been going so well lately too. Why did this have to happen now when I was just starting to enjoy life again?

I must have fallen asleep because the next thing I know there are lots of voices around me speaking all at once and I am placed on a rolling bed and hustled away into the depths of the hospital before I can protest.

"They're just taking you for x-rays. We'll be right here waiting," Ethen says firmly, probably seeing the panic on my face. "We won't leave you."

But part of me doesn't believe him. I will probably never see any of them again. I will be shuffled to some foster family or group home in a different city far away from Three Sisters. And, in a few months, they'll forget I even existed.

The nurses speak to me kindly as they set me up for x-rays but I don't respond. I just close my eyes and wait for it all to be over.

"Lena, can you hear us?' The doctors keep asking me the same annoying questions over and over while they shuttle me to get a CT scan and an MRI as soon as the x-rays are done.

I hear a few scattered words. Head trauma, cracked ribs, bruising. But I don't care. Nothing they do matters much anymore.

At least they've given me some pain control to take the edge off things, though. And it also has the side benefit of reducing some of my overwhelming panic too.

At some point, I'm taken to a private room that has a window overlooking a little courtyard. There is nobody else there and, for the first time, I feel a tiny sense of peace. This feels like a place where I can rest and be safe for a little while.

———

"Lena?"

I open my eyes to see Kira's dad looking down at me, a kind expression on his face.

"Hi," I say, struggling to sit up a little.

"Just rest," he says. "I won't stay long. You need to gain your strength. I just want to ask you a quick question."

"Okay," I say, gulping nervously.

"Would you like to stay with us temporarily, until this is all sorted out? Kira insists that you do but I wanted to check with you first."

I freeze, not sure if I'm hearing him right.

"You want me to stay with you?" I ask cautiously.

"Yes, Kira has been pretty insistent that you're coming home with us. At least until you decide what you'd like to do next."

"Really?"

"You'll still need to talk to a social worker, but I'll get the paperwork started to be your temporary guardian. I just wanted to be sure that there wasn't anywhere else you'd prefer to stay."

"Wow, okay." I offer him a tentative smile. "Thank you."

"You're welcome. Now get some sleep. They want to keep you for a few days for observation. You've been through a lot."

Tears sting my eyes and I have to look away when I see the sympathy on his face.

"Lena…" he says quietly.

I glance back to where he's standing, one hand already poised on the door handle, ready to leave.

"What your mother did is criminal and we're going to make sure nothing like that ever happens again. I hope you know that none of this is your fault. You've been very brave. Braver than a person should have to be."

I look away again, not daring to breathe until the door clicks shut behind him.

I'm not brave. I'm just…. Stupid. I think. *Stupid for staying too long, stupid for misjudging Natalia's mood. I should have gone right to my room when I knew she was drunk. Or made a run for it back out the front door. I should have guessed this would happen. It was at least partly my fault.*

The door clicks open again and I'm surrounded by smiling faces.

Ethen comes over and takes my hand gently. "See, we told you we'd be back."

"The nurse is going to chase us out so we have to be quick," Oliver says. "You look so much better without all the blood."

"Um, thanks." I start to laugh but stop abruptly when my ribs constrict painfully. "The nurses cleaned me up. I guess my nose broke and that's where all the blood was from."

There's an awkward silence.

"I'm so glad you get to stay with us," Kira says softly. "I was so scared when I first saw you in that place. You never have to go back there, Lena. And, now that you're living with us we can carpool to the barn together. Actually, you can teach me how to ride the bus."

She sounds so excited that I laugh again, this time more carefully. Then I remember the part about the barn.

"Um, I think I've been fired."

"What?" Ethen says. "When? Why?"

I look away, mortification creeping over me. I can't tell him about what Alice's dad had said to me. I can't have him thinking that any of this is because of him.

"It was a mistake," Kira says, sending a meaningful look at Oliver. "Don't worry about that now. Anna said that it was all a misunderstanding and it's being fixed."

"Oh, okay," I say in surprise. "That's great."

"You can go back to work as soon as you feel ready."

She reaches down and I see that she has my backpack. And a decorative gift bag with something else in it.

"I thought you might like this," she says, setting Jax on the table beside the bed. "I hope I got the colour right."

"Oh, Kira, he's perfect," I say in astonishment because he looks just like the Jax I remember when he was shiny and new. All the broken parts have been put back together and you can't even see the scars.

"Come on, Kira," Oliver says, "it's almost time to go, let's give these guys a couple of minutes alone."

"Why?" She looks at him in bewilderment. "Lena is *my* best friend."

"Because maybe they want some privacy to talk."

Kira rolls her eyes but follows Oliver outside, muttering something under her breath.

"Lena, are you really all right?" Ethen is looking down at me like I'm this precious, breakable thing that might disappear on him at any second.

"Yes, I mean I'm sore but I'll live. Do you know what happened to my mom?"

"No." He shakes his head. "But my brother said the police took her away somewhere."

I sigh heavily, wondering if she's going back to jail. I also wonder how long Kira's dad will let me stay at their place, if it will be long enough for me to graduate high school and maybe save up enough money to move out on my own.

"Lena, I can't tell you what it felt like when I saw you hurt like that. I should have never let you go back there at all."

"It was my choice. I knew the risks."

"Yeah, but Lena…" He breaks off and I look up to see him staring at me with this wide-eyed, starry look on his face. "I will never let something like that happen again. I will protect you from now on, understand? I will do anything to take care of you."

I know he's sincere, I know he means well. But that look on his face is exactly the same way Natalia's many boyfriends looked at her. Like she was this shining sun that their world revolved around.

I pull my hand away from his, fighting the feeling of nausea in my belly.

I will never be like Natalia, I promise myself fiercely. I never want to have that power over someone. To have them lose themselves in me completely until they don't even know who they are anymore. To give me money and take care of me. To have them hang on my words and watch their expressions fall when I crush them. I have seen it happen so many times and I want nothing to do with it. Especially not to Ethen.

"Sorry, I'm really tired. I'm going to get some sleep," I say, turning over abruptly and closing my eyes.

"Right, of course." I feel him touch my hair gently and then a soft kiss on my forehead that makes me want to start crying again.

But when he's gone, I feel a terrible sense of loneliness; like I've lost something precious that I can't get back.

Chapter 33

Lena

Things are a bit of a blur after that. I have to talk to the police, twice, to tell them what happened. And I learn that Natalia has a court date set for the fall that I might be asked to testify in. Which is something that terrifies me, but I'm going to put off worrying about it until I have to. Whatever happens, she will never get custody of me again; that part of my life is over.

Before I know it, I am whisked from the hospital and set up in a guest bedroom in Kira's fancy house. And I am suddenly eating three solid meals a day and being waited on hand and foot by both Grace and Kira, which is a little overwhelming.

It has been the most surreal week of my life. I have gone from struggling just to survive to living in the lap of luxury in such a short period of time that my head is spinning.

My body begins to repair itself and my bruises fade, although I doubt that my memories of that night will heal as rapidly.

Nobody has told me how long I can expect to stay here yet. But Kira introduced me to her nosy neighbour, Mrs. Harris, as "my new sister, Lena," the other day, so I had the feeling that I didn't need to worry about leaving quite yet.

Ethen continues to visit me every night after work, even though Kira's dad seems a little suspicious and grumpy when he's around.

I still feel torn around Ethen. On one hand, he feels like he's my other half and I can't live without him. But, on the other hand, sometimes I feel that he likes me way too much. That his happiness is dependent on me and that is a terrifying amount of responsibility.

It isn't until the end of the week that something happens to change my mind.

It was after Ethen had just left that Kira's dad found me pensively staring out the living room window onto the rolling golf course out back.

"Everything all right, Lena?" he asks, sitting down on the couch. "How was your visit with Ethen?"

"Oh, it was good," I say, but it doesn't sound completely convincing.

"Lena, I didn't want to say anything before. But I did a little digging on Ethen's family and I'm not entirely sure that they're the best connections for you to have right now. His dad did some prison time and his brother Owen has been in juvenile detention twice. And his uncle is a rough character."

"You investigated them?" I ask, turning to face him in surprise.

"Well, no. It's all on the public record."

"Maybe, but what's not in the public record is how sweet his mom and his younger siblings are. And how they took me in and fed me so many times without question."

"I'm not saying they don't have good qualities…"

"Or how Ethen's dad went to work for his uncle just one

time because he needed the money. And that was the night he was shot when the police raided the garage. And now he has to suffer every day in a crappy wheelchair because they can't afford a better one."

"Lena, I…"

"Or, how the little girls love horses and would kill to ride one but they will probably never get the opportunity because of where they live and who they are."

"Okay, okay, I just…."

"Or how Ethen is the kindest, most gentle human being on the planet. He literally saved my life this summer. And, honestly, I can't imagine him ever not being in my life. So, if you're about to suggest that I don't see him or his amazing family any more, then I'm going to have to leave. Because I don't think I ever want to live in a world without him."

Kira's dad stares at me, open-mouthed, and I prepare to be told to go to the guest room and pack my bags.

But that doesn't happen.

"All right," he says, nodding at me. "Well, maybe I was wrong. How about Ethen comes for dinner tomorrow night? That might give us the chance to get off on a better foot."

"Oh." I huff out a breath, still in fighting mode even though he's already given in and there's nothing to argue about. "Okay. Thank you. That would be great."

And after that argument, things are less tense between me and Ethen too. Because I realized that, no matter what happens in the future, I am going to do my best to make this relationship work. And sure, I'm probably going to mess up sometimes, as people do, but at least I owe it to us both to try.

Chapter 34

Kira

"Are you sure you want to do this?" I ask, kicking my feet out of the stirrups. Flicker may not have pulled anything dirty during our rides in the last few weeks but he hasn't been easy either. He's questioned pretty much every request I've made of him.

"Yep," Oliver says, raising an eyebrow at me in challenge. "I can handle this."

"Okay," I sigh and jump to the ground. Oliver has been working hard for the last few weeks. He's cooled Flicker down after almost every ride and has been taking lots of extra lessons on Bluebell.

But I'm not sure if either of us is ready for this next step.

"All ready to go?" Lena asks, leading out Tessa and Bluebell from the barn. She smiles at us excitedly, her expression relaxed and happy.

It is so good to see her looking like this. Her bruises are nearly all gone and she is planning to start back to work next week to help Samantha with the summer camp kids. She'd even managed to get camp scholarships for Ethen's little sister and cousin who'd already been out twice to meet the horses and see where Lena works.

Surprisingly, Tessa had loved the kids and they'd spent over an hour fawning over her and feeding her carrots.

"Yep," Oliver says. "More than ready."

He grins at me and swings easily up onto Flicker's back. Flicker's ears swivel around like he's plotting something, but right now he's more interested in Bluebell and Tessa.

"I'm so excited," Lena says. "I haven't been on a trail ride in ages and I can't wait to meet the foal. Thanks so much for letting me ride Bluebell, Oliver."

"Any time. Bluebell is as trustworthy as they come so you don't need to worry about her playing up."

Lena doesn't look worried, though. She is smiling from ear to ear as she climbs slowly onto Bluebell's back and then reaches down and pets the mare softly.

We let Tessa take the lead, with Oliver and Flicker in the middle, and then Lena at the end. Hopefully, Flicker will be less inclined to pull anything silly if he's sandwiched in the middle.

The air is warm but there is a faint breeze and I inhale deeply, some of my usual anxiety melting away.

We climb up the hill past Barn A and I wonder idly where Isla is and if she's found a new barn to ride at. Or if she's just given up riding now that she is no longer welcome at Three Sisters. She hadn't seemed to actually enjoy horses for a long time, anyway.

She hadn't given a great explanation for what she'd done. I hadn't been there when Anna had asked her to leave. But she'd told Anna to apologize to everyone for her and then had left quietly, without putting up a fuss. Maybe even *she* was shocked at what she'd done.

And I think she felt a little responsible about what had happened to Alice too, since it was all the stress that had finally pushed Alice's condition over the edge. After lots of tests, Alice had been diagnosed with a tumour on her brain and they'd taken her right to surgery. She was still in recovery and I'd been asked to start schooling Jiggs since nobody else wanted to ride the pony.

Finally, I have all the horses I want at my fingertips. I'm going to be hard-pressed to find time to ride everyone once school starts back up. But at least this time I won't be so alone at school. This time Lena is going to be there with me, and I have the feeling that this year is going to be much better than last.

And now that my dad is on board with me making horses a career, we are going to figure out if I can use my riding and training time as extra credits at school.

After what I'd seen at Lena's place, all the worries I'd been stewing over in my own life suddenly hadn't seemed so insurmountable. I'd had a meeting with my dad the afternoon we came back from the hospital and had told him flat out that I wasn't going to go to university to study anything boring. I was going to work with horses for a living either with or without him.

And, it had actually turned out all right. He'd listened to me and been supportive. And he'd even confessed that he'd been thinking about switching from corporate law to environmental law now that I was older and didn't need so much support. It looked like it was the right time for all of us to follow our dreams.

The trail to Fina's place is well beaten down by this time since Oliver and I have been riding there a few days a week. We have loved helping out with the draft horses but today is special.

Because Beatrice has finally had her baby.

We pick up speed the closer we get, all of us eager to see the new foal.

"How's he doing?" I ask, turning to look over my shoulder at Oliver, but I barely need to ask. Flicker has his neck stretched out and his eyes half closed like he's a seasoned ranch horse. Apparently, trail riding suits him.

We turn the horses out in the paddock that we always use and hurry to the little field where Beatrice is happily grazing.

"She is perfect," I whisper, leaning against the fence rail and peering through the gap at the little bay filly. She looks just like her mom with a fluffy chocolate coat and white leg markings. Her scruffy little black tail flicks back and forth as she goes in for another snack of milk from Beatrice.

"I know," Fina whispers back. "I can't stop watching her. I come out here and just stare for hours. My grandfather and Dale are over the moon, of course. Everyone has been crossing their fingers for a filly."

"What are you going to call her?" Lena says softly from my other side.

"Don't laugh, but we've named her Mabel. It just sort of went with Beatrice somehow."

"Aww, that's adorable," Lena says. "Are you going to keep her?"

"Oh definitely. She's going to be part of the breeding program here eventually. She has pretty amazing bloodlines. But for now, she just gets to be an adorable baby. We'll get to show her in halter classes next year though. That is, if you'll help me get them ready, Kira," she says, throwing me a grin.

"Oh, I'm in."

I lean my chin on the wooden fence rail and dreamily watch the baby.

"Are we still all on for tonight?" Fina asks, rubbing her hands together eagerly. "I haven't been out to a restaurant in ages. Someone will have to stop me from ordering only desserts."

"Yep, we're in," Oliver says before I can answer, looking over and grinning at me when I glower at him. He'd used all his vast powers of persuasion to convince me to go to dinner and the movies with them all tonight.

It was the fact that he'd printed out the entire menu for me and circled all the foods I liked that had finally swayed me.

"Ethen's excited that he doesn't have to dress up in anything fancy," Lena laughed. "A restaurant on the beach is exactly up his ally."

I turn my attention back to the baby, my stomach fluttering a little in excitement despite my nerves. It wasn't a date night exactly, since Isabelle was coming and so was Fina's older brother, but it still felt kind of grown up and new.

This summer certainly hadn't turned out anything like 'd expected. I feel like I lived an entire lifetime in just a few short months. And I am sure Lena feels the same way.

But I have to admit that I am the happiest I've ever been in my life. I have new friends, one who is nearly a sister to me; a sense of purpose; and a feeling of actually being in control of my own life. I feel different somehow. More like an adult. And more comfortable in my own skin.

It feels like all the missing puzzle pieces in my life are suddenly clicking into place one by one. And the picture unfolding is looking pretty darn good.

Acknowledgments

Big thanks to my editor, Shannon Page and to James at Go On Write for designing the cover.

Thanks to the Advanced Reader Team for being the first eyes on the page. And special thanks to Helen Cartwright, Mariko Brown and Honey Johnston for the support and excellent feedback.

And a huge shout-out to the patient, saintly horses of my childhood who let me gallop around bareback and barefoot and refrained from bucking me off too often. I was very lucky to have grown up with such amazing teachers.

About the Author

Genevieve McKay is the author of over a dozen books, and most of them are about horses. She was allowed to free-range as a child and spent many hours riding (and reading) in the woods. She lives on the west coast of Canada with her family, her horses, and an assortment of barnyard animals such as dogs, cats, sheep, chickens and two half-tame ravens.

Also by Genevieve Mckay

There is more to come! Make sure to check out book three of the Three Sisters Farm series. Casting Shadows will be coming soon.

Casting Shadows

The October Horses series

The last thing Bree Connor expected, after being diagnosed with a terminal illness, was a second chance at life. But, somehow, that's exactly what she got.

When a fateful encounter at the hospital introduces her to the world of horses, Bree is determined to make them a part of her new life. Things quickly spiral out of control when she becomes the caretaker to a pair of misfit thoroughbreds who also need a second chance.

Will her strength and willpower be enough to beat the overwhelming odds that are stacked against them all?

The October Horses

Facing the Fire

Keeping Chilly

Defining Gravity series

Astrid never breaks the rules; she's much too terrified of her overbearing father to step out of line. He controls her weight, her friends, and even her career path. And he doesn't approve of anyone in their family thinking for themselves.

When one impulsive decision ends in disaster, Astrid is grounded for the summer, forced to put her archery career on hold and take a menial job cleaning stalls at a posh dressage barn. It takes a little horse named Quarry and a quirky cast of characters to banish Astrid's unhappiness and show her that she is worth something. But when her father steps in, once again, everything Astrid has grown to love is threatened.

Defining Gravity

Flight

Freefall

Riding Above Air

Touching Ground

<u>Short Stories and Collections</u>

Sarah Lawson has given up making Christmas wishes for herself. When her parents died in an accident she had to push all her dreams of a family and horses aside. Her only goal this holiday season is to find a permanent place for her baby sister Amy. Their latest foster home has everything Sarah could hope for; a farm in the country, a nice foster-mom, and the kind of stability that creative, scatter-brained Amy needs. The only problem; it's temporary.

When imaginative Amy finds a lost horse she's convinced is a unicorn, Sarah is dragged on an adventure she'll never forget.

This could be the Christmas that changes everything. But is Sarah ready to take a leap of faith?

The Horses of Winter

<u>Greystone Manor Mysteries</u>

All Jillian Harrington wants is to live a predictable, ordinary life. One where she can ride her horses and read books in peace. And for her haunting memories of the past to stay buried.

But, when life throws her a curveball in the form of her reckless cousin Xander, Jilly is dragged into a deadly adventure. Not only is she forced to face the secrets of her eccentric family, but the creepy mansion they're stranded in has a dark past of its own; along with a resident ghost or two.

With her best friend Gilbert, and her four-legged side-kicks, Morris and Bally at her side, Jilly will have to fight

harder than she ever has to make it through this adventure alive.

The Curse of the Golden Touch

The Sting of the Serpent's Blade

<u>The Wayfarer's End Series</u>

The Opposite of Living

Good Bones

Wayfarer's End

Visit my website at www.genevievemckay.com

Follow my pics on Instagram: @mckaygenevieve

Or join my Facebook author page: www.facebook.com/authorgenevievemckay

If you are enjoying reading my books I'd love it if you'd take a moment to write a review on Amazon, Goodreads or any of the platforms where they are sold.

I also have a mailing list where you can stay up to date on new releases, promotions and giveaways.

https://landing.mailerlite.com/webforms/landing/d2s9l0